Last of the
Blue and Gray

Also by Richard A. Serrano

One of Ours:
Timothy McVeigh and the Oklahoma City Bombing

My Grandfather's Prison:
A Story of Death and Deceit in 1940s Kansas City

LAST OF THE BLUE AND GRAY

OLD MEN, STOLEN GLORY, AND THE MYSTERY THAT OUTLIVED THE CIVIL WAR

RICHARD A. SERRANO

Smithsonian Books
WASHINGTON, DC

This book may be purchased for educational, business, or sales
promotional use. For information, please write: Special Markets Department,
Smithsonian Books, P. O. Box 37012, MRC 513, Washington, DC 20013.

Published by Smithsonian Books
Director: Carolyn Gleason
Production Editor: Christina Wiginton
Editor: Duke Johns
Designer: Mary Parsons

Library of Congress Cataloging-in-Publication Data

Serrano, Richard A.

Last of the blue and gray : old men, stolen glory,
and the mystery that outlived the Civil War / Richard A. Serrano.

p.   cm.

ISBN 978-1-58834-395-6 (hardback)

1. Woolson, Albert, 1847-1956. 2. Williams, Walter Washington, -1959. 3. United
States—History—Civil War, 1861-1865—Veterans. 4. Impostors and imposture—
United States—Biography. 5. Veterans—United States—Biography. 6. United States—
History—Civil War, 1861-1865—Centennial celebrations, etc. I. Title.

E467.S43 2013

973.70922—dc23

[B]

2013028772

Manufactured in the United States of America

18 17 16 15 14 13   5 4 3 2 1

Come tell us old man ...

WALT WHITMAN, "The Wound-Dresser"
From his Civil War poems, *Drum Taps*

CONTENTS

⟨ ◆ ⟩

1

·············

TWO OLD SOLDIERS

A lbert Woolson loved the parades. For Memorial Day in Duluth, Minnesota, he rode in the biggest car down the widest streets of his hometown. The city etched his name in the Duluth Honor Roll, and he was celebrated at conventions and banquets across the North. Even the president wrote him letters on his birthday. Because everyone said he was the last surviving member of the Grand Army of the Republic, a fraternal organization of Union veterans once nearly half a million strong, they erected a life-size statue of him on the most hallowed ground of that entire horrible conflict—Gettysburg.

Though deaf and often ill, he was still spry enough that, even at 109 years of age, he could be polite and mannerly, always a gentleman. He was especially fond of children and enjoyed visiting schools and exciting the boys with stories of cannon and steel and unbelievable courage on the fields around Chattanooga. The boys called him "Grandpa Al."

But Woolson could be fussy. His breakfast eggs had to be scrambled and his bacon crisp. He continued to smoke; he had probably lit up more than a thousand cigars just since he had hit the century mark. And no one kept him from his half-ounce of brandy before dinner.

His grandfather had served in the War of 1812, and when guns were fired on Fort Sumter in 1861, his father went off to fight for Lincoln. He lost a leg and died. So, as the story goes, young Albert, blue-eyed and blonde-haired, a mere five and a half feet tall, took his father's place.

With just a year left in the war, he enlisted as a drummer boy with the 1st Minnesota Heavy Artillery Regiment, rolling his snare as they marched south to Tennessee.

But that had been long ago, more than 90 years past. Now Albert Woolson's days were fading, the muffled drum of his youth a softening memory. At St. Luke's Hospital in Duluth, his health deteriorating, he would sometimes feel his old self, quoting Civil War verse or the Gettysburg Address. But then on a Saturday in late July 1956 he slipped into a coma. Just before he drifted off, he asked a nurse's aide for a dish of lemon sherbet. She gave him some soft candy too. As she shut the door she glanced back at her patient. "I thought he was looking very old," she recalled. For a week he lay quietly in his hospital bed, awaiting death.

Down in Houston, old Walter Washington Williams had sent Woolson a telegram congratulating him on turning 109. "Happy birthday greetings from Colonel Walter Williams," the wire said.

Williams was blind, nearly deaf, rail-thin, and confined to a bed in his daughter's house. He had served as a Confederate forage master for Hood's Brigade, they said, and now he was bound and determined to be the last on either side still alive when America's great Civil War Centennial commemoration began in 1961. "I'm going to wait around until the others are gone," he said, "to see what happens."

Williams had ridden in a parade too. He was named in presidential proclamations and tributes in the press. *Life* magazine devoted a three-page spread to the old Rebel, including a photograph of Williams propped up on his pillows, a large Stars and Bars flag hanging on the wall. An American Legion band serenaded at his window, and he tapped his long, spindly fingers in time with "Old Soldiers Never Die." But Williams was a Southern boy deep in his bones. He would have preferred "Cotton-Eyed Joe" on the radio:

> O Lawd, O Lawd,
> Come pity my case.
> For I'm gettin' old
> An' wrinkled in de face.

Like Woolson, Williams could be cantankerous. On his last birthday, when he said he was 117, they served him his favorite barbecued pork, though his daughter and a nurse had to feed him. His bed was piled high with cards and telegrams, but he could not read them. He could hardly pick them up. "I'm tired of staying here," he complained in his son's ear. The son smiled and told visitors how they had hunted deer together when his father was 101. "He rode a horse until he was 103," the son said.

Williams's last public outing was in an Armed Forces Day parade in Houston in May 1959, when he rode in an air-conditioned ambulance. As he passed the reviewing stand, he struggled to raise his arm in salute. Then they took him home and put him back to bed.

Four times he suffered bouts of pneumonia; twice they hung an oxygen tent over his bed. His doctor was doubtful, and his daughter feared the worst. "There's too many years; too many miles," she said.

And so the clock ticked down, not just on Albert Woolson and Walter Williams, but for a whole generation, an entire era, the closing of a searing chapter in American history: four years of brutal civil war. Like the old soldiers, memories of the North and South and how they had splintered and then remade America were slowly dying out too. Starting in the 1920s, '30s, and '40s, Civil War soldiers began passing away in rapid numbers, nearly three a day. The glorious reunions of proud veterans at Gettysburg and the cities of the South were coming to an end; there were too few healthy enough to attend. The Grand Army of the Republic closed its last local chapter. The Rebel yell fell silent. The campfires went dark. Echoing down the years were Gen. Robert E. Lee's last words: "Strike the tent."

By the start of the 1950s, about sixty-five of the blue and gray veterans were left; by 1955, just a half dozen. As their numbers dwindled they became artifacts of a shuttered era, curiosities of an ancient time, sepia-toned figures still inhabiting a modern world from their rocking chairs and oxygen tents. They had gone to war with rifles and sabers and in horse-mounted patrols. They had lived off hardtack and beans. Now they seemed lost in a new American century that had endured two devastating world wars fought with armored tank divisions, deadly mustard gas, and atomic bombs that fell from the sky.

Bruce Catton, long a chronicler of the Civil War, could recall his boyhood in the "pre-automobile age" of rural Michigan and how a group of old Union veterans in white whiskers and blue greatcoats had delighted his young eyes. He remembered one selling summer berries from a pail he hooked over the stub of his forearm, an arm he had lost in the Battle of the Wilderness. A church deacon had fought with the 2nd Ohio Cavalry in Virginia's Shenandoah Valley, burning barns and killing livestock. Another had returned to Gettysburg for the fiftieth anniversary there, and when he arrived back by train and his buggy was late, the seventy-year-old simply hoisted his bag and walked the five miles home. "They were grave, dignified, and thoughtful," Catton would write of his home-town heroes. "For the most part they had never been 50 miles away from the farm or the dusty village streets; yet once, ages ago, they had been everywhere and had seen everything.... All that was real had taken place when they were young; everything after that had simply been a process of waiting for death." Eventually, one by one the old men were carried up a small hilltop to the town cemetery. "As they departed," Catton wrote, "we began to lose more than we knew we were losing."

By the close of the 1950s, as the nation was preparing for the 100th anniversary of the Civil War, much of the pubic watched transfixed, marking the passing of each of the final veterans, wondering who might be the last, wondering if any would make it to the centennial, curious how anyone could live so long. Could anyone be so old?

That question seemed never more poignant than when a Confederate veteran from Georgia disrupted a Civil War museum and jabbed his cane in sudden bayonet thrusts, threatening the portraits of Yankee soldiers hanging on the wall. "Let me at him!" he yelled at a painting of Union hero Gen. William Tecumseh Sherman, the scourge of Atlanta. Sadly, the old Rebel appeared a pitiful figure, a misfit, more a caricature of himself than a gallant hero from an epic time.

Because it turns out that many of the men were not so old after all. Many who claimed to be well over 100 and survivors of that great war were really imposters, some flat-out frauds. In truth they had been mere children and too young to march off to war in the early 1860s. Or they had not even been born. Yet as they grew old, they fabricated stories about past heroic adventures and brazenly applied for Civil War pensions during the long, lean years of the Great Depression. Some backdated their birthdates. Some made up the names of comrades and commanding officers. Some lied to their friends and neighbors and to newspapers and government officials. Over the years, some accepted so many accolades as Civil War veterans that they never could muster the courage or the humility to own up to the truth, even as they lay near death. Many ended up believing their own fabrications. Driven by money, ego, or a craving to belong to something grand and glorious, these men defrauded a nation. They especially dishonored those who had served, those who had been wounded, and above all those who had died. Many of them fooled their own families. One fooled the White House.

The last veteran who said he fought for the Union was Albert Woolson; Walter Williams said he was the last Confederate. One of them indeed was a soldier, but one, according to the best evidence, was a fake. One of them had been living a great big lie.

....

REUNION

The great fiftieth reunion of the blue and the gray was being held in July 1911 in Manassas, Virginia, half a century after the first Battle of Bull Run, and the president of the United States was running late. In a gesture signifying that much had changed since the two sides had clashed so long ago, that the age of the horse was ending and the wagon and locomotive too, William Howard Taft decided to drive from the White House to the Virginia countryside in his flashy new motor car, a sporty White steamer.

He brought with him his trusted assistant, Maj. Archibald Willingham Butt. A son of the South born just five months after the Civil War ended, Butt restlessly sought new adventures. He had enlisted in the Army and saw action in the Philippines and Cuba. He never married, giving his all to his career. Eventually he was appointed a White House military adjutant and worked closely with Taft in the White House.

But the art of politics and statecraft bored Butt. He was a man who thrived on danger. A year after this "Peace Jubilee" in Manassas, he would take a rare vacation to Europe. Sailing home in April 1912, his ocean liner struck an iceberg in the North Atlantic. Ever the soldier, Butt was seen by survivors on the deck fighting with men trying to sneak onto the precious few lifeboats. Some accounts have him with drawn pistol, firing at passengers frantic to push their way onto too few rafts. For Butt, it was always chivalry, and always women and children first. He went down with the USS *Titanic*.

Major Butt did indeed nurture a flair for the theatric. The afternoon drive with the president to Manassas became an adventure as well. They almost never made it.

Along the way, Butt wrote to his sister Clara a few days later, "we met with every obstacle which nature could provide." They started out at half past noon, four vehicles in a sort of miniature presidential motorcade. They reached Falls Church, Virginia, and stopped for a reception with some fifty attendees. The president drank lemonade and offered a few short remarks. They then drove to Fairfax City and the lawn of the Fairfax County Courthouse. The mayor and other dignitaries met them, but storm clouds suddenly opened up and everyone hurried inside. "It seemed as if the bottom had fallen out of the sky," Butt wrote.

They pushed on, braving the driving rain, and reached a state senator's home for lunch. A big man, President Taft was not going to miss his meal. It was the perfect Southern feast: fried chicken, Virginia ham, and hot crisp corn bread. When they had eaten, the sun reappeared. The clock said a quarter to three, and they were due in Manassas in an hour and fifteen minutes. So they drove on, turning onto the Manassas Pike, where they "were bumped and jolted over the worst road I have ever seen," Butt recalled. They climbed a small hill and spotted a stream below, the water rising. The current was strong and wheel-high. Cross it, or not? Butt hopped out, pulled off his boots, and waded in, testing its depth, searching for a shallow lane. At some points the water reached his armpits, but he found a passable route, and the White steamer huffed through the muck, mire, and the roiling water.

Two miles on they reached Little Rocky Creek, swollen the size of a torrent. Several farmers warned them not to chance crossing it. The president called on the major to wade into this one as well. Off again went the boots, and in he plowed. Too deep, too dangerous, he called out. So they circled back, crossed the first stream again, found an alternate route ten miles out and headed for Centreville. Butt hung his wet socks over the dashboard to dry. No rain had fallen here, but heavy swirling dust picked up and coated the entourage. Still they persisted, finally reaching Manassas at a quarter to six, nearly two hours late. Tired, sweating, dirty, worn, and thirsty—and likely hungry again—the president stepped out of his car and into the crowd.

The throng was ten thousand strong, a sight like none of them had seen before. Here the skies were clear and the air steaming, a blistering 90-plus degrees. Red dust kicked up around town. But the air of peace was afloat. Teenage girls waving small American flags wore white gowns and banners, each representing one of the reunited states. The town's business district near Grant and Lee avenues was decorated with patriotic bunting, and much of it proclaimed "The New America." A huge banner heralded Gen. Ulysses S. Grant's famous words, "Let us have peace." Alongside it was a saying from Gen. Robert E. Lee, "Duty is the sublimest word in the English language." Hotels were jammed, and other guests took rooms in private homes. More guests crowded into two large dormitories at Eastern College, opened just a year earlier. The nearby Prince William County Courthouse, a red brick Romanesque Revival structure also still fairly new, seemed to pitch and sway as the crowd pushed closer and the president climbed to the dais. Peering into the vast audience, he could make out a good number of the 350 faces that had fought a half century ago for the South, and half that many for the North. Many came dressed sharply in old battle uniforms, some with medals pinned to their chests. They were stern, disciplined old men, but hard of hearing. The president would make just a brief address, and he would have to speak loud. But the veterans heard him. Major Butt knew that. Even at a distance, he could see the tears in their eyes.

The president did not need to remind these brave souls that the fighting along Bull Run, in fields, groves, and a line of trees just up the pike from Manassas, became the first major encounter of the Civil War. The Confederates routed the Union army and sent the men in blue retreating pell-mell, following much the same route (in reverse) that Taft and his party had driven that day, fleeing east across the Potomac and home to Washington, D.C. Walt Whitman had chronicled the panicked, distraught, defeated Union army: "The men appear, at first sparsely and shame-faced enough, then thicker, in the streets of Washington—appear in Pennsylvania Avenue and on the steps and basement entrances," the poet wrote. "They come along in disorderly mobs, some in squads, stragglers, companies. Occasionally a rare regiment, in perfect order, with its officers marching in perfect silence, with lowering faces, stern, weary to sinking, all black and dirty."

President William Howard Taft addresses Union and Confederate veterans at Manassas, Virginia, in July 1911, fifty years after blue and gray soldiers fought one another in a nearby field. "You who have suffered war," he told them, "will appreciate what peace means." (Courtesy of the Manassas National Battlefield Park)

Everyone had predicted a quick finish to this conflict. Instead, the war wore on for four more bloody, agonizing years.

"I deplore war," the president told the veterans. "I wish it could be abolished entirely. But we may all rejoice that in that awful test the greatness of the American people was developed. There we showed our ability to fight out our differences to the very death and to make the greatest nation in the world after having had the greatest civil war the world had ever witnessed."

Speaking directly now to those old men in the crowd, he said, "When we look back to that period, a feeling of sadness must overcome us, for that is a period that we dislike to look back upon, a period of discouragement and sorrow, reviving in our minds all the great strain and trial of that awful struggle.... You who have suffered in war will appreciate what peace means."

More of the veterans cried, leaning on their wooden canes or unable to stand at all. Some raised a feeble whoop and the Rebel yell. Those in blue tipped their black, gold-corded hats in a round of cheers. The applause grew louder when the governor of Virginia, dressed in Confederate gray, rose and shook the president's hand. William Hodges Mann was the last Confederate soldier to serve as governor of the commonwealth. The president, by contrast, was a Northern man from Ohio, who had been just three years old when the guns sounded at Manassas. The symbolism was lost on no one. The two sides had officially reunited.

The great Peace Jubilee that summer was the brainchild of George Carr Round, a Union officer who at war's end had moved to Virginia. He came up with the idea after reading a letter to the *Washington Post* from a South Carolina Confederate who had argued that the fiftieth anniversary of the Civil War should be honored as one of "peace and reconciliation." Now practicing law and serving on the Manassas school board, Round suggested that the place to pay tribute to the shrinking ranks of blue and gray soldiers who had fought that war was where it began. By the time of the Jubilee, Round was already seventy years old. He would not live to see eighty.

The son of a Methodist preacher, Round was born in Pennsylvania and raised in New York. He left college before graduating to join the 1st Connecticut Artillery in 1862. After two years he was transferred to the Signal Corps and commissioned a lieutenant. The war proved a long slog for Round, as it did for many during those years of battle, retreat, and battle.

"Dear Mother," he wrote home in October 1864. He was then at the Signal Corps camp in Georgetown, just blocks from the White House. "It is now ten o'clock in the evening. I have been on the hill close by here all day ... in charge of a signal station. It was quite cold and *very windy*, although the sun shone brightly all day. But I bundled myself in my overcoat and had a first-rate time talking with a man down at the Provost Marshal's office in the city of Washington."

Round also served as signal officer for Gen. William Tecumseh Sherman as he carved the last of his famous march up the coast of North Carolina. Round climbed atop the high dome of the capitol building in Raleigh, now held by the Union army, the perfect spot to fire his signal flares. From that perch, he heard below the click of horses' hooves. Maybe drunken cavalrymen out of camp, he thought. But as the horsemen drew near, he could make out their yelling. Then a lookout shouted, "Hurrah!" Round, a small, young man with a thin beard, a Yankee officer sitting atop the highest point in a captured Southern capital city, knew instantly what it meant. The South had surrendered; the fighting was over. He aimed his signal rockets heavenward, lighting the night sky with what became the last Signal Corps message of the war: "Peace on Earth, Good Will to Men."

Round returned to civilian life and college and moved to Manassas. He lived in a large antebellum home, and each day around 11 a.m. his wife would step out on their porch and watch for him to depart his law office on Center Street. (If he waved a handkerchief, it was his signal that he was headed home for lunch.) He built community schools and lined the town streets with shade trees. He pushed for a national preservation battle site where Confederate Gen. Stonewall Jackson made his famous stand near the copse of trees. But his greatest passion was seeing the Jubilee underway. Just as he had done as a signal messenger, he sent out the word. He had ribbons sewn up and honorary badges struck for the veterans. He persuaded the Northern president and the Southern governor to attend. He commissioned poems, prayers, and songs to be sung.

A new peace anthem was drafted. Food, water, and other accommodations were arranged. But the two sides had once been bitter enemies, and not all came together without controversy. Three days before the Jubilee, the Grand Army of the Republic's chapter in Brooklyn, New York, adopted a resolution of protest and sent it to the White House. They asked President Taft to refuse to appear if the Confederate battle flag, the old Stars and Bars, were unfurled and flown there: "Speaking in the name of the comrades who are living and more earnestly and solemnly for the million maimed and dead comrades of the armies of the Union, we protest most emphatically against such an act and demand that the President of the United States take such action as may be proper to prevent it."

The Grand Army's resolution demanded that the Confederate banner be ceremoniously vanquished once and for all, and what better time and place than the Jubilee reunion. "Dig a grave, broad and deep, in the soil of the battlefield and publicly bury the Confederate flag," the Yankees demanded.

That set off howls from the Southern side. The *Manassas Democrat* newspaper editorialized that the Union veterans were missing the point of the reunion. The paper lamented that "such sectional feeling still exists and that it should be expressed at the inauguration of a great peace movement, at a time when the North and the South are being united in friendship with all differences cast aside, is indeed regrettable."

George Round, ever the messenger, sent an urgent press dispatch to the nation's wire services and told his Northern friends that both blue and gray would be recognized. "The Jubilee decorations floating from every part of our town include a thousand square feet of the National colors to every ten square feet of the Confederate colors," he wired. "The Confederate battle flag works beautifully into the prevailing design. Abraham Lincoln loved to hear 'Dixie' and I love to see the battle flag which represents one of the greatest military powers in the world's history nestling so quietly and lovingly in the folds of the Stars and Stripes." "I invite my Brooklyn comrades to come and join our Jubilee," he added.

Pickpockets were another nuisance, and they smoothly worked the swelling crowds. B. C. Cornwell told police he had lost his pocketbook, including cash and a $25 check. Gone were Wilber Clark's wallet with $20 and his train ticket home to California. After the celebrations, nine pocketbooks were found wrapped in a discarded newspaper under a warehouse on Railroad Avenue—all were empty.

But except for these minor distractions, the Peace Jubilee of July 1911 went mostly without a hitch. And while speeches and political hoopla played out on the courthouse grounds, the most somber and memorable moment came earlier in the day at the battle site. There, forming a double line, the 350 ex-Confederates faced north. A dozen yards away, 150 Union veterans faced south. On cue at precisely noon, they advanced toward one another, not with rifles and fixed bayonets but with outstretched arms. Above the Southern line one solitary Virginia state flag waved in the air, the only banner held by either group. They shook hands and patted backs. They recounted old battle tales, and many agreed that their war had been a complete "misunderstanding."

Next followed the speeches downtown and, that evening, after the politicians were gone and the air was quiet again, the clanging of the dinner bell. The old men shuffled up, headed for long tables filled with plates of fried chicken. At nightfall they sat around the campfire. As the light sputtered out, one of the Rebels sang:

> I'm an old Confederate veteran,
> And that's good enough for me.

Another voice heard that night was that of James Redmond, a former slave who lived on the Manassas outskirts, a mile or two southwest of the battlefield. Back in July 1861, when much of this ground was blackened by fire, he had been pressed into burying the dead at Bull Run.

"The Southern soldiers were going about the fields picking up dead men and burying them, but the bodies were still lying around thick," he recalled. "I saw lots of wounded men, crying for water. So I took a bucket and filled it and carried water to what I could. There were a lot of soldiers and colored men doing the same thing. There were about as many wounded of one side as the other, but it didn't make any difference to any of us which side they were. They all got water just the same."

Redmond, now ninety-seven years old, shook his head. "No sir," he said. "I don't ever want to see any more war."

There was another man named James at that Jubilee. He was a white man and a Northerner, and he said he was a Yankee veteran who had come to the reunion from his hometown of Erie, Pennsylvania. James E. Maddox complained to the *Washington Post* that many of the Manassas women refused to give water to thirsty Union veterans at the reunion.

"If Manassas is typical of the hospitality of the South, then I don't wonder the Union soldiers ran for Washington in 1861," he boasted. "It was the best thing they ever did.... From everything that was told me by Confederate veterans, it was plainly evident that the women of Virginia are as bitter as they were ten or twenty years ago. In the midst of this scene, where men were greeting each other and forgetting the wrongs of other days, the women maintained an icy attitude." He said one Confederate told him that "we men who fought against you are willing to forgive and forget. As far as we are concerned, the friendship we pledged today is real and sincere. But our women will never forgive the North."

The locals, led by the Jubilee chairman, wasted no time in firing back. George Round posted an open letter "to my fellow citizens of Manassas," calling the allegations "fabricated and false." He said it was "Satanic malignity" designed to "fire the Southern heart." He called for a retraction from the *Post*. How dare someone, especially a Yankee, impugn the dignity, grace, and gentility of Southern women, the flower of the old Confederacy? He hired H. A. Strong, a leading attorney in Erie, to find out what he could about this "alleged Yankee." Get to the bottom of James E. Maddox, he instructed.

Strong checked the Erie city directory but could not find Maddox listed. He interviewed three members of the local chapter of the Grand Army of the Republic (GAR), all Union veterans of the Civil War. None had heard of Maddox. The quartermaster of the GAR post checked the membership rolls as far back as twenty-five years, but "no such name appeared." Strong inquired at the Pennsylvania Soldiers' and Sailors' Home in Erie. "They never heard of this war veteran," Strong wrote in his report to Round.

Strong visited all three of the Erie daily newspapers and talked with the editors. None knew a whit about James E. Maddox. The editors did, however, advise Strong that no out-of-town correspondent had been in

Former Confederate soldiers, their hats doffed, reenact Pickett's Charge during the 1913 Gettysburg reunion. For the South this was the turning moment in 1863 that ultimately brought defeat. (Courtesy of the Gettysburg National Military Park)

the city to interview anyone, so this Maddox must have been interviewed at the Jubilee in Manassas.

In finalizing his report, Strong urged the Jubilee committee to find Maddox and unmask his true identity. The Manassas newspaper also called for swift vindication. "Let us have this man's name, please!" the paper cried. But the investigation turned up no further details. At a time when the old warriors had come together in peace to heal the wounds of war, to shake hands and pat backs, this one man had singularly managed to mar their triumph. They dismissed him as a fraud.

THE NORTH HOSTED THE SECOND great reunion. Two years after Manassas, the remnants of the two armies gathered for the fiftieth anniversary of the Battle of Gettysburg, at a rural Pennsylvania crossroads between Baltimore and Harrisburg. Here Lee had invaded the enemy's home, hoping to encircle Washington, cut off recruits and supplies, and force a truce. But the Union forces beat him back, especially after Confederate infantry wildly dashed across a sun-dappled peach orchard at one o'clock in the afternoon, led in part by Maj. Gen. George Pickett. This time it was the men in gray who turned and retreated back across the Potomac.

"I went down the Avenue and saw a big flaring placard on the bulletin board of a newspaper office, announcing, 'Glorious Victory for the Union Army!'" wrote the poet Whitman. "The Washington bells are ringing."

The Gettysburg of July 1863 would best be remembered for names such as Meade and Longstreet, Cemetery Ridge and Little Round Top. First to arrive for the reunion amid these old monuments, what the South would later call its high-water mark in the war, was a veteran who gave his name simply as P. Guibert. He said he had fought at Gettysburg as part of a Pennsylvania regiment. Not wanting to miss the reunion, he had left his home in Pittsburgh on May 26—walking. He strode into Gettysburg on June 13, two-and-a-half weeks early.

President Woodrow Wilson, born in Virginia and schooled in New Jersey, delivered the chief address. His earliest childhood memory was hearing that Lincoln had been elected and that war was afoot. Like Taft at Manassas, Wilson challenged the veterans to become symbols of peace rather than relics of war: "We have found one another again as brothers and comrades in arms, enemies no longer, generous friends rather, our battles long past, the quarrel forgotten. We shall not forget the splendid valor, the manly devotion of the men then arrayed against one another, now grasping hands and smiling into each other's eyes. How complete the union has become."

Also like Taft, Wilson's remarks were not the highlight of the day. The spotlight fell on the veterans, especially when a group of grays reenacted Pickett's Charge. Feebly, with canes and walkers, some holding onto one another, they limped with backs bent across a small portion of the orchard and joined hands with their old adversaries in blue.

"It's jest about as hot as the last time we all charged," said one of the Confederates. A Yankee remembered gunning them down as they raced at him: "We shattered their lines with our fire, and every time they just closed up and closed up again as if nothing had happened and kept right on."

The old veterans gathered like brothers now around the Bloody Angle, the spot where Confederates had fought desperately to break the Union line. "The place is right here," recalled one of the Rebels. "I was shot right here where I stand now. I would have died if it hadn't been for a Union solder who saved my life. I've often wished I could see him but I never saw him after that day."

A Union veteran turned sharply around. "That's funny," he said. "I was at the Bloody Angle too, and there was a Rebel there who was pretty badly hurt. I first gave him a drink of water, and then I took him upon my back and carried him out of the line of fire to the field hospital."

"My God!" cried the Rebel. "Let me look at you."

The Confederate stared deeply into the other man's eyes. He grabbed the Yankee by the shoulders. "You are the man!" he shouted. They hugged and traded names. The Confederate was A. C. Smith of Virginia; Albert N. Hamilton of Pennsylvania was his Union savior.

That Pennsylvania summer of 1913 some fifty thousand veterans gathered at Gettysburg. The youngest, who had been a drummer boy at Shiloh, just nine years old when the war broke out, was sixty-one now. The oldest claimed he was a spry 112.

The state legislature authorized $500,000 to help fund the reunion. The money also paid railroad fare for any Pennsylvania Civil War veteran

Comrades now, veterans in gray and blue shake hands at the 1913 Gettysburg reunion, much of the old animosity healed after a half century of peace. (Courtesy of the Gettysburg National Military Park)

strong enough to make the trip. And they came, 22,103 from the home state alone, including 303 who had fought for the Confederacy. In the South, the Virginia chapter of the United Confederate Veterans supplied UCV uniforms for their war heroes.

Army engineers tramped around the fields of Pickett's Charge and chose that crucible spot for the main campground. The army built hundreds of tents, benches, and boardwalks, in all encompassing some 280 acres of battlefield. More than 500 lamps lit up the night, and thirty-two water fountains slaked a massive summer thirst. Two thousand cooks and bakers ran 175 open-air kitchens. For old men, the veterans ate well: 14,000 pounds of chicken and 7,000 fruit pies. Pork roast sandwiches proved a particular favorite. Ice cream helped beat the heat.

Makeshift hospitals and first-aid stations were stationed nearby. Boy Scouts escorted the weak and unsteady. But the reunion took its toll. Nine of the old men died during the weeklong festivities; the heat and humidity as much as their age did them in. August D. Brown of Maine was the first to pass, succumbing before an Army surgeon could reach him. Edgar A. Bigsley from Wisconsin died in his sleep in his tent. At the close of the week, H. H. Hodge of North Carolina dropped dead among the crowd headed home from the train station.

News also arrived of veterans who had died at home, too ill to join their comrades and adversaries at the Gettysburg reunion. Gov. Louis B. Hanna of North Dakota, in one of a series of testimonials during the encampment week, told how a Confederate veteran had just passed away in one of the Northern states. He was buried by ex-Union members of the Grand Army of the Republic at a GAR cemetery. At the gravesite, the GAR commandant told the assembled, "We cannot understand why this man fought for the Stars and Bars while we fought for the Stars and Stripes. But it is enough to know that each man fought for the right. And now, in the spirit of charity and fraternity, we lay him to rest, the Gray beside the Blue."

In Gettysburg they finally broke camp and groups of old men started for home. But as they departed, the peace and goodwill that had sounded throughout the Jubilee was suddenly shattered. In the packed dining room of the Gettysburg Hotel on the town square, seven men were stabbed when a veteran in blue overheard some unkind words about the martyred Lincoln. The fight started suddenly and ended quickly. Knives flashed and bottles were thrown. Women fled for the exits; other ladies raced for the windows, trying to squeeze out. Should there ever be another reunion, they all agreed, let us please close the saloons.

ONE MORE LARGE-SCALE REUNION was to come.

Paul L. Roy, editor of the *Gettysburg Times* and executive secretary of yet another reunion committee, labored hard to pull off a seventy-fifth anniversary encampment in July 1938. He faced several obstacles. How old and feeble were the men, and how many were left? And would those still living join hands yet again?

"In my years of preliminary preparation and planning, I failed to reckon with certain unreconstructed factions in the South," Roy wrote afterward, "and equally stubborn and irreconcilable forces in the North." He found pockets of Confederate and Union veterans "together with allied groups who, for some time, had been trying to guide" their own separate destinies.

The early 1930s had seen a series of state reunions in the South, in places such as Shreveport, Louisiana, and Jackson, Mississippi. In the North, the GAR staged its own get-togethers. What Roy wanted was one final joint reunion of the two colors. The Confederates invited him to discuss it at their meetings, but they always turned his idea down unless they could be assured their flag would be welcome. The Northern men, however, did not want the Rebel flag anywhere near them.

So Roy traveled often to the South, hoping to broker a compromise. In Jackson, at a meeting of Southern veterans, he urged one more joint commemoration, and again the South said no. Then the United Confederate Veterans organization endorsed his compromise of separate sections for separate flags. About to leave the auditorium, Roy at last felt hopeful. Then he stepped outside.

"Several women blocked my way and started to harangue me as a 'damn Yankee' who was 'trying to kill our veterans,'" he recalled. "Two women scratched my face and tried to tear my coat off, all while shouting and shrieking unprintable accusations. But I managed to elude their clutches and escape to my hotel room."

The flag issue continued to vex veterans from both sides. James W. Willett, a ninety-one-year-old former GAR commander in chief from Tama, Iowa, said, "I won't vote yes if they are to have their flag on display."

"They can go to hell," exclaimed his Confederate veteran counterpart, Rice Pierce.

M. J. Bonner, a national leader with the United Confederate Veterans organization, worried that if the two old armies met again without the flag controversy settled, "the war would be renewed."

David Corbin Ker, the last surviving Rebel in Richland Parish, Louisiana, was so angry that his wife had to hold him back from going to Gettysburg and flying the Dixie flag in defiance. Ker had enlisted at fourteen, he said, in the second year of the war, and had served under both Stonewall Jackson and Robert E. Lee. He said he hailed from a family of "fightin' Texans," and that his father and two grandfathers had seen duty in the War of 1812. Ker liked to boast how his father was a major in the Battle of New Orleans. As for himself, he served mostly in Virginia. But "all through the war I tried to get with the Bloody Texans, where I belonged but couldn't make it. I would have much rather been with them because they knew how to fight and didn't mind it. Oh, I got a few scratches during the war. Maybe some people would call them wounds, but a fightin' Texan wouldn't." Now he was going on ninety-one and was still ornery. He kept a small farm near the town of Mangham, after moving to Louisiana to be near his daughter. Asked why at his age he still had rosy pink cheeks, he admitted that most of the heavy work around the place was done by an "ancient Negro." But Ker still got around okay, and he was determined not to go anywhere where the Stars and Bars was banned. "My wife don't want me to go because she thinks I'll get in another fight with them d–– Yankees," he said. "And maybe I would."

Harry Rene Lee, even older at ninety-eight and adjutant general of the national UCV, firmed up the Southern position when he warned, "No flag will ever lead ours. The American flag can be on the right, where it belongs, but it must be even and even."

The standoff eventually was resolved with Roy's compromise. Each side would fly its own banners in their own camps at Gettysburg.

There still remained the larger question. By 1938, Civil War veterans were passing away at the rate of 900 a year. It was guessed that a little more than ten thousand were still alive, and no more than two thousand could be expected to make the final trek to Gettysburg, given that all but a few of them were well over ninety.

Organizers found little problem locating and verifying Union veterans. Their service records were intact and many belonged to the GAR, the fraternal body of state chapters for former Yankee soldiers. Finding Confederates proved more difficult. Many records were lost or incomplete, file folders gone altogether. Southern home guards and guerrilla units had enlisted soldiers for short periods to protect communities, and those service rolls had long been misplaced or destroyed—if there ever were records. So the reunion committee's ground rules stated that if no records existed, or a man was not a member of a veterans' group or did not receive a Civil War pension, he would not be invited.

Formal invitations were mailed to 10,500 men. In 2,243 cases, the letters were returned marked "deceased." Others sent regrets. "I am very deaf and my sight is failing, but if I am able I will be glad to come," William Perrine of the 1st New Jersey Cavalry wrote to the committee. His daughter, Gertrude Van Nest, mailed a follow-up letter the next month to Gettysburg. It would be too much for him, she said. "The excitement of going has upset his mind. He is ninety-four years old and never traveled very much, as he has been very deaf since the war."

About 1,845 blue and gray veterans eventually crowded into Gettysburg for the final hoopla. The vast majority were Yankees, if only because Pennsylvania was closer. Albert Woolson, the former Union drummer boy who by the 1950s would lay dying in Duluth, was on hand. Walter Williams, his Confederate counterpart, stayed home in Houston, though most of the men in gray who did make it to Gettysburg hailed from Texas.

Roy and his committee set up first-aid stations and wellness centers around the battlefield. A regimental hospital with 140 beds was opened in the dormitory at Gettysburg College. Wooden walkways were installed, and wheelchairs rolled out. Boxes of soap, brushes, and other toiletries were carted in. Sewer lines were dug. Barbers clipped beards short enough to beat the July heat. Each veteran in every tent was given a cot and mattress, and handed a pillow, sheets, and a wool blanket. The tents came equipped with electric lights, wash basins, soap and towels, canes and walkers, and in some cases stretchers. Many of the men dressed smartly in their old battle regalia (if they could still fit into the pants and jackets) and sat on lawn chairs to pass the long afternoons. Most fell asleep.

The keynote speech was again delivered by a president. Franklin Delano Roosevelt phrased all the right sentiments about peace and brotherhood for a once divided nation. An Eternal Light Peace Memorial was set aglow, and the president proclaimed that all the old men in their old colors "stand together under one flag now."

Perhaps more poignant were the words from Dr. Overton H. Mennet of California: "I see here before me a beautiful national military park where once men lay in agony." The commander in chief of the GAR and a former Indiana infantryman, he appeared resplendent in his double-breasted blue Union jacket, gold-corded, broad-brimmed hat, and bow tie.

The Southern cause's words were put to music, as the bands played "Dixie."

Suffering aches and arthritis, ears that did not hear and eyes that could not see well, legs no longer sturdy enough to manage their failing, ailing bodies, many of the veterans nevertheless had arrived in Gettysburg in high spirits. John Milton Claypool, a ninety-two-year-old retired preacher and Confederate commander of the UCV post in Missouri, joked that "since the Lord has put up with the Yankees all this time, I guess I can also for a few days." Alvin F. Tolman, a ninety-year-old Union man who still drove his own car, motored up from his home in Florida, arriving early at the encampment. He teased that he wanted "to get my pick of the Gettysburg women." Charles W. Eldridge, wounded five times by Confederates, celebrated his 107th birthday during the reunion. "Never had an ache of pain," he claimed. "I'll feel good for another ten years at least."

From California 121 veterans had boarded special trains and headed east to Pennsylvania. From Arkansas, Texas, Louisiana, and Missouri came 450, mostly Confederates. Louis Quint drove down from Minnesota at ninety. Ninety-two-year-old A. G. Harris, once a Confederate major general, was escorted by his son, Homer, who had soldiered in World War I. Warren Fisher of California, a Union soldier in two dozen engagements, was ninety-two years old and brought Daisy, his sixty-four-year-old wife. A North Carolina man brought his bride too; he said he was 105, and his wife thirty-eight.

Many of them achieved incredible feats of endurance. Ninety-six-year-old M. A. Loop from Sacramento, California, climbed the stairs to the top of a seventy-foot steel observation tower on Oak Ridge. The ex-Yankee wanted a panoramic view of the battlefield and encampments, but also to escape the autograph seekers down below. He came down the steps without stopping to rest. James Handcock, who had traveled to Gettysburg from the Confederate Home in New Orleans, snuck off for a day of sightseeing in Philadelphia. Police found him sound asleep at a ball game, his pipe in his mouth. He told the police he was 104.

Despite all the health precautions, by the time the reunion ended five of the veterans had died in Gettysburg. One was John W. Weaver Sr., a Tennessee cavalryman during the last year of the war, who later farmed, ran a saw mill, and shoed horses. He had married twice and outlived both wives. He was eighty-nine now, and his heart gave out in a Gettysburg hospital. Another veteran died on the last day of festivities at a hospital just outside of town. Six more collapsed returning home.

Rumors floated about plans for an eighty-fifth reunion. "I wouldn't put anything past this crew," said ninety-seven-year-old Samuel B. Hanson of Philadelphia, a Union veteran. "Some of the boys are struttin' around here like they're fifty."

Some veterans did not want to leave the reunion at all. A small band led by William W. Banks of Alabama refused to depart the federally owned battlefield park. They sent a telegram to the quartermaster general's office in Washington asking permission to stay for as long as they wanted, or at least until the Lord sent his angels. "We have been the humble guests of the greatest nation on the earth and as such have walked on and viewed again the sacred ground and shrines at Gettysburg made Holy by the blood of patriot martyrs, North and South," they wired. "We desire to remain here on this hallowed hill till Gabriel shall call us to that eternal party where there is no strife, bitter hate, nor bloodshed. We are one for all and all for one. Please wire immediate that we shall stay."

Washington did not respond, and the veterans returned home.

3

OLD AGE AND STOLEN VALOR

Eighteen years after the veterans departed Gettysburg, police found an old woman from Georgia wandering the streets of a small town in New York State, just over the Pennsylvania line. She was stooped, wrinkled, and incoherent. The authorities drove her to a hospital in Binghamton, New York, for examination and began searching for her family.

Helen Dortch Longstreet was ninety-five years old. Born in the year of the Battle of Gettysburg, she would die during the Civil War Centennial, living just a year short of 100. She was the widow of Confederate Gen. James Longstreet, whom many held accountable for the bloody failure that was Pickett's Charge, and once she had been revered both as the "Belle of the Post-Confederacy" and the "Fighting Lady of the South." She preferred the latter, a title she grandly wore in her lifelong efforts trying to salvage her husband's reputation from what went wrong in that peach field. She married him when she was thirty-four and he was seventy-six at a ceremony held inside the Governor's Mansion on Peachtree Street in Atlanta. He died seven years later, and she then set out to resurrect his image. Now, in the spring of 1956, she was found lost and confused in Elmira, New York.

In Atlanta her brother, John Dortch, had been waiting for word from a friend of his sister's who was supposed to check on her condition up north. The New York authorities located Dortch, and they exchanged telegrams. She had left Augusta, Georgia, about a week earlier, taking a bus to New York for reasons unknown. At Elmira the bus company's staff was amazed at the vitality of the old woman, but for good measure they put her in the care of the local Travelers Aid Society, which took her to the Elmira YWCA. Then she walked off.

Dortch brought her home to Georgia and placed her with the Milledgeville State Hospital. She died there a pensioner, frail and hard of hearing, alone and nearly forgotten. Her death came on the ninety-eighth anniversary of the Battle of the Wilderness, where her husband, part of Gen. Robert E. Lee's top command, was fired on by mistake by his own troops.

When she had met Longstreet, she was immediately touched by his "wounds and sadness." He was four decades her senior, quite ancient in any young woman's eyes, yet in Helen he stirred a "poetic interest." She was a student at Brenau College in Gainesville, Georgia, and a friend of his daughter from a previous marriage. Helen had been studying about General Longstreet in her history class and writing essays about his exploits against the Northern invaders. Her father had opposed the war. Her mother, "a noted belle of the period," had "danced the hours away through the stormy years of the war on a great plantation in the picturesque Georgia mountains," as Helen would later write. But the young girl had three uncles in uniform, and she swooned at the sight of a man in Confederate gray. Longstreet's gallantry melted her heart.

They settled at his farm near Gainesville. The scuppernong-covered cottage was small, on a slight rise of red clay, and many of the general's detractors sarcastically derided it as "Little Round Top." It reminded them of that small bloody rise at Gettysburg. Indeed, Helen soon learned that her husband was all but condemned by many in the old Southern aristocracy, and by the rising generation as well. When he died, the United Daughters of the Confederacy in Savannah voted not to send flowers.

The Widow Longstreet knew full well what the others thought, especially after he died in January 1904. "The supreme hours with my husband were all too fleeting," she wrote. "When I closed his eyelids in death and faced the barren years, it was not easy to gather up broken threads and begin life over."

But that is exactly what she did. Helen Dortch Longstreet outlived him by fifty-eight years. She became the first woman to hold state office in Georgia, as an assistant state librarian, and was the first woman to have her portrait hung in the state capitol. She fought efforts by the Georgia Power Company to turn the famed Tallulah Falls into a power source. She wrote essays and books about her husband, working hard to salvage his name. She appeared at newspaper offices around the South, always bearing something new to share about her long-gone husband. She tirelessly pushed for memorials, tributes, and statues of General Longstreet commemorating his honor, constantly firing off letters to raise funds.

The *New York Times* hired her as a special correspondent to cover the two great Gettysburg reunions in 1913 and 1938. "I am writing an answer to all the unfair and false statements made against Gen. Longstreet. His judgment saved them from worse defeat," she wrote from the national battlefield, twice filled with blue and gray veterans. "Gen. Lee relied on his advice, and took the whole blame for defeat at Gettysburg after the battle."

She sat in a little wooden chair in a small tent on the battlefield grounds, bent over a manual typewriter on her lap, dressed in high heels and a swooping flowered hat. Her purse dangled from the arm of the chair. Two small Confederate flags flew nearby. Unbowed in ninety-two-degree heat, she tapped away, her fingers flying, determined to redeem her husband.

With gusto she glorified not just the men who had served under her husband but those in blue as well. "Gettysburg's bugles echo today over a reunited nation," she wrote. "Standing on the borderland of eternity with its shadows touching their bent forms and silvered heads, these last survivors ... have gathered here."

She returned to Georgia and was appointed vice president of a Catholic group called the Army of Prayer. During World War II she worked as a riveter for Bell Aircraft in Atlanta. "I was at the head of my class in riveting school," she told *Life* magazine. "In fact I was the only one in it." Each morning she left her trailer home and drove her Nash coupe to the plant. Along with other women supporting the war effort, she pulled the 8 to 4:45 shift. She was already eighty years old, yet still full of heart and vinegar. "I'm going to assist in building a plane to bomb Hitler to the Judgment Seat of God," she proclaimed. A *Life* photograph showed her in the plant's break room at lunchtime, perched atop a long table, a sandwich in one hand, a Dixie cup in the other, regaling a young admirer with stories of Lt. Gen. James Longstreet. She wore a black visor cap, black sweater, black pants, and white socks. She may have been eighty, but to land the job she had listed her age and background as "50 plus, centuries-old experience, and between 17 and 18 in mind and body." She insisted on doing her part to win the war. "I couldn't stay out," she said. "The thought of American boys dying on the battlefields."

The Bell plant was criticized for hiring Helen. The local labor union complained it was a publicity stunt to trade on her famous name. They said her job should have gone to some out-of-work Georgian more deserving of a paycheck. They also complained that the company had hired someone so old.

Helen bristled. "Who is still alive who can recall when I was born?"

When work slowed, more questions were raised, and dozens of fellow employees gathered to gaze at the old riveter, she carried on undaunted. She boasted she could outwork them all, that her eyesight was as clear as when she was twenty, and that she had not seen a doctor in two decades. "Now if you don't mind," she announced, "I'll go back to my work. We're holding up production."

Long a liberal, she ran for governor of Georgia in the early 1950s, hopelessly trying to unseat the enormously popular Herman Talmadge. Her campaign stationery included a top hat with stars and stripes and her motto, "United We Stand." But Helen was disastrously defeated, and her legend faded.

Her death in May 1962 left 136 Confederate widows in the state, but almost all of them were much younger because they had been born long after the war had ended. Elsewhere in the South, the widow closest to her in stature was "Mother Pickett" from Virginia, the wife of George.

LaSalle Corbell Pickett was a writer too, and she also spent much of her postwar life trying to rehabilitate her husband for that ill-fated dash at Gettysburg. She had married the major general two months after his command was decimated in Pennsylvania. The postwar years were hard on Mother Pickett. For a while the couple lived in Canada, where he sold insurance and she sold jewelry. The second of their two sons, seven-year-old David Corbell Pickett, died of measles one Easter Sunday. Scarlet fever took her husband. Then she set out on a highly romanticized promotional tour to redeem her husband's legacy. She also sought to reinvent herself. She fudged her age and claimed to be twenty years younger, dubbing herself the "Child-bride of the Confederacy."

She moved to Washington and worked for a time as a nameless government clerk in the Federal Pensions Office. Like Helen, she too ended her days inside a sanatorium; hers was in Rockville, Maryland, outside of Washington. The walls of her tiny apartment were decorated with documents and photographs of Civil War heroes, the ghosts of her past. She broke a hip, her arteries hardened, and she grew weary from a long illness. She died on the first day of spring in 1931. Her correct age, when best sorted out, put her close to ninety.

And that is what endeared LaSalle Corbell Pickett and Helen Dortch Longstreet to much of the country, North and South. It was the sheer length of their days. To live that long, to approach the century mark, was a marvel in a time filled with the agonies of war, the struggles of Reconstruction and the Great Depression, and the long lean years when many endured poverty, hard labor, and incurable disease. A common cold could put a man down. A cut or a scrape could mean gangrene. Doctors and hospitals often were far away. Medicine was not so modern. Not only were there measles and scarlet fever, but also smallpox and diphtheria and a run of epidemics—including a deadly scourge of influenza. Who could hope to make it to old age, much less 100?

In 1959 Dr. Paul D. White of Boston, tackling the medical question of longevity, provided the *New England Journal of Medicine* with the story of his remarkable patient, Charles W. Thiery. Born in 1850, Thiery had died in 1958 at the age of 107. He was born of "sturdy Huguenot stock" in Cambridge, Massachusetts. At the age of two his parents feared him "almost fatally ill" with pneumonia. When he died in Boston, he succumbed to bronchopneumonia. Otherwise, he had rarely if ever been ill. He did suffer normal childhood ailments, and he broke an arm falling from a tree. At twenty he came down with typhoid fever. Other than that, "he had very little illness until his final pneumonia," Dr. White wrote. "There were occasional colds or attacks of grippe, one of which was rather severe in his 104th year and required a good many weeks of convalescence. He also for many years was bothered somewhat by 'nervous indigestion,' which, he said, prevented him from eating as much as most of his friends who died at much younger ages. His only other complaint was that he was somewhat hard of hearing which, however, was not very evident most of the time following my first examination of him three days after his 100th birthday."

Thiery exercised daily. He would fly up and down the stairs. He took off on long walks, sometimes twenty-five miles in five hours. He never married, never smoked, and never drank. He stayed away from eggs but ate more than his share of ice cream. "He enjoyed life, liked company, and spoke easily and wittily with a cheerful twinkle in his eye," the doctor wrote. "Occasionally Mr. Thiery would reminisce about the American Civil War. Lincoln and Grant were heroes of his."

But he had missed serving in the war. A mere eleven when a Confederate battery fired on Fort Sumter, he was just fifteen when Rebel soldiers stacked their rifles in defeat. His father had taken him out of school in 1861 anyway, putting him to work as a messenger in a watch case factory across from Boston's Old South Church. Two years after the war, he joined the Boston Light Dragoons. For eight years he served in its 1st Brigade, earning the rank of sergeant.

Afterward Thiery lived mostly alone, voting the straight Republican ticket every four years, from General Grant to General Eisenhower. His mother had died at thirty-eight, a sister at twenty-one. But a brother, whom Thiery remembered as a "puny boy" in childhood, lived to ninety-two. If longevity was embedded in the family genes, no one would have guessed. A modest man, he cleared a century and more, thinking maybe there was a biblical explanation. "A good many people would live to be my age if they followed the Book," he counseled. "Go to God. You'll get the right answer."

For eighty-two years he worked in silver- and goldsmithing, retiring at ninety-three. In that first medical examination with Dr. White, shortly after Thiery turned 100, the physician found an "elderly man with white hair, beard, and moustache, short (63 inches) and slight (115 pounds) in build." His eyesight was good; his heart was strong, his pulse and blood pressure near perfect.

At the century mark, Thiery wrote a letter to Dr. White:

For nearly a year I have had some cream with my crackers and milk for my supper two thirds of the week, and bread and butter with perhaps a little cake. Eggs I don't eat in any form unless in something already cooked. They do not agree with me. Butter seems all right.

I have to be careful about going up stairs after dinner now, or my heart is affected. In the middle of the day I can eat a fair sized dinner with other people. If I eat a fairly good meal, just before retiring I use my back rest to sit up the first quarter of the night, and lie down the rest of the night. I am not a good sleeper generally. I seldom go out of an evening.

My strange start in life was because my parents were poor but honest and my mother lived mostly on brown bread until she gagged, so she said.

In 1957, at 106, he was still exercising and averaging a mile or more on his daily walks. In 1958 his elderly landlord died. The landlord's wife, who had been frail for years, suffered a fall and later died. Thiery had tried to help her, but then he fell too. Taken to a nursing home, he was diagnosed with pneumonia. He died on March 16.

"There is little to add to this account in the way of discussion," Dr. White summed up in his clinical history. "Every centenarian is asked why he lived so long. Usually the answer is 'by the grace of God,' which was also one of Mr. Thiery's several answers. Such a reason is, of course, a combination of the influence of heredity, an escape from serious accidents and fatal infections, and the effect of the ways of life.

"Doubtless all of these factors were operative in Mr. Thiery's case. We cannot credit any one for the entire responsibility—his abstinence from the use of tobacco or alcohol or the fact that he never married, or even his nervous indigestion which prevented him from eating as much as some of his friends who died a generation earlier."

The physician made one final observation, this one perhaps the most astute of all. "Old age doesn't kill a person," he wrote. "It may doubtless make a person more susceptible to strains. But my idea is that a person doesn't die of old age. He has either pneumonia or something like it."

THE CIVIL WAR DID NOT LACK centenarians. Henry Dorman was cited in the *New York Times* in 1910 as the first veteran to live to be well over 100. Maybe the oldest, even—the paper put him at 111. But that would have made him sixty-two when the fighting broke out in 1861 and sixty-four when he said he enlisted. According to his story, four of his sons joined the Union army, and when one of them died in prison, Henry signed up too. He said he served with a western cavalry unit for two years and was discharged after being severely wounded in the left hand. By 1910 he was "very feeble and helpless" and living with a daughter-in-law in tiny Liberal, Missouri.

Union records show that a Henry Dorman did serve with Troop F, 7th Michigan Cavalry. But that Henry Dorman saw action throughout the war—at Gettysburg and South Mountain and Spotsylvania, and fighting around Richmond at the close of the war. Those battles were held along the Eastern Seaboard; none were waged out west. There also was no mention of a gunshot wound or a shattered left hand.

Nevertheless Dorman became quite the celebrity in Liberal, especially to J. P. Moore, a young newspaperman covering the small community for the *Liberal News*. In a book he wrote years later in 1963, at the time of the Civil War Centennial, Moore recalled his newspaper days meeting the older men around town. "Wylie S. Van Camp, who usually used only the initials, W. S., and by these initials he was generally called, was one of the first comers to Liberal," he wrote. "He was a well educated man, a veteran of the Civil War, a lawyer, and had been a school teacher in his younger days. Here he practiced law and made brooms for a livelihood."

Van Camp served as a city clerk and also played the fife, an instrument he had picked up in the army. On summer evenings he would sit outside the door of "the small shack where he lived on Main Street and blow the fife for his own amusement, and probably hoping to be heard." But, Moore recalled, "with all his ability, Van Camp was something of a derelict. Strong drink was his failing. He loved his liquor, and to see him soused was not an uncommon sight on the streets of Liberal."

Henry Dorman moved to Liberal in 1903. Moore found him fascinating, and he strongly disagreed with the big city newspapermen who visited Dorman during his last years, primarily to speculate about how old the man really was. They often filed stories suggesting he was not telling the truth. They thought he seemed eighty, if a day.

But Moore believed the old man was 115 in 1914. "Mr. Dorman was a Civil War veteran and received a pension," Moore wrote. "In those days it was required that a pension check be signed before a notary public. I was a notary public then and went once a month to Mr. Dorman's home to notarize his check during the last years of his life.... To gaze upon the aged man's countenance was to be filled with awe. Words can hardly describe his ancient-appearing visage—to such a vast age did he appear to be. One's thoughts turned to the catacombs of old Rome. He was very feeble in his last days."

There was one problem, though. When the out-of-town reporters came to Liberal, they brought a camera and one of them snapped the old man's picture. It later was made into a postcard that circulated around the country, and over the years it became a bit of a collector's item. It shows Dorman a year and a half before he died, lying on a Jenny Lind bed, the sheets pulled up to his chin, his head propped on a pillow. All that can be seen is his scowling face and his left hand, the hand he said a Rebel gun had blown apart in the Civil War. But the photograph reveals no visible scar. His left hand looks perfectly fine. So do his long fingers. Not one of them is missing.

Another curious old man appeared in another small Missouri town in the eastern part of the state, just south of St. Louis. In March 1950 inside a courtroom in Union, 250 lawyers and spectators watched as J. Frank Dalton was carried in on a stretcher. Long white hair sprawled atop his head; gray whiskers covered most of his face. One set of fingers gripped a pearl-handled revolver, while the other hand held a tomato can he used for a spittoon. Dalton claimed to be as old as the Ozark hills. He said his real name was Jesse James.

The two-day trial would determine whether Jesse James the outlaw ever took that bullet years ago in St. Joseph, Missouri, or instead lived on in the person of bedridden J. Frank Dalton. The real Jesse James rode as a Confederate guerilla and bushwhacker during the Civil War. To many he was acclaimed the "last Rebel" of the lost war because he had carried the fight into the tough and lean years of defeat and Reconstruction.

Dalton, claiming he was 102 years old, knew there was a lot of money riding on a court judgment that he was Jesse James. This was 1950, after all. There might be a book deal or a Hollywood movie. He was willing to offer sworn testimony about those desperate years riding with Quantrill's Raiders in the border skirmishes around Missouri. Two years earlier he had started telling his neighbors in Lawton, Oklahoma, that someone else was shot in April 1882 in that house in St. Joe, and that it was not Jesse James straightening a picture on the wall who died. The real Jesse escaped alive, he said. It was all a scheme to fool federal authorities and Pinkerton detectives into thinking he was dead.

Dalton did know a good amount about Quantrill and the James and Younger gangs. He could spin tales about train robberies and bank heists and other midnight banditry that had terrorized much of the Midwest. So the Oklahoma reporters put him in the papers, and soon enough the story spread and eventually landed in New York.

Robert C. Ruark, a popular columnist for the *New York World Telegram*, headed straight for Stanton, Missouri. Dalton by then had moved to a modest rustic home there because, he said, he used to hide out in the dark, dank caves nearby to keep federal marshals from finding him after he staged his killing.

Ruark wrote three columns in July 1949, trying to separate the Dalton myth from the James legend. He called his first column "Dead or Alive." He found "the old man who says he is Jesse James lying all day in a cabin under tall trees close to the Meramec caverns in which history says he once hid out from the law." He was bedfast from a broken hip, but his mind was still "whip-sharp." He was a touch deaf and nearly blind but "full of scrap." Everyone around Stanton called him "Uncle Jesse."

"Even at his age, his resemblance to the authenticated photos of the outlaw is amazing," Ruark wrote. "There are the cavernous eyes, the same sharply cut nostrils, the same sweep to his hair, the same scraggly growth of beard, the same set to the ears. Jesses James was supposed to have lost a fingertip in a gun accident. Old man Dalton's left hand shows a ruined, twisted nail."

But Ruark was not sure. Like any good reporter, he had his doubts. "I don't know whether the old gent is in reality the man he claims to be. But his story is remarkably tight." He told his readers "at this point I am 60 per cent sure he is the old outlaw, and in tomorrow's piece I will probably convince myself of the other 40 per cent."

The second installment was headlined "Uncle Jesse's Proof." Here Ruark presented the evidence. "He is still a cagy old man. He will admit directly to no robbery or murder, but he can give you some magnificent first-hand details that would be pretty hard for a man 102 years old to parrot for the purpose of carrying off a hoax. When Uncle Jesse—now I'm calling him Uncle Jesse, too—speaks of the past, he sounds exactly like my grandpa used to sound when he was telling of his life in the Civil War."

Dalton told Ruark he joined Quantrill's Raiders when he was fifteen, and he spoke vaguely about how his Civil War enlistment first drew enemy blood. "It is the only killing that he will admit," Ruark wrote, "because he does not construe it as murder." The war was still fresh when Dalton said he and Cole Younger rode to Independence, Missouri, to file some papers at the Jackson County Courthouse. He said he waited with the horses when a Yankee patrol with two lieutenants and a captain drew up. They demanded the horses. Dalton said no. They accused him of stealing the horses. Dalton unholstered and shot the captain and killed one of the lieutenants. "His hatred of the damn yanks is still immense," Ruark wrote of Dalton. "He says that when he tried to surrender at the end of the Civil War, he was ambushed."

The old man recalled several secret passageways into the Meramec Caverns. He knew about a schoolhouse fire that had never made it into the James legend. "Bit by bit he has convinced all the people around him of authenticity, and I suppose that includes me," Ruark wrote.

The final column ran the next day: "Jesse James? Hmm." Dalton said a friend named Charlie Bigelow, "who looked enough like me to be my twin," was the one shot dead by Bob Ford in St. Joseph. Dalton said he heard the gunfire, then found Bigelow on the floor and Ford standing over him. He told Ford, "This is my chance, Bob. You tell 'em it's me you killed. You tell my mother to say so.... I'm long gone."

Ruark looked into the old man's face, searching for truth. Dalton stammered. He started to describe once walking out of a movie theater because he did not like the way the picture portrayed Jesse James. "I left after

15 minutes," he told Ruark. "That damn silly business about me standing on a chair to hang a picture. You've all been in that house in St. Joe.
You know what a low ceiling it's got. Why would a man as tall as me be
standing on a so-and-so chair to hang a picture when I could do it easier
standing on the floor?"

Ruark summed up Dalton this way: "If the old man has not been
proved he has not yet been disproved, and there is certainly a chance
that he is all he says. I prefer to hope that he is telling the truth. For Jesse
James or not Jesse James, that old boy in the Ozarks cabin had a tremendous life.... If the old man wasn't there, he was certainly thereabouts."

In the Union courtroom, Dalton tried to convince the judge to declare
him the one and only Jesse James. But Circuit Judge Ransom A. Breuer,
himself just turned eighty, wanted to see some evidence and hear a little
testimony. He allowed the matter to proceed.

"Cut out that damned picture taking!" Dalton hollered at photogra-
phers as he was carried into court. He drew an old frontier model six-
shooter from beneath his blanket and waved it about. Everyone reeled
back. But Dalton did not fire, nor did he lose hold of a ten-gallon hat resting on his stomach. They set the stretcher down near the witness stand
and propped Dalton up on two pillows. His goatee and sideburns were
coated with thick tobacco juice, what he called his "eatin'."

First to testify was an old pal, 109-year-old Col. James R. Davis, a self-
described former Confederate officer from Nashville. He told the court
he had known Jesse James in the old days and frequently met him "by
accident" as far away as Kansas and Tennessee. He said Jesse had faked
his death in order to steer clear of the law. "I'm just as sure of him as I am
of myself," Davis said.

He said it was Charlie Bigelow who was killed, not Jesse James, and
that he had arrived at Jesse's rented home in St. Joseph about an hour
after the shooting and recognized Bigelow's body. "I've got one foot in
the grave and the other on the brink," he proclaimed. "But I tell you now,
once and for all, this man is the real Jesse James." Davis was right about
that first part—he died the next day.

Dalton testified from his stretcher. He said he was outside the house
in St. Joseph when the fatal bullet ended someone else's life. "I was at the

stable currying the horses when I heard a shot," Dalton said. "I went in the house and found Bigelow on the floor." He seethed at the faces of disbelief. "Jesse James is not dead!" he hollered. "I'm Jesse James!"

But another witness, John Roach, reported that he was standing in a yard behind a St. Joseph funeral parlor when they brought the body in. "I pulled back the sheet from his face and said, 'You've sure got him. That's Jesse James.'" He said he recognized the Confederate outlaw's birthmark. "Looked exactly like a tater," Roach said.

Judge Breuer had heard enough. He looked down upon Dalton lying on the stretcher. "There is no evidence here to show that this gentleman, if he ever was Jesse James, has ever changed his name," the judge ruled. "If he isn't what he professes to be, then he is trying to perpetrate a fraud upon this court." And if he was Jesse James, then he should "ask the good God above to forgive him."

Case dismissed.

MONEY AND FAME WERE NOT ALL that drove a fraud. Sometimes it was nothing more than a hot meal and a warm bed. Soon after J. Frank Dalton was exposed as a phony in Missouri, another old man was recuperating in a hospital in Nevada. He too said he had fought in the Civil War.

In July 1951 he was hitchhiking with a thirty-pound bag over his shoulder on a highway outside of Reno when he fell to the pavement. A truck driver gave him a lift into town, dropping him off at the local Red Cross shelter. The drifter told the manager of the shelter that he had been discharged in March 1865 from the Pennsylvania 184th Regiment. He stayed the night at the shelter, and in the morning the manager arranged a hotel room for him. But the old man said he was restless and wanted to push on. He was trying to find his long-lost great-great-grandson. He also said he was hungry and wanted breakfast. So he hoisted his bag and stepped out onto Virginia Street, looking for a diner. Then he collapsed again.

This time they whisked him to the Washoe General Hospital and treated him for a heart attack. They placed him under an oxygen tent. He slept a few hours and when he awoke he told the staff he was J. W. Boyer, 104 years old and a former lieutenant in the Union army. Soon enough he had a private room with a private nurse. The next morning the local newspaper ran his picture on the front page—sitting up in his hospital bed, knife in one hand, fork in the other, about to start in on a big piece of steak. After dinner he enjoyed a cigarette. Then he smoked another. Night nurse Frances Cunningham fluffed up his pillows.

He seemed talkative and cheerful, though the staff worried that his condition was precarious. He weighed less than a hundred pounds. It was hot outside, and he had been lugging that heavy backpack. He scratched his beard a lot; he said it itched.

All of his accommodations were provided free of charge by the Washoe County Medical Association. His story also moved the Ladies Auxiliary of the Grand Army of the Republic (GAR) to send him flowers. He said he had been thumbing his way from a retirement home in San Diego to northern Nevada to hook up with the great-great-grandson he thought was living in or near Carson City. He said the great-great-grandson, Robert Dawson, was his last remaining relative, and Robert had sent him a letter post-marked from the state capital. So he assumed Robert lived in Carson City.

Everyone started looking for Robert Dawson, but no one in Carson City had heard of him. Yet Boyer persisted. He has to be around here, he said. His great-great-grandson had recognized him in a group photograph of GAR members published in a national magazine. Robert had written to the magazine and was given an address for a Lieutenant Boyer in San Diego. Dawson then wrote Boyer in San Diego but left no forwarding address. Now Boyer had come looking for him.

The Veterans Administration pored through War Department files and other records in Washington, and officials located a Lt. John Boyer who had served with the Pennsylvania Volunteers. But this Lieutenant Boyer was dead, and the remaining Union veterans from that regiment were all accounted for. Hearing the news, Boyer suddenly felt another heart attack coming on. The doctors placed him under an oxygen tent.

"I'm just looking for the last of my kin," he cried.

The newspapers said the old man seemed delusional and might be dying. Officials soon decided he was not a veteran of any war, and not eligible for any veterans' benefits. He then said he must have been con-fused, and maybe he meant to say he had served with an Indiana outfit during the Civil War. But GAR headquarters in Indianapolis had nothing on him either. From out of his bag Boyer produced some old, yellowed War Department papers, but they did not match him.

The hospital discharged him, and Veterans Administration authorities revealed that in truth he was Walter Engle Urwiler, a mere sixty-nine years old, notorious for pretending to be a Civil War veteran. His habit was checking into hospitals with fake heart attacks. He had a condition known as a "diaphragmatic flutter" and could make his heart speed up to 300 beats a minute.

He was widely known in medical case histories. "In various hospitals," reported the journal *Psychosomatic Medicine*, "he has assumed the role of a deep-sea diver, trapper, miner, retired army or navy officer, and sheriff. He has identified himself with the Civil War, Spanish-American War and World Wars I and II. More recently he has grown a full beard, and favors the Civil War.... He has entertained fellow patients with his exploits as a drummer boy during the American Civil War."

In the *Journal of the American Medical Association*, Urwiler was dismissed as "a pathological liar" who had "greeted each of his medical examiners in recent years with fantastic life stories which agree only in their incredibility. He has been traced to a number of hospitals in different states under different names and has given widely dissimilar versions of his personal and medical history."

Chased out of Reno, Urwiler showed up within a week at a hospital in Susanville, California. He was taken there after "collapsing" on the street once again. He put on his dying act and told the nurses that this was going to be his "death bed."

Then Dr. Arthur Bachelor walked into the room and told Urwiler he knew the truth about his wandering ways and forty aliases, his lies about the Civil War, and how he could manually manipulate his heart to fake a heart attack.

Urwiler shot bolt upright. "That's all newspaper talk!" he cried.

Dr. Bachelor said there would be no more hospital meals and no more fluffy pillows. It was time to leave. Thereupon Urwiler leaped out of bed, scooped up his bag, and cleared the door.

A few days later he staged another collapse on a downtown street in Tacoma and was rushed to the county hospital. In the emergency room he gasped that his name was Robert Larson and that he had fought in the Civil War. He said he also had a pension from a Pennsylvania railroad company. The hospital gave him a room, and nurses took a stethoscope recording that put his heart rate at about 200 beats a minute. But then a follow-up electrocardiograph examination clocked his true rate at sixty beats—about normal for a man aged around seventy.

The hospital summoned the police, and Urwiler's next bed was a cot in the city jail. In court he kept switching his story, saying first he came from Chicago, then Pennsylvania, and then Idaho. The court sentenced him to sixty days for vagrancy. "It's clear we can't let you go on wandering around the country at your age—irrespective of your apparent abilities," Judge Frank Hale told him, grinning as he scanned the long police report listing Urwiler's travels. "But of course I have no quarrel with a man who can get in and out of a hospital for free these days, like you do. You really should have a medal for that, too."

They led Urwiler away but still he protested, telling detectives that the railroad company had honored him with a special pension years ago for helping prevent the wreck of a train traveling from New York to Washington for President McKinley's inauguration. He showed them a medal, but it turned out to be nothing more than a cheap trinket from a 1949 Chicago railway exhibition.

"But I was in the Pennsylvania Volunteers!" he shouted, insisting he was a Union man from the Civil War and rolling up his sleeves to show army tattoos—a floral wreath on one arm, an American bald eagle on the other.

"Okay, Dad," said one of the weary detectives. "Now tell us the real reason you came to Tacoma and put on that phony spinner."

Walter Urwiler knew he was beaten. "Well," he replied, "I wasn't satisfied with hospitals anyway." He pointed to his skinny arms. "You can't get fat on a hospital diet. Look, what I need is some steaks."

Two months later in San Antonio, a former Union soldier from the Civil War was rushed to a local hospital suffering from what appeared to be a heart attack. He had arrived in town that morning looking for his great-great-grandson....

ALBERT WOOLSON

lbert Woolson said he went to war because his father had gone to war and his grandfather before that. The boy who lived past 100 and became the last of the blue soldiers hailed from a family steeped in military service. Well into the 1950s, as he lay in his room at St. Luke's Hospital in Duluth, his thoughts could drift back to images of Civil War horror and gallantry and the turbulent decades that followed. He remembered bright parade uniforms and veterans marching bent and stooped, and the glory that once was the Grand Army of the Republic. Nothing excited him more.

But by his own account, Woolson never fired at the enemy or fought them with raised bayonet. Rather, he said, he was but a blue-eyed teenager when he enlisted in the last year of the war, seeking a paycheck to help his mother. He was mustered into an adult man's army and served safely behind the front lines. He did not carry a rifle but instead hoisted the company's drum and bugle; he woke the soldiers in the morning and sometimes helped bury them at dusk. One of his greatest thrills as an old man was delighting schoolboys and Civil War historians with tales not about the whirl of combat but how one day an officer let him practice on the company cannon.

"The colonel handed me the end of a long rope," he would recall at school assemblies in Duluth and veterans reunions around the North. "He said, 'When I yell, you stand on your toes, open your mouth, and pull.' First time the cannon went off, I was scared to death."

Woolson said he was born on February 11, 1847, the same day as the inventor Thomas Alva Edison. James K. Polk was president, and the country was more focused on Mexican atrocities and Manifest Destiny than on the fracturing of its sacred Union.

His mother's family was English and Scottish and they settled in upstate New York two years after American revolutionaries published the Declaration of Independence. His grandfather farmed, cut timber, and grew apples. They built a large eight-room house and four barns, and dug a cement-floored kitchen. David Baldwin, his grandfather, lived to be 103; his grandmother, Betsy, 100. They were buried in the cemetery at Antwerp, New York, near the little brick school house young Albert occasionally attended. As he remembered and recorded in a brief account he called "My Reminiscences," in those days "there were panthers, or what they call mountain lions out west nowadays. They used to scream in the night ... and were very destructive to cattle."

David and Betsy's daughter, Caroline, married Willard Woolson, and they became Albert's parents. Willard's father was William Woolson of New Hampshire. William had served as a private in the War of 1812, and his oldest son, Roswell, served with him as a drummer boy. The other son, Willard, was born in Cambridge, Massachusetts, and his marriage to Caroline Baldwin in 1839 almost never came off.

"He was employed as a cabinetmaker, painter, and builder of fine furniture," Albert recalled of his father. "He was a violinist before he was married and had been a member of Allan Dodsworth's Military Band and Orchestra, a highly popular, largely brass ensemble of up to 100 members based in New York City." But, Albert wrote, "my grandfather [Baldwin] did not approve of him because he was a fiddler and a rover and a no account. But my father had many good qualities, just the same."

His father often left the family for long tours with a military troupe or a traveling circus. Sometimes he amused audiences by claiming to be related to naval hero John Paul Jones. During other long absences he managed a combination hotel, horse barn, and tavern on the old plank road to Carthage, New York. The stopover, which included a large ballroom and banquet area, was popular in the winter, mostly for sleighing parties.

Growing up with just one younger brother, Albert saw little of his father. He even was away when word first reached him from Felts Mills, New York, that Albert had been born. "The nurse sent word up to my father, who, with his orchestra, was furnishing the music for the dance," Albert wrote. "They and a large number of visitors came down with wine and congratulations to mother and the new citizen, Albert Woolson."

In the spring of 1859, his mother sent twelve-year-old Albert to live with her cousin, William Warren, in a community near Oswego, New York. "They had a beautiful fruit farm where I was installed as chore boy to feed the chickens, collect the eggs," Woolson recalled. "This family consisted of Mr. and Mrs. Warren and two daughters who were a little older than myself. Here I spent two happy years."

Charles B. Thompson and his wife, both university teachers, enjoyed winter and summer breaks with the Warrens too, and "they established a school for all of us young folks, with Divine service on Sundays," Albert remembered. "During this period I obtained about all the important education I ever received. I was busy at that time reading the immortal book entitled *Uncle Tom's Cabin*."

His father did stay with the family in 1860. He worried over Abraham Lincoln's election to the presidency and the South's threats of abandoning the Union for a renegade form of government. Lincoln left his home in Illinois and headed east, determined to reach Washington and keep the Union whole. To garner support along the way, he visited various state capitals and addressed state legislators. When he stopped in Albany, New York, Woolson and his father rode over to see the president-elect.

"There was a meeting there," Albert wrote, recounting the trip many years later, when he had reached the age of 107. "One man was tall and had large, bony hands. It was 'old Uncle Abe,' and he talked about human slavery. What he said I was too young to comprehend."

Lincoln was inaugurated president and the war came. By the spring of 1861 Albert was hearing stories spread by "loads of men" headed south. In his hometown, Charles Thompson Jr., the son of Albert's teachers, had enlisted as an artillery captain and hurried off to Manassas. "He was sent home in a pine box," Albert remembered. "I thought his mother would lose her mind."

The boy's father, Willard Woolson, left for Minnesota. He settled around Lake Elysian, hoping the war would blow over with the Union restored. But the fighting tore through the summer, and in November 1861 he enlisted and joined Company I, a unit out of Warsaw, Minnesota. They were sent to the Benton Barracks near St. Louis. In May 1862 they marched through the streets of the city and at sunset boarded a steamboat headed down the Mississippi and Tennessee rivers. Plans were to join with Union armies moving south, but just before Brown's Landing on the Tennessee, their boat the *Gladiator* ran hard onto a shoal and splintered. One man died, and fifteen others crowded on the two decks were injured. A shattering staircase smashed Pvt. Willard Woolson's knee.

His family heard nothing of him for more than a year. Then startling news arrived that he was hospitalized in Windom, Minnesota, and may actually have been wounded during the Battle of Shiloh. Alarmed, Albert, his mother, and younger brother Frank hurried to Minnesota by Great Lakes steamer and coach. "His left leg had been amputated," Albert wrote. "That was the condition we found him in, on crutches." Eventually the wound would take his father's life.

The family united in Minnesota, and the Civil War seemed far away. Closer to home were the Sioux. "We began to see unusual lights in the sky west of us at night," Albert remembered. "This continued for a short time and we were told that the Sioux Indians, 70 miles from us, had gone on the warpath against the white settlers." He recalled military forces rounding up 320 Sioux and marching them to nearby Mankato, for trial. "Thirty-eight of these big chiefs were hung by the neck. I was a witness to this." Another three thousand Winnebagos were confined on a reservation along the Blue Earth River. Albert said one of them named Winneshake taught him to shoulder and fire a rifle.

After two more years passed and the fall of 1864 arrived, with the Woolson family still struggling, Albert decided it was his turn to take the uniform. He said he signed up in early October of that year, just seventeen. Attached to the 1st Minnesota Heavy Artillery, Woolson fell in with a 1,800-man call-up of soldiers requested by Lincoln and the War Department to defend the fortifications around Chattanooga. He came into the army asking for a rifle, explaining that he had learned to handle the weapon from old Winneshake. But his commanders decided he would roll on a snare while the older, trained soldiers engaged the enemy.

Southward they marched, first to Nashville, then to Chattanooga. He served, he said, through April 1865 and then some additional months beyond the Confederate surrender. In his rakish blue forage cap, lined up with other drummers, he beat out the march step and learned to blow the bugle too. He pounded his drums for assemblies and company marches, he said, and played "Taps" at night and at burials. He returned home tired, sweaty, and hungry from war, and thankful he had never hurt anyone.

Woolson repeated his stories over the years, stretching his adventures to dazzle his listeners. In later versions he claimed he was acquainted with some of the North's legendary leaders, including Maj. Gen. George H. Thomas, the "Rock of Chickamauga," and Col. William Colville, who had organized the Minnesota volunteer regiment. In a radio interview late in his life, he told the following tale:

> One day we was marching by General Thomas' headquarters. He was sitting out on the porch with a companion. We found later that it was Col. William Colville.
>
> We was going by this mansion … playing buffalo drums out to the cemetery to bury one of our comrades. On the return we come back playing "The Girl I Left behind Me." And a colored lady, an elderly woman, come out and held her arms in front of us.
>
> "Why, that's tasteless," she said.
>
> Finally Major Lewis said, "Why lady, what does this mean?"
>
> She said, "I just want to know, when you go by just a while ago playing so sorrowful, and now you come back playing … like the devil."
>
> "Why," he says, "we go out in respect for the dead and then return in respect for the living."

Woolson loved telling his stories. He shared them whenever a crowd drew near in school uniforms or battered old veterans' jackets. He would work himself into quite a lather, feeling young and full of grit all over again, delighted that he could find a lighter side to the suffering in war.

> Thomas called us in, [and] give us a glass of lemonade.

Colonel Colville says, "Who, what organization is this?"

John Lewis said, "This is the regimental drum corps, 1st Minnesota.... We know you."

"Why, really I didn't recognize you. God bless you boys."

Woolson would smile broadly and shake with laughter. "We hopped in and drank lemonade! Where they got the ice, I don't know."

Another favorite story concerned a doctor near Knoxville, Tennessee. Woolson's artillery regiment was reduced to half rations with orders to keep their hands off any local livestock or other private sources of food. But that doctor was a Southern sympathizer who "seemed to have it in for us." So, Woolson would say, "We decided one night to help ourselves to his chickens. The doctor had his chickens in a coop. We decided that to keep the chickens from making too much noise we had better take chickens, coop and all, and we did."

Now he was grinning. "We dug a hole in the ground and lined it with rock to hold the heat and used the coop for fuel and roasted those chickens."

Now he was laughing. "Man, that was the best meal we had since we left Minnesota!"

But much of Woolson's war was monotonous drilling, practicing, and waiting for maneuvers. Bored for days, he often sat idly around camp tired and hungry, sometimes lonely, and often scared. It was not until October 1865 that the 1st Minnesota Heavy Artillery returned home, a year after Woolson had marched away. His parents still waited in Mankato, and Albert moved back into the home. His father, minus his leg and any heart for more song and dance or another traveling minstrel troupe, died two weeks after Albert's return. He was just forty-five.

Albert started scouring for jobs. He worked as a fireman for the Chicago and Northwestern Railroad, still supporting his mother. One day his crew was snowplowing tracks when they hit a drift so high the engines were tossed into a barren cornfield. "That ended my railroad career," he said.

His mother remarried, his brother Frank died, and Albert was cast on his own. He married Sarah Jane Sloper in June 1868 in South Bend, Minnesota, and they moved to St. Peter. For sixteen years he worked as a wood turner in the cabinetmaking business, much like his father. He labored in the grain mills too. For a while Woolson and a friend, Robert Rhodes, once a bandmaster in a Minnesota company of Union volunteers, formed a twenty-member ensemble. Woolson beat on his old Civil War drum, and he learned the guitar and the cello too. Like his father, he sometimes traveled the circuit. "We played fine lively music," he recalled. "Nothing sad." Memories of the war grew distant, but music still coursed through his veins. "Our single young men had a happy time dancing with the frontier ladies," he wrote after one performance. "We sure had a happy time."

His wife died in 1901, and Woolson moved to Duluth. Three years later, at fifty-eight, he married Ann Haugen and found work as an electrician for the American Carbolite Company. But he was restless; he kept moving about the city and changing jobs. He returned to woodworking, then hired on at the Scott Graff Lumber Company and helped build the columns supporting the local Crawford Mortuary. He ran machinery for the Clyde Iron Works; then he built washing machines for the Hirschy Company.

And that was his last job. He retired to enjoy his already grown family: in all, fourteen children from the two marriages, minus a child who had died in an accidental drowning. His family was so large and sprawling and many of them lived so long that, when Woolson died years later, six daughters and two sons survived him.

At the eighty-year mark, Woolson suddenly joined the local Gorman-Culver Post No. 13 of the Grand Army of the Republic (GAR). It was another man's death that drew him in. Ninety-year-old Henry Theodore Johnson lived just two blocks from Woolson up East Fifth Street in Duluth. He was a former Yankee too, who had enlisted in the 1st Minnesota Infantry in 1864. He served his final months in Georgia as Gen. William Tecumseh Sherman swept to the sea. Later he worked as a Northern Pacific Railroad man and was active in the GAR. By 1928 he was the local post's second oldest member.

On Armistice Day 1928, the holiday celebrating the end of the Great War in Europe, Woolson walked over to visit Johnson. With no answer at the door that afternoon, he peered in the window and then stepped through the doorway. His friend Johnson was dead inside. Duluth and the GAR honored the old warrior with a military funeral, and the pomp and pageantry sparkled in Woolson's eyes.

The Duluth GAR post had been chartered in 1882 as a place for local Union veterans to gather and reminisce, to support one another in old age, and to relive their shared memories of the Civil War. Nationally the GAR had been founded by Dr. Benjamin F. Stephenson, an Illinois infantry surgeon who served as its first provisional commander in chief. He helped open the first post in Decatur, Illinois, and in April 1866, the first meeting was called to order in a flag-decked Indianapolis opera house. Post No. 1 was christened with just twelve members. But the organization caught on and the ranks grew rapidly, spreading with new chapters around the North and later including a National Women's Relief Corps and a Ladies of the GAR auxiliary. By 1890 its rolls topped 400,000 members. They staged annual state and national encampments, offering opportunities for veterans in blue to gather, boost civic pride, and swap battlefield stories. After it dissolved with the death of its last member in the 1950s, the group's records were sent to the Library of Congress. Its flags and official seal were donated to the Smithsonian Institution.

By the time Woolson joined the GAR in 1928, the lists of Civil War veterans were already thinning. Nationwide, a thousand veterans from the 1860s were dying every month. In Duluth a second chapter of the GAR, the J. B. Culver Post No. 128, was so spare it had been merged with another to create the Gorman-Culver Post No. 13. Woolson was elected its last commander in 1929. Six more men died in 1930; two years later, only six others still stood sentry.

Those half dozen, including eighty-five-year-old Woolson, decided it best to cancel any more official gatherings. Only three were strong enough to make it to their last formal meeting at the Memorial Hall in Duluth. W. W. Huntley was appointed for life as quartermaster and post adjutant. Once a group 500 strong, the last three Duluth Yankees adjourned their meeting, furled their banners, and returned home.

Then in 1938 the great seventy-fifth reunion of the blue and the gray descended on the fields of Gettysburg. Only Woolson and Frank Clemmons from the Duluth GAR were able to journey to Pennsylvania. When they returned, Woolson (now ninety-one) told friends how Confederate Gen. George Pickett's widow, LaSalle Corbell Pickett, had addressed them at Gettysburg and insisted that her husband would have taken that Yan-

Albert Woolson, the last of the blue in his
hometown of Duluth, then the last in his home
state of Minnesota, ultimately became the last in
the nation to wear the uniform of the Grand Army
of the Republic. (Courtesy of Whitman College and
Northwest Archives, Walla Walla, Washington)

kee position across the wheat and peach lanes if he had only been given ten more minutes to prepare.

"Like hell they would!" a Union veteran had shouted back.

Woolson loved that story, but he clearly was confused, embellishing his memories, or just plainly not telling the truth: LaSalle Corbell Pickett was already seven years dead.

He also told of Yankee veterans singing "Tenting Tonight on the Old Campground," and he recalled the "rather peculiar" dispute at Gettysburg over whether Confederates should fly their Stars and Bars. Finally a group of wives, widows, and daughters from both sides exchanged flags among themselves.

"The old Confederate soldiers, regular Johnnies, had been vindicated in what they believed to be right. Tears were streaming down their cheeks," Woolson recalled. "I was strangely affected at that spectacle. One of them said, 'If the women of America from the South and the North had combined and talked this thing over, there would never have been any Civil War.'"

When his comrade Clemmons died, Woolson became one of just two Union veterans left in Duluth. When Huntley died, he stood alone. Once a solitary man, he suddenly was elevated to local celebrity, a curiosity to youngsters and a hero to their grandparents. He kept on telling the stories of his war, though many of the tales no longer tracked or made much sense. In a taped interview he claimed that he and his father had visited Ford's Theatre in Washington a week before Lincoln was assassinated. But Woolson had also maintained he was serving in Tennessee when the president was shot. Nevertheless, he held to his story. "Poor old Abe," he lamented.

Woolson continued to keep busy with GAR activities around the state. Often he dictated letters on stationery from GAR headquarters in St. Paul, addressed to the "family of our late comrade" whenever another Civil War Yankee passed on. "My dear friends," he wrote in July 1943 to the children of Dr. Albert Sweet, a GAR member in Hopkins, Minnesota. "Please accept the deepest sympathy of not only myself but of the department of Minnesota Grand Army of the Republic also, for truly we mourn with you in the loss of our true and loyal comrade and your beloved father.... As the stars light God's heavens, so will He give you comfort and strength in this hour of great sorrow."

He also kept a firm hold on GAR affairs. When renegade member Orrin S. Pierce of Minneapolis was suspended from a local post and tried to attend GAR functions anyway, Woolson locked him out. A former honor guard in Lincoln's funeral who now was 100, Pierce sued. Woolson refused to budge. The case went to the state supreme court. The newspapers called it "the Battle of the Centenarians." It was still unresolved when Pierce died in the Minnesota Soldiers' Home.

Soon Woolson was grappling with larger problems. The statewide GAR moved in 1947 to disband the entire outfit. By then only Woolson and two other Civil War veterans remained as bona fide members in Minnesota. So the trio agreed to surrender their charter to the national GAR organization and close the state posts. But first they paraded through the streets of St. Paul for one last time. Bands played marches, and Woolson rode in a place of honor, his head held high. At the parade's end he asked the bugler to blow "Retreat" rather than "Taps." "Retreat," he said, signals only that day is done and night has fallen. Yet to all in Minnesota, an era was ending. Everyone sensed it. "I feel like I'm going to a funeral," a city official riding in the last car said.

As the last state commander that last day, Woolson wore his blue uniform with all his medals and ribbons coloring his chest. When they assembled at the St. Paul city auditorium, an audience of three thousand hushed as he stepped to the podium. They could see the tears in Albert Woolson's eyes. "It is my hope that there will be no more cruel and inhuman wars," he told them.

In an official letter to the GAR headquarters, Woolson said the Minnesota branch would now be folded in with the national organization. "After due consideration we voted to close the Department of Minnesota and become members at large under the national umbrella," he wrote. "Appropriate ceremonies were conducted for the closing of the department." He signed his note, "yours in fraternity, charity, and loyalty."

On the national stage, the glory days of the Grand Army of the Republic were slowly fading. Yet only a dozen years earlier, 350 ex-Yankees had been strong and hardy enough to march down Washington's streets in a GAR reunion in the nation's capital, thrilling a crowd of 100,000 as they traced the same steps Gen. William Tecumseh Sherman and his proudly victorious Union Army had paraded for two days after the war was won in 1865.

The Union gathering in Washington in 1936 had experienced a troubled start. The original idea was to draw Confederate veterans to Washington too, convening a joint reunion of the two former adversaries, much like the galas at Manassas and Gettysburg. Many in blue and gray thought it might be a fitting tribute if held in the nation's capital. But once again the Confederate flag issue irked Northern veterans, and that prompted Gen. Harry Rene Lee of Nashville, adjutant and chief of staff of the United Confederate Veterans, to call it an "obnoxious order that we furl our flags." The Rebels stayed home.

So that September the Yankees put on their own show, complete with a viewing stand in front of the White House for the veterans to pass one last time down Pennsylvania Avenue. They were called into line when an old drum (once beaten at Lincoln's second inaugural) sounded "Yankee Doodle." At the sticks was 90-year-old R. D. Parker of Illinois, who, like Woolson, had served as a Union drummer boy.

And the old men marched.

"This is different from what it was when I rode along here in 1865," said Ira Wildman of Michigan, sporting the same snappy white hat he had worn while proudly prancing with General Sherman so many years ago. "That was a parade, two days of it. But what a street then—every minute you'd sink up to your knees in a mud hole, and you had to kick sows suckling their pigs out of the way so you could go on. Those were grand days, though. I was in General Custer's corps. There never was anything like it."

In the Ohio line walked Sam Yoho, who had run off on his sixteenth birthday to join the fighting around Nashville. "We're just a lot of boys," he said. "Once a man, twice a child, you know. I'm keeping up my pep."

I. W. Johnson of West Virginia displayed the longest beard in the parade; it swung against his belt buckle. But Bryon Johnson of Ohio stole the spotlight when he noticed some pretty young women standing outside the Washington Hotel; he quickly made a pass at them. The men around him broke ranks for the curb too.

Despite the high spirits, a cloud hung over the festivities. One GAR official from Iowa, John P. Risley, announced that he had conducted a study of pension records and census and insurance data, and had projected that the last Union soldier would be dead within four years—by 1940. It was a dire prediction. "The average age of our survivors of the Civil War now is past 91 years," said Risley. "Insurance statistics show that by 1940 the last of them should be gone and the Grand Army of the Republic will be mustered out for all time."

The Yankees were unnerved. They elected a new GAR national commander, C. H. William Ruhe of Pittsburgh, another former drummer boy and a youngster at eighty-seven, who announced more conventions in the years ahead. "Gosh," he said, "we can't quit when we're all feeling so spry."

Ninety-year-old, white-bearded J. L. Hussey of San Francisco spoke for them all when he mentioned the inevitable. He had loved the parade in Washington, but it left him all the more tired and worn out. "I'll go soon. That's certain," he said. A. O. Williams, eighty-nine, of Toledo was more optimistic. He had been injured in a car accident the year before and surprised his doctor with a speedy recovery. "I told him my time just hadn't come yet."

They defied the odds, these hardy old bricks. In 1941 they met again in Columbus, Ohio. "As long as one member of the Grand Army of the Republic remains, there will be an annual encampment," vowed Katherine Flood, the Washington secretary for the national GAR. "Actuarial figures furnished by insurance companies predict that there will be two Civil War veterans alive in 1952," she said. And then, after a short pause, she added, "But these men have been smashing actuarial figures for years."

Only eighty-nine veterans made it to Columbus. Many sat around the lobby of the Deshler-Wallick Hotel, a glazed terra-cotta–tiled building, once one of the world's largest towers. A fife-and-drum band entertained them. At the Memorial Hall they were presented with a marble sundial and a bronze tablet bearing the Gettysburg Address. They accepted $3,800 in contributions and gifts to keep the nearly insolvent GAR afloat.

They met in Des Moines three years later, but only twenty-five in blue coats and brass buttons came this time. Many of the expenses for the national group were paid by the few state posts still operating. The meeting was called to order with a gavel whittled from part of a wooden banister in Lincoln's Springfield home. The veterans sat in a small line of chairs at the memorial service, some cupping their ears, others falling asleep. The local Crocker Post No. 27 dedicated a park boulder to the GAR.

In the lobby of the Hotel Fort Des Moines sat ninety-five-year-old Fred Fisher Jr. of Humeston, Iowa, alone and dejected. He had been told he could not wear the GAR insignia, even though he insisted both he and his father had served under fire in the Union army. Amy Noll, secretary of the Iowa GAR, said Fisher's name had been dropped from the rolls because only a Fred Fisher Sr. truly had enlisted. Junior mistakenly had been allowed at the Columbus gathering, but not this time in Des Moines.

Fisher claimed he had gone to war at eleven, accompanying his father at the first and second battles of Bull Run, and at Chancellorsville and Nashville too. Ray Aten, commander of the local American Legion post in Fisher's hometown, vouched for him, reporting that Fisher often took part in war memorial ceremonies there: "We always have considered him a Civil War veteran, and he now is the last one in Wayne County. There is not a more highly respected man in the community, and his integrity is above reproach.... We always have heard that he went with his father into the Civil War, that he shouldered a gun, but that there had been some sort of a mix-up about papers."

Nevertheless, Noll and Flood, the Iowa and national GAR secretaries, would not permit Fisher to join the ranks of the blue in Des Moines. "We all have sympathy," Noll said. "But membership lines must be strictly drawn."

In the fall of 1945 the veterans were back in Columbus, if just a handful. Only 161 Yankees were believed still alive; only fourteen came to Columbus. It rained and it was chilly, yet the bands played, and twelve men posed for a group picture. They paraded up High Street, albeit in cars. Among them was 100-year-old Fred Pfiester, though he had fallen a few days earlier in his bathtub in Cincinnati.

In August 1946 it was Indianapolis—with just a dozen on hand. Robert M. Rownd of Ripley, New York, at 102 the organization's chaplain in chief, waved away the microphone and with a deep husky voice roared to the group inside the Murat Temple. "When the last man is gone, the GAR is gone too," he bellowed.

President Truman had sent them a letter. "Time has thinned their ranks," he wrote, "but time can never erase their proud record of service to our country." Rownd held the letter aloft. "Let us look to the future!" he proclaimed.

Off to the far left sat Albert Woolson, in shirt, tie, and vest, shouldering a drum and a pair of sticks, his slouch cap atop his head. He had ridden with them in the parade along the downtown streets. And for the first time he had been elected to a national office as the GAR's "patriotic instructor." The honor earned him another badge and ribbon.

At ninety-nine, Woolson had taken the train from St. Paul to Indianapolis. He brought with him his GAR secretary, Marian G. Jewell, who worked out of a small office in Room 321 of the state capitol. Fremont Power, a longtime Indiana reporter, columnist, and executive editor, interviewed him in Indianapolis. To the reporter, Woolson seemed a lot younger than he said he was.

"Albert Woolson was rather the 'Gay old dog,'" Power wrote. "We had a bottle of beer in the Claypool Tavern, and he smoked one of my cigarettes. Some of the others took a bit of shepherding and mothering by the women of the various auxiliaries. But not Mr. Woolson. He was his own man. You didn't have to yell to make him hear, and his answers to your questions were sharp and concise. He was a quotable man. Mr. Woolson poured himself a glass of beer and stated his views on the atomic bomb."

Woolson told his war stories again, including one about a lieutenant who had whacked a boy soldier with the flat end of a sword when the youth stood frozen in battle, his hand covering his mouth. The lieutenant had promised the boy's mother he would look out for the youth. Now, in the thick of the fighting, the boy appeared to have lost his nerve. "Go on there, lad," the lieutenant called out. "That's not the way a hero fights." Suddenly the boy's hand dropped, and he fell to the ground, dead from a bullet that had torn open his neck.

"Now," asked Woolson, "what would that lieutenant tell his mother?"

The 1947 encampment was held in Cleveland. A picture of a huge cross was projected upon the west wall of the grand ballroom of the Hotel Cleveland to honor dead comrades. Floral arrangements were displayed to commemorate the nineteen who had died in the last year. "They rest in our hearts," said the Rev. A. Dale Fiers, the grandson of a Union soldier.

At the dais, Rownd again refused the microphone. "As the years have ripened in my life, the spirit of comradeship is still alive, and will remain forever with me," he thundered to his brethren.

Only forty-seven Yankees still lived; only five were strong enough to participate in the parade. Eagle Scouts posted along the route checked on them as they were driven past.

Woolson had stayed home, but he joined five others the following year in Grand Rapids, Michigan, at what all assumed would be their last farewell. Two of the veterans brought their canes; one was pushed in a wheelchair. The talk was about disbanding the old fraternity, just letting it go. Too many years, they said.

Then, in the summer of 1949, 102-year-old Woolson headed again to Indianapolis, the site of the GAR's first national convention and what now would become its last gathering anywhere. Only six made it. Woolson left his home on East Fifth Street for the Duluth depot and the 8:15 train. The Moose Lodge drum and bugle corps performed in his honor. He boarded and flashed a smile. His blue eyes sparkled, much like a seventeen-year-old heading off for another war to win. He chomped on a big stogie, and the smoke filled the railcar.

When his train chugged into Union Station in Indianapolis, he was the second veteran to arrive, and he found a wheelchair waiting on the platform. In fact, a whole team of nurses and Red Cross workers were at the ready. He reluctantly sat down in the chair. He had brought with him his sixty-nine-year-old son, Robert Woolson, a druggist from Dayton, Washington, and Robert started pushing the old man to the Claypool Hotel headquarters.

The final meeting was understandably somber. All six GAR attendees, minus ten other Yankees too frail to attend, were over 100 years old, which John Mason Brown, writing in the *Saturday Review*, called "an age which is abnormal." One of them was blind; some were unable to walk; others could hardly stand. "All of us pass daily, without recognizing them, older people whose presence are forecasts of what our futures will be like, if only we last to their age," Brown wrote. "We seldom see ourselves in these passers-by. We do not want to. We live nourished by the illusion that each of us is somehow different."

These six men, who in their youth could have known old soldiers who had fought with George Washington, now were themselves the ancient relics. "They came home from combat full of youth and impatience with the old, only to grow old themselves," Brown wrote. "Their bodies age, sag, soften, fatten or shrink.... Where once these men of action were capable of scaling walls, charging up hills, or trudging through miles of mud, they dwindle into men of inaction, no longer able to climb stairs. Their rifles are replaced with canes."

In Indianapolis they formed a decrepit final unit, sporting worn blue coats and dangling brass buttons. The blind veteran said he was a former slave. Another fainted as he tried to step into a Red Cross wagon. Every night they all retired early.

It was raining when Woolson was rolled into the Indiana Roof Ball-room in a wheelchair, guided by a military policeman. The band struck up "The Battle Hymn of the Republic," and each veteran was introduced.

But old Woolson seemed confused. He started talking about a recent bear attack in Duluth. He said he had been eating dinner at his daughter's home when a 300-pound bruin was shot in the street. A group of ladies presented him with a bouquet, and he motioned for a photographer. He wanted his picture taken. "My wife loves flowers," he beamed. "She'll think more of that than she would a $20 bill." Next Woolson was saying that just yesterday he had ridden to Hibbing, Minnesota, to inspect the ore mines there.

The group had little business to conduct; nothing much was left to say. Rownd was dead, so Theodore Augustus Penland of Portland, Oregon, officiated as the group's last commander in chief. The talk was low, respectful, and brief. They dedicated a new GAR postage stamp in a ceremony at the city's Monument Circle, one of the nation's first elaborate Civil War memorials to the common soldier. They rode in a short parade in open cars, and Nancy Baxter, a wide-eyed teenager, watched them from a second-floor window. What she saw, she never forgot: "The old guys rode around in convertibles," she remembered, "their bald heads with a few white hairs on them, glistening in the late afternoon sunlight."

The Yankees gathered for a final "campfire" in the hotel ballroom, all six of them pinned with new ribbons and medals. Woolson was promoted from national chief of staff to junior vice commander. They furled their flags and tucked them away. There would be no more parties, no more reunions, no more Grand Army of the Republic. One of them, the senior vice commander, asked to hold the GAR wooden gavel one more time, if only "for just a little while."

The oldest of them, 108-year-old James A. Hard of Rochester, New York, said he wished that one or two of the last Confederates could have joined them for this roll call. Maybe, he said wistfully, they all could hold one more reunion in Washington to celebrate the blue and the gray. Maybe next year, he thought. He looked around the room, but all was quiet. "It's just a suggestion," he said.

These last six Union veterans were as stubborn as they were old. Before they departed, they decided to never officially disband the GAR. Let it live, they said, some of them in tears. As a fraternal organization, let it continue until the last of them passed away. Then fold the tent.

Off to the side, Woolson, wearing a shirt, tie, and vest, picked up an acoustic guitar and started strumming. He flashed a big smile and lit up his bright blue eyes. "Feeling fine," he said.

5

WALTER WILLIAMS

For most of his long life, Walter Washington Williams never fussed much about his stint as a Confederate forage master in the Civil War. He occasionally mentioned it around his rural Texas community, and his neighbors understood him to be a veteran of that war. But rarely did he attend a Civil War reunion, a Soldiers' Day parade, or a Confederate veterans' encampment. He never joined fraternal organizations dedicated to honoring the Lost Cause. He did seek a Confederate pension and he did fly the Stars and Bars, but in the postwar South that hardly set an old man apart. In truth, it was not until he was a long retired farmer and cattle herder that the world sought out Williams as the last of the soldiers in gray.

By that time he lay crumpled in a bed in his daughter's house in Houston. He was blind, deaf, and barely able to speak, a shriveled old body that could eat or drink only when his daughter fed him from an eyedropper or a bottle. There was little more for him to say by then, anyway. His time foraging with John Bell Hood's fabled brigade in the Confederate army was a distant memory. He said he had only served for eleven months, and for a man who in the end claimed to be 117 years old, those eleven months seemed like a mere trickle of time. It was all so long ago.

Unlike Albert Woolson, the last of the blue veterans in Minnesota, Williams never abandoned his country roots nor moved to the big city—at least not until he was forced to in old age. Rather, for nearly seventy years he quietly spooled out his retirement in a three-bedroom cabin with a porch out front and a garage around back. He built his home at the end of Shiloh and Eaton roads, deep in a patch of woods outside Franklin, Texas, and he set the wooden frame structure up on bricks to keep the floors dry when it rained. For years he made do without electricity, a telephone, or running water.

He had been born before Texas became a state, and he died at the dawn of the space age. "Uncle Walt," most called him. He was bright, blue-eyed, and cheerful, an elf of a man with a friendly chuckle. When attention swerved his way, he preferred to tell stories about herding cattle on the Chisholm Trail rather than stealing food for Hood's Brigade. But even still, some of the farmers and townspeople around Franklin remembered him as an old Confederate, and it was that memory they held when in the mid-1950s Williams was driven down to Houston to be cared for by his daughter. By that time he was far too old and feeble to fend for himself. Twice a widower, he required constant care. Yet even during those last years as his body was shutting down, he still hung on for another birthday and another birthday and then another. He clearly enjoyed living beyond the span of a century. "I'll be around when you are all dead and gone," he liked to chuckle to visitors from Austin, Washington, and Hollywood too. "I'm just sticking around to see what will happen." He said that over and over until he could no longer speak, and then he just lay quietly in the bed in the house on West Twenty-Third Avenue in Houston.

Williams said he was born November 14, 1842, in Itawamba County, Mississippi. According to family history, he was the son of George Washington Williams and Nancy Marcus Williams. He claimed his father lived to 119—or maybe it was his grandfather, as he changed the story often. Yet even as a country boy Walter told friends he was going to live even longer than his forefathers. He was going to top 120, he said.

The Williamses were a farm family, and Walter and his brothers shared the chores. In 1862, when he said he was twenty, he joined Company C of the 5th Regiment of then-Colonel Hood's Texas Brigade. As a forage master, it fell to him to scrounge for cattle, fresh crops, and anything else to eat as the brigade took on new enlistments and scurried about the state.

John Bell Hood had been to West Point. After Fort Sumter fell and his native Kentucky could not decide whether to fight for the North or secede with the South, an exasperated Hood abandoned the Union army and embraced the Rebels. With a reputation for dash and daring, he distinguished himself at Antietam. He was wounded at Gettysburg when an artillery shell blasted his left arm, and he lost his right leg at Chickamauga. He was promoted to general in 1864. He was desperately trying to make it back to Texas to rally another brigade when Lee surrendered in Virginia. Hood himself was cornered in Mississippi. But all those exploits came after Hood had earlier swung south through Mississippi and plucked up young men like Walter Williams from their farms in the Delta to get to Texas and organize that first brigade. Walter never took any credit for following Hood up into Maryland and Pennsylvania and the hotbed of the war. In fact, the most Walter Williams did—according to what he said—was to forage for food as Hood and his men passed through Mississippi and headed for the Lone Star state.

"I stole food," he would explain, trying to describe how, atop his horse Willie, he had scoured the town depots and farm fields for something to feed the men. "I never fired a shot at Yankees, but I heard a few bullets whine when Unionists fired on me once while I ate breakfast." He later would claim he was part of a battle that killed 100 Union soldiers. Another time, he said, "thirty of our men was killed. A bunch of Yankees come ridin' round a mountain right into us. We fired into 'em. I remember one Yankee horse bolted, and he run smack through the middle of us. Didn't get a scratch."

Other times he insisted that he only had fired his rifle when he was sent out hunting for stray cattle. "I had to kill twenty of them a day," he said of the cattle. "I killed them all along the road when I could find them."

He also bragged that Willie was the best horse in the outfit, and that he had trained his mount to halt whenever he raised his rifle as if to fire at something. He said that after the war he rode Willie home.

When Williams's eleven months under Hood clocked out, he was "free to go home," he said. But he claimed he also rode briefly with Quantrill's Raiders. "I wasn't discharged," he maintained. "We just broke up." It seemed an odd assertion, given that Quantrill and his guerrillas spent their part of the war far away in the Kansas and Missouri region during the border conflicts there. But, like Hood, the name Quantrill in the years of defeat and Reconstruction became quite a legend. Maybe in his later years the old Confederate forage master Walter Williams simply was mistaken. Memories lose their hold after a while.

Soon after the surrender, Williams married his first wife, Florence Humphries. As he told it, they moved to Texas in 1870 and settled in Brazos County. They raised seven children, and he opened a meat market. But Florence died, and in 1888, when he said he was forty-six, he married Ella Mae Holliday. She was just eighteen, yet he outlived her too. Together they raised twelve children of their own, and for nearly seventy years the family planted crops and gathered eggs on their twenty acres of woods and flatland next to the cabin outside of Franklin in Robertson County— largely isolated from the rest of the increasingly modern age. Williams loved to fox hunt, and he kept a passel of twelve hound dogs. He raised a pet deer in his cabin. Occasionally he hired himself out as a cattle herder on the Chisholm Trail, he said. But other than that, the world outside of rural Texas spun busily along without any thought of Walter Williams, the old Confederate.

In August 1932, during what proved for many to be the leanest year of the Great Depression, Williams applied for a Confederate pension. Under a Texas state law passed in 1889, pensions were paid to any "bona fide" Confederate veteran who lived in the state. And while for more than forty years he had never raised his hand as a Confederate veteran and asked for the money, Williams evidently thought some state assistance would see him through the hard times.

In his application, written in longhand by a friend, Williams mentioned Hood's Brigade and Quantrill's Raiders. He was eighty-six, he reported, and he needed help. "My occupation is a farmer but I am unable to farm or do any of this kind of work at this time," he told the pension office in Austin. Unable to read or write much himself, he signed the application with his "X."

A county judge in Franklin, Joe Y. McNutt, mailed his own letter to the state capitol supporting the application. He told George H. Sheppard, the state comptroller of public accounts, that he completely vouched for Williams. "I believe Mr. Williams is a very deserving old Confederate soldier

and trust that you will grant him a pension at your earliest convenience."
He also identified two longtime citizens and merchants around town
who had known Williams for years and also were ready to testify to his
good character. "Both of the witnesses swear upon their oaths that Mr.
Williams is a creditable [sic] person and that they believe the statements
enabling him to a pension are true."

The application arrived in Austin, state officials read it over, and the
pension was granted.

The outside world continued to know little of Walter Williams until
1949, when Frank X. Tolbert Sr., a feature writer for the *Dallas Morning
News*, drove down to the cabin in the woods. Williams told the reporter
about his daily mundane tasks of milking cows and chasing chickens, and
his more adventurous years of herding cattle. This was the year of the last
GAR convention in the North, but up to now Williams had spoken little
of the Civil War.

"I never et much," he said in his southern drawl, the newspaperman
taking it down in his spiral notebook. "I get up for breakfast, turn around
for dinner, and go to bed for supper. When I was riding up the Chisholm
Trail, the range cooks sort of held it against me because I was a light-
eating man. I've always drunk lots of coffee, chewed plenty of tobacco,
and haven't tried to avoid any of this good Texas weather."

Sometimes he ventured out, if just to take a peek at what was hap-
pening outside his cabin door. In 1937 he showed up in Corsicana, Texas,
for what became the last state reunion of Texas Confederate veterans. It
was his first and last formal outing among soldiers in gray. Six of the old
warriors convened in the town square, all in their nineties, and they took
rooms at the Commercial Hotel. Confederate veteran M. H. Wolfe proudly
fingered a long scar across his face. He told a Corsicana reporter it was a
souvenir from "a Yankee saber thrust." The reporter also briefly met Williams on the square, but the encounter left him perplexed. Williams, the
reporter noted, "did not look as old as the other veterans."

"He has been living in the neighborhood of Franklin for more than
60 years," Franklin's *Texan* newspaper reported in November 1950, just
after Gov. Robert Allan Shivers, an army major in World War II, knighted
Williams as an honorary colonel on the occasion of his 108th birthday. By

then, the paper noted, Williams had over a hundred descendants spread across five generations. "Most of these years were spent farming and raising cattle, and he still lives on his farm and directs the work on the place." Williams attended a short ceremony at the courthouse in Franklin to receive the honorary title and accept a testimonial accompanying the military commission. He looked at the papers and studied the words, but he could not read them.

A year later, he made the cover of the September 1951 *United Daughters of the Confederacy* magazine. The photograph showed him with sunglasses and a broad grin, accepting a large cake from one of the Daughters at a get-together in his cabin. The story said he was born on November 14, 1843 (a year later than he had claimed), and in another county in Mississippi. It reported that he had been twenty-two rather than twenty when he joined Hood's Brigade. But otherwise the feature was quite positive about Walter and his wife, Ella Mae.

"Mr. Williams attributes his long life to hard work and clean living," the story read. He "stated his most enjoyable pastime was fox hunting, which he has had to forego for the past two years. The Williams are taken to prayer meeting occasionally, when weather permits. The Colonel and his wife still think that many of this world's problems could be solved, if people would attend prayer meetings and turn for guidance to the Lord."

"At 77," the magazine added, "Mrs. Williams milks the cows, tends the chickens and horses, does her own planting and still finds time to raise flowers. If she needs help, she blows a few blasts on a cow horn, and a son who lives near or some of the neighbors come over and lend a hand."

Two years later a photographer for *Life* magazine knocked on the cabin door, and Williams posed for him on the porch. He sat in a small rocker, a fedora hat slanted atop his head. He was dressed quite formally for the occasion, in a white shirt and black jacket and pants. He wore black-and-ivory cowboy boots and a stick pin in his right lapel. His thin eyebrows and narrow moustache had long ago turned gray. He had rather large ears for his small head. He did not smile or chuckle. Ella Mae stood behind him, leaning her hand on a large covered chair to steady herself, dressed in a bonnet, striped dress, and wool sweater. She did not smile either.

He started every morning "with a toddy of whisky, a chew of tobacco and a cup of coffee," he said. The porch floor was fashioned out of splintered wood planks, and the roof was made of tin. Most days he sat there in that rocker and snuggled in until the sun dropped beyond the trees. His plan, he told the magazine, was "to live until everyone else is gone, just to see what'll happen."

He went down to Houston for a medical checkup in August, and Dr. Russell Wolfe declared him "surprisingly good" for a man his age. "Frankly, we were medically curious about him," the doctor said. "You don't get a chance very often to study a man that old." Williams exclaimed that he felt more like sixty, but he needed help sometimes to walk. Yet the doctors said his blood pressure was good, and the cardiogram tests came back "remarkably normal." They fit him with a truss for a hernia and urged him to take plenty of mineral oil. Take vitamins too, they recommended. Other than that, they saw no need for a special diet.

He told the doctors, "My grandfather lived to be 120"—different from his earlier accounts that it was his father who had lived to be 119. But old age plays tricks. And Williams still was feisty. "I'm going to beat that," he vowed. Then he hurried home. "I don't like towns," he grumbled.

He told reporters around Franklin that "I could hit 120 easy if I keep feelin' way I do." He said, "Way I feel now I'll never die. There ain't a thing wrong with me 'cept my hearing." He said the state legislature had hiked his bonus pay a bit, and that he "might get me a new car. If I could see I could drive the thing myself."

Asked about the Civil War, Williams turned serious. "It was a wide mistake," he said. "Looks like we've always got wars goin' but they don't ever seem to settle nothin'."

In October he toured the Texas State Fair. A wealthy benefactor flew him to Dallas in a private plane. "I like it better than riding a horse," he said. He also went down to Galveston for a television spot and then to Houston where he stayed at the Shamrock Hotel. He ran into some attractive young women in the lobby. "Wanted to take some home with me," he said.

For his birthday in November, at 110, he told well-wishers that he started every day with a "big chew of tobacco." His preferred brand was Beechnut. About a hundred of his descendants, including a brood of great-

great-grandchildren, filled the porch and crowded into the cabin. He looked spry and alert but talked little about the past. New gimmicks, especially TV consoles, were what interested him now. "I never have seen that television," he told his family. "Seen a lot of other things. But I'd like to see television."

The next year they brought out a five-tiered cake with three candles to mark his 111th birthday. The family feasted on barbecued hog, beef, and venison, all of the old man's favorites. Asked to speak a few words, Williams talked about the war this time. While before he had always maintained he never came close to any fighting, this time he recalled that one morning he and his fellow Confederates had ambushed some Yankees. He said they killed a hundred of them.

He insisted that Grant's army had prevailed at Appomattox only because General Lee and the Confederacy were famished, worn out, and tired. They lacked both food and shoes, he said. "We didn't get beat. We was starved out." His eyesight was beginning to fail, and his hearing was going too, so he spoke louder. "We quit just five minutes too early," he griped. "They [the Yankees] was getting ready to stack arms, and we beat 'em to it." Then he warned his relatives that "I'm still going to be around after everyone here is gone."

In the spring he climbed aboard for his second airplane ride, flying to Bergstrom Air Force Base in Austin, where he was named an honorary commander for the day. The band played "Dixie" and the crowd whooped up a Rebel yell. Hollywood was on hand, and actor James Stewart read the orders of the day. Williams was dressed in a military uniform brought from a movie set. He had been asked to bring his old Confederate uniform, but he said that it had been destroyed years ago in a fire. Ella Mae, who said she did not like airplanes, waited for him on the ground.

When Williams turned 112, two hundred relatives and guests jammed into the cabin. He wore a tie and jacket for the affair, and they set him out on the porch in a wheelchair and presented him with another fancy birthday cake. He scanned the well-wishers and repeated, "I will live after everyone else goes." Ella Mae also spoke up this time: "I just hope and pray the Lord will give me strength to take care of Papa as long as he lives." She suffered from heart trouble and kidney disease but still managed to

In November 1957 Texas's Walter Williams celebrates another birthday and another year closer to becoming honored as the South's last living Confederate soldier. (Courtesy of the *Houston Chronicle*)

milk the cows and tend to chores. A son and daughter-in-law had moved in to help. From Minnesota, the old Yankee drummer boy Albert Woolson sent birthday greetings.

A big Chicago firm with an office in Houston gave Williams a free hearing aid. He slipped it in and said, "You won't have to holler now." A box of cigars arrived from Florida, and the shipper promised more for as long as Williams lived. In December he attended Confederate Day ceremonies at the state fair, where they passed around box lunches at the picnic pavilion. He danced—sort of wriggled, really—for a television camera.

At 113 he was presented with a Civil War medal by the Pentagon. By now he was blind, nearly deaf, and often ill. He suffered from dropsy, and his legs and feet were swollen. One of his daughters, Willie Mae Bowles, said "I'm afraid he won't last long." But he managed to sit up and take food, and he soon improved. "They are trying to make out that I am a heap worse than I really am," he complained.

To boost his spirits, a Houston furniture store presented him with a brand-new rocker. He took to it right away, especially enjoying the padded straw seat bottom. "He's just been rockin' ever since he got it," Willie Mae reported. His Civil War pension was raised to $300, but the increase did not immediately kick in because of a legislative mix-up. Willie Mae worried that the household might not make it; she said they were down to just $1.30 in the bank and behind in mortgage payments.

A newspaper reporter stopped by hoping to snag an interview. When the family helped the old man understand that the newsman was at the door, Williams barked, "I'll be here when you're gone!"

It seemed that maybe the old man was right. He became ill again in 1957 with a dangerously high fever of 103 degrees, but it was another Rebel veteran who died that year in Florida. "I am sorry to hear it," Williams said. Told there was yet one more Confederate still alive, 111 years old and living deep in Virginia's Appalachian Mountains, Williams vowed to "still outlive that other one" too.

Then Ella Mae, his second wife for all those years, the mother of his second round of twelve children, the bride who was almost thirty years younger than he was, passed on. Williams was just twelve days short of his 115th birthday when she died. His family moved him to Houston and put him in the back bedroom of daughter Willie Mae's house. There they thought the old man would soon die peacefully. But Williams hung on stubbornly.

Reporters and Civil War buffs came looking for him at the home on West Twenty-Third Avenue, just as they sought out Albert Woolson on East Fifth Street in Duluth, especially now that the Civil War Centennial would soon be under way. Much of the public hoped that the last of the blue or the last of the gray—both if possible—would stick around for the centennial ceremonies.

MAYBE IT WAS JUST SOMETHING ABOUT the Confederacy itself that kept old Walter Williams going. The Rebels lost the war, but they never surrendered their pride. Each state in the South boasted its own Confederate honor guard, and Louisiana offers a notable example of how the veterans in gray, by their strength and fortitude, helped the region endure defeat and Reconstruction, and pick up the shattered pieces of Southern society.

The national United Confederate Veterans (UCV) was born in New Orleans in June 1889 so that men could shake hands, slap backs, and swap war stories. More important, it helped them deal with the loss of confidence that came with defeat, to struggle against the spreading poverty that followed the surrender, and to support relief agencies trying to heal the stricken South. One of their first efforts, even before they formally organized, was to raise money for a Robert E. Lee Monument in the heart of New Orleans. The symbol would demonstrate that the South had its heroes too. Set atop a giant obelisk in the center of the Crescent City, the statue lifted citizens' hopes.

Even as local chapters opened in other Southern states, memories of the war were replaced with nostalgia and what eventually flowered into the cult of the Lost Cause. Some 100 ex-Confederate cavalrymen gathered in New Orleans to form the national organization, and the excitement of brotherhood filled the downtown shopping district and the Vieux Carré.

They elected John B. Gordon to be their first commander in chief. He had served as a major general in the Civil War, had afterward gone to Washington and a seat in the Senate, and then moved into the governor's mansion in Atlanta. Gordon had led a final lunge at Appomattox, and he used his fame to stoke fresh energy in the New South.

The veterans gathered in hotel ballrooms and outdoor tent sites. They played the old tunes, sang the old songs, and raised the old banners. In 1903 a crowd in New Orleans swelled to an estimated half million to applaud some twelve thousand whiskered Rebels who paraded down Canal Street and then bivouacked on the fairgrounds.

If they could not boast of victory, they could warm themselves in the cherished code of their war: duty, chivalry, and sacred honor. In 1915, with the Great War aflame in Europe, they designated Confederate President Jefferson Davis's birthday a legal holiday. They called it Memorial Day in Louisiana. "By this observance," said *Confederate Veteran* magazine, "we hope so to inspire the children with our love for the Southern cause that they will for all time preserve the memory of the Confederate soldier."

In 1911 they had gathered in Little Rock, Arkansas, at the half-century mark after the war's onset, praised by letter from President Taft in Washington. "The men of the Confederate army fought for a principle which they believed to be right," he wrote, "and for which they were willing to sacrifice their lives, their homes—in fact all those things which men hold most dear."

New Pension Bureau records now showed Confederate veterans were dying at a rate of six thousand a year. (For those from the larger Union army, it was thirty-five thousand Yankees per year.) Less than twenty-five years after the war, in 1888, W. P. Parks, an Arkansas artillery captain at Vicksburg, had written to Jefferson Davis about how the "many thousands, in the past two decades, have passed over the river." And Davis, in remarks that same year in Mississippi, urged his former troops to look past the war. "The past is dead. Let it bury its dead, its hopes and aspirations," he said. "Before you lies the future."

At a 1928 reunion in Little Rock, no more than three thousand turned up. "The snap and dash of the old men was gone," lamented *Confederate Veteran* magazine. "Nearly all of them are hard of hearing and are feeble in body. There was no Rebel yell to excite the people and to quicken their interest." An elderly veteran was asked how many of his company still survived. "Thirty-five years ago, I could call the roll of thirty in my company," he said. "But now, I am the only one living. They are all dead, and when a man dies, he drops out of thought or recollection." In an editorial, the magazine challenged the South to honor its hobbling, doddering veterans. "Let the world know how few remain. Let us keep in mind the glory of their achievement during four years of military struggle against heavy odds."

In 1933 a mere twenty-seven met for a Louisiana reunion in Baton Rouge. They doled out honorary commissions and new promotions. When one man was mistakenly referred to as a "colonel," he stood and insisted, "Call me general, or call me nothing!" They sported broad-brimmed hats made famous by General Lee. Veteran J. St. Clair Favrot welcomed them with an inspiring invocation. "The South has remained true to the ideals set by her wartime citizens," he said. "Out of the crucible of defeat and Reconstruction, the South came back." At a grand luncheon, the women decorated the tables with small Dixie flags and large baskets of scarlet dahlias. The men bowed graciously to the ladies. After dinner they gathered as usual for cigars and tales of approaching cannon.

At another reunion five years later in Baton Rouge, fifteen veterans met on the roof of the Hotel Heidelberg and clamored for back pay they said was due Confederate pensioners. "They've got the money, why don't they give it to us?" demanded ninety-two-year-old S. T. Seagrave from Lake Charles, Louisiana.

Minnie Booth Kernan of New Orleans, assistant adjutant general of the UCV, explained that the state had fulfilled its obligations of $60 a month and cautioned the veterans against agitating for more. It was unwise to keep "touching on any sore spots," Kernan urged.

Tempers cooled, and soon smiles were flashing again. W. E. "Uncle Billy" Dark of Dodson, Louisiana, pranced a little jig to the strains of "Dixie." At ninety-one, he had been married three times and fathered twenty-two children. How many great-grandchildren he had, he could not say. "I don't know them when I meet them," he laughed.

Only ten veterans convened at the state capitol in Baton Rouge a year later. They dined on oysters and eggs for breakfast, addressing one another as "general." Uncle Billy Dark stood up to dance again, telling his comrades he still could cut a pigeon wing. All he could manage was one foot off the ground.

Every year their numbers dwindled. Twelve were counted in 1940, in hats, ties, and beards. Several repaired to the Heidelberg bar for a morning toddy and then stayed much of the day. "We're going to get drunker 'n hell," roared "General" O. R. Gillette of Shreveport. "They ain't no better way to get drunk than to drink beer and smoke cigars." He turned to his pals. "Here, drink up!"

Angry words were hurled around too. The veterans condemned a man who had set up shop outside the front of the hotel wearing the insignia of a Confederate soldier and asking for nickels and dimes. A panhandler and a "fake," they called him. "No real old soldier has to beg," scoffed one veteran.

In 1942 only four in gray mustered to Baton Rouge. The business session was brief; they simply elected themselves as officers. The parade was just a few blocks. By 1945, of the thousands of men once listed on the state Confederate pension rolls, only nine were still alive. Finally there was but one: William D. Townsend of Olla, the last of the Louisiana gray.

William Daniel Townsend, also called "Billy-Dan," "Uncle Eli," or plain "Grandpa," said he gave two years to the war. He grew up in Meridian, Mississippi, and the Confederacy took him when he was just fifteen. He said he saw action in Louisiana and that a bullet tore open his right arm at Vicksburg. Captured there by Yankees, he said he was paroled in 1863 because of gangrene from that wound. He settled in Olla, farmed, and married four times: to an Annie, two wives named Frances, and a Maggie.

Like Walter Williams, he could rock for hours in his porch chair. Never having learned his letters, his stepdaughter read him the *Shreveport Times*. When he neared 100, he could barely walk to the corner; the single block to the town square was too much. But when he felt up to it, he would have someone drive him to the hospital in Shreveport to entertain the patients with a little fiddle playing.

Thinking back to the war, he described standing guard up to thirty-six hours because "there was no turning back." He had been young and strong then. Food was scarce, and they often ate "old poor beef." Or they fed on "mule meat that tasted awfully good during the bitter days of the Siege of Vicksburg." Reporters asked to see the scar on his arm, and he rolled up his sleeve. But it was faint and nearly gone; as a reporter for the *Shreveport Times* wrote, it was "hardly noticeable except by close examination."

Over Memorial Day weekend 1951, at a final reunion of Confederate veterans in Norfolk, Virginia, Townsend dressed in a fedora and double-breasted dark suit and got into a squabble over his pension pay. "Yes, I been ailing a long time," he told the Norfolk mayor. "Didn't think I could make it. Wasn't fit fer nothing till I got here." He invoked the legendary former governor, senator, and populist boss of Louisiana: "Yes, sir. I knew Huey Long's daddy. I did all I could fer Huey, but you know, Huey never did think of me. In fact, it took me five years to get my pension straight. I believe if Huey had lived he'd have remembered me." Townsend leaned in to the mayor. "If you see them fellers," he said, "see if you can do something.... It's mighty tight on a small pension."

As with Walter Williams in his rustic Texas cabin, the postwar years were hard on Billy-Dan Townsend. To earn a little cash he once posed for an ad for Southern Maid Cream Mixed Glazed Donuts. He wore a slouch hat and raised a coconut pastry to his mouth, a cup of coffee at the ready. But that kind of money never stretched far. So in 1935, when he said he was a year short of ninety, he applied for a Confederate pension. He claimed he had been captured on the Fourth of July 1863 after the forty days of Vicksburg, when the Confederate garrison surrendered. He identified his commanding officer as a Capt. Gus Cobb.

Louisiana pension officials could not find a Captain Cobb. They also wanted evidence of Townsend's exact age. So they turned him down. "Evidence of your Confederate service is not sufficient," pension commissioners told him. They suspected he was trying to take credit for another man's military record: "One W. or William Townsend was a private in Co. B, 27th Louisiana Infantry, but he enlisted at a time when you were only thirteen years of age."

Townsend did not give up. John Coats, a politician in Townsend's home parish, wrote to Baton Rouge that there must be some mistake, that a government clerk must have made a "typegraphel" error in Townsend's birth date, that he actually was fifteen when he enlisted, and that "from his size could easily have passed for older. He ran away from home to join." Coats added, "The old man has no edication [sic], and after talking to him I sincerely believe that what he states is true. Of course all dates are given from memory, and [with] a man of his age his memory is not always good."

Townsend tried to clear up the discrepancies. But he stuck to his story about Vicksburg. "I was sick at the time I was captured and wounded," he wrote to the pension commission. He gave five witnesses as former Confederate comrades—John Orr, Jim Orr, Lum Knox, B. Russell, and Dave Seats. But the commission could not find any of them, and Baton Rouge rejected him again: "The evidence of your service in the Confederate Army is not sufficient."

Townsend persisted. A ninety-two-year-old veteran, Alf Fuller of Dubach, Louisiana, signed a notarized affidavit swearing that he remembered a Willie Townsend from Company B of the 27th Louisiana Infantry Regiment. At long last, probably well beaten down, the state awarded Townsend $60 a month. But first they instructed the state Public Welfare Department to drop his name from the relief rolls. They did not want him double-dipping.

That did not satisfy Townsend. Now he demanded all the pension money he would have pocketed had his application not been held up. "You promised to pay us old soldiers our back pay," he insisted. The state denied him any back pay. So his wife, Maggie, wrote to Public Welfare officials and requested that they put him back on the relief rolls. She complained that Billy-Dan was squandering his $60 a month and not sharing it with her. "When he get [sic] his check he will get mad and leave and just waste [it], and leave me without food and anything and never give me a penny," she wrote. "I want to no [sic] if there would be any chance for me to get a part of it as I feel I am due half of it."

When that did not work, she wrote to the Veterans Administration in Washington. "I would furnish [our] home with a cow for our milk if he would give me half of the check to carry it on. He could do as he wished with his part ... [but] it is winter time. I haft [sic] to buy wood [and] feed and food." The VA officials said no. "Would [it be] possible for you all to grant enough money to buy Mr. Townsend a suit of clothes [and] a pair of shoes for his birthday?" Maggie then asked. No again.

Townsend died in February 1953. The governor praised him, and they lowered the flag at the state capitol. At his burial in Shreveport, they blew "Taps" and fired twenty-one rounds in salute. "Dixie" was played as they eased him into the red clay. He returned to the earth in an ash-gray uniform with polished brass buttons. A badge with the seal of the Confederacy was pinned to his coat.

And Maggie finally received some compensation. Every sixth day of the month, the postman brought her a widow's pension check for $48.39. She collected it for another fifteen years.

THAT IS HOW IT GOES SOMETIMES, when men age, memories blur, and stories get stretched. Sometimes the state can be cold and unforgiving when records are lost or incomplete. Were many of these old men truly veterans, or just warriors in their own minds? Those were the questions soon raised about Albert Woolson in Minnesota and Walter Williams in Texas, the last of the blue and the gray. But as symbols of honor and bravery, no one dared ask them directly.

"I'm so glad, Mr. Hoar, you haven't forgotten Dear Dad, Gen. Williams," Willie Mae Bowles wrote years later about her father, Walter Williams, to Jay Hoar, a writer who devoted years tracking down descendants of Civil War veterans. She described how each day she had cared for him in those last years in her home in Houston as her father lay slowly dying in her back bedroom:

5:00 a.m.	Coffee.
9:00 a.m.	Two soft scrambled eggs and milk.
Noon	Strained baby food, usually green beans or peas.
4:00 p.m.	Applesauce or custard.
9:00 p.m.	Strained peaches or pears.

"He got vitamin shots every Tuesday and Friday," Willie Mae wrote. "A night nurse made it possible for me to rest. So many people want his things, but I just can't turn them loose. How nice of you to seek my remembrances of him while I yet may share. What I have of Dad's I love and everything of his makes me feel he is closer to me. I have blood clots and am not over well myself these days. It was my privilege to be his daughter."

OLD MEN IN BLUE

The snow falls early in Duluth. Anchored along hills that shiver up from Lake Superior, the cold turns ashen white, the sky gray like iron. The mercury drops to zero and below, and it lodges there for months. The freeze hangs on so long they call it the "Air-Conditioned City."

The cold did not deter Albert Woolson. Early each February he was out on his ten-foot sidewalk, cigar in his teeth, shovel in hand, clearing a path for the mailman. He would put on heavy wool pants and a Grand Army of the Republic (GAR) cap, and head out the front door. He was especially diligent in the days before February 11, his birthday, because that meant the mailman would be hoisting a large satchel of cards. Woolson liked to keep the path at least a foot wide, large enough for the postman to maneuver to the mailbox at 215 East Fifth Street, where he lived with his daughter and her family, just blocks from the water, the wind, and the winter freeze.

"He's worried about the mailman having to walk through the snow to deliver birthday cards," explained the daughter, Mrs. John Kobus. "He plans to keep the walk cleared at least until his birthday."

Woolson appeared as strong and as hardy as a man half his age. Little dulled his spirit, nothing dampened his grit. He showed no sign of slowing down, even at 105, 106, and 107. He was so robust that nearly every afternoon on his birthday, when the cards and letters filled the parlor and the dining room table, he dressed formally in shirt, tie, and vest and settled into a favorite chair. Pen in hand, he would start answering the well wishes and tributes, though his hand at times shook a bit. To keep pace with all his letter writing, he often whistled a tune he remembered from the battlefields in Tennessee, the music of the Civil War still pulsing through his hardening arteries: "The Girl I Left behind Me."

> Though many a name our banner bore
> Of former deeds of daring,
> But they were of the day of yore
> In which we had no sharing.

Other times he devoured histories of Minnesota and stories of the American Indian tribes that for centuries had roamed the Lake Superior hills. The Ojibwas called the area "the little portage" after they rousted the Sioux from the bay and drove them out, less than a hundred years before Woolson was born. He could recall the names of some of those warriors, and he knew their descendants well; one had taught him to fire a musket.

Among his well-thumbed volumes was *Minnesota in the Civil and Indian Wars*. With a small slip of paper he had bookmarked the page where he was listed as a member of the 1st Minnesota Heavy Artillery.

At family dinners he led the prayer, a Divine blessing he called it, as his children and grandchildren gathered around the table. His face was deeply wrinkled, but that highlighted his sparkling blue eyes. His white hair had thinned somewhat, but it still covered most of his head. His appetite remained as strong as his muscles, and while he required no special diet he did usually avoid fatty foods. Whenever a plate of sauerkraut and spare ribs was served, Woolson dug in eagerly. "We can't stop him," said his daughter.

If the weather was fair, he would step out with his cane for a short stroll, maybe try a block or two. Or he might find a ride to a friend's house to pass an afternoon. Most evenings he was in bed by 7 p.m., and each morning he rose with the sun, usually around 6:30 a.m. He shaved with a safety razor, bathed himself, and then dressed for the day. Without any help he clomped down the stairs from his upstairs bedroom, read the morning paper through shell-rimmed glasses, and waited for breakfast.

He always took his eggs scrambled and his bacon crisp. Then he was comfortably back in his chair and armed with his books, in the front room with the floral wallpaper and the burgundy carpet, and he passed the rest of the morning until he heard the steps of the mailman. On most days throughout the year he received up to twenty-five cards and letters. Most of them dealt with GAR matters or inquiries from Duluth school kids wanting help with history projects. Many letters came from curious strangers. At birthday time, thousands of pieces of mail were delivered to his door. When he turned 106, an avalanche of eight thousand cards and letters arrived. He stayed up then to near midnight, just trying to keep ahead of the correspondence.

"Dear Rob and all," he wrote in September 1950 to his son and his family in Dayton, Washington, "just a line to inform you I am still alive and kicking. We all and the Johnsons packed up our lunch [and] went up the north shore some 45 miles from here to what is called Gooseberry Falls, a most beautiful park of some 35 acres right near the Big Lake. We had a jolly good time." He told his son that "my hearing is improving and usual good health much better." He said there was "quite a sum of cash in the GAR treasury," and "I hope I get some of it."

In February 1951 he again wrote to Rob: "This has been a very hard cold winter. It's still with us." He described being feted as the honorary guest at an American Legion banquet, with nine hundred members and their wives in a Duluth ballroom. "I have received a very large number of greetings from all parts of this country. $5 from an old man in Kentucky. Another old chap in Indiana, he sent $2."

Cora Gillis, secretary at the national GAR headquarters in Washington, wrote to Woolson a month later. She told him that Union veteran Hiram Gale of Washington State had just died. "This cuts us down to 7 members now," she noted, "and our colored comrade [Joseph] Clovese of Michigan is now in the veterans hospital in serious condition so [I] am looking for a message about him most any time. They had a big public celebration on his 107th birthday and I guess it was too much for him. I wonder if people will ever realize that men past 100 cannot stand these things any more. I read in the *National Tribune* about your birthday and am glad that you spent it with your family and not a big public affair. We want to keep you with us as long as possible, and these public appearances take so much out of men of your age."

Gillis bragged a bit about Route 6 in Nevada being renamed the Grand Army of the Republic Highway. And she complained that some state GAR organizations had not closed their staffs and sent their files to Washington once their last member had passed on: "I have just this morning been writing to the Kansas lady and told her if she didn't complete her records and turn them over that I would have to come and do it myself. Her last man died three years ago, and there is no excuse for this delay in closing." She added: "Hope you are keeping well and that soon you will be out of your terrible winter.... I think of you every time I hear of a new storm out there."

Woolson wrote to his son about the weather, too: "This has been a long cold winter and very much snow. Drifts 7–8 feet high all over the city." The American Legion had invited him to another banquet, he said, and "I have very many requests for my autographs on postage stamps recently. It has kept me quite busy. I am as well as usual. My hearing improving lately."

He wrote to Rob again after his birthday in 1952, what he called "another milepost in life's long journey." He delighted in all the gifts— twelve boxes of cigars, six quarts of "fine liquor and wine," and $100 in cash. "I was about tired out," he said. He always signed his letters "Father."

A. B. Kapplin, an admirer in Washington, D.C., wrote to Woolson: "Time moves on, as another year rolls by and another birthday. This must be a great day in the Woolson household." He closed with a wish. "May the good Lord spare you for many more years to come and that I may have my often-mentioned dream come true, that Albert Woolson of Duluth would someday be the last living veteran of the Civil War in America."

Woolson wrote to Rob that Union veteran James A. Hard in upstate New York had just turned 111, making him the oldest of the Yankees. As for himself, he boasted about a recent country outing in a "Nash car that makes the trip 52 miles in one hour." But he added, rather ominously, "If I live until Feb. 11 next, [I'll] be 106, which I think doubtful."

But the old drummer boy did make it, and on that February 11 came a letter from President Eisenhower, congratulating him at 106 and wishing him "many birthday anniversaries in the years that lie ahead."

By 1954 Woolson's letters to Rob were short, his handwriting scrawled, his thoughts often scattered. "Still alive," he scratched in one message.

Cora Gillis continued to write from Washington, warning Woolson of internal squabbles among competing Sons and Daughters organizations that honored Union veterans: "The Sons have the idea that because they are the men in the family that they should run everything, and we don't agree with them." She also spoke of a third generation: "Still getting many requests for records from folks who had grandfathers in the Civil War. It seems strange to me how little so many know about their grandfathers. Mine died when I was but five years old, but I still know about his service record." She closed with: "Hope you will be careful and not get a bad cold this year. We want you to stay with us for several years yet."

Too often over these years the mail brought sad news to the little house in Duluth. Theodore Augustus Penland died in September 1950. At 101, "Daddy" Penland had been the GAR's national commander in chief. He had attended more than eighty encampments; he missed only two. He enlisted late in the war, and years later, after the attack on Pearl Harbor, he had tried to re-up for a spot in World War II at the age of ninety-two. When Woolson learned of Penland's death, he dashed off a note to son Rob. He always thought Penland had joined too late and missed the fighting. "Mr. Penland was a kind old man, but it has been proved that he entered in with an Indiana regt. in 1865. That was when I was mustered out of U.S. Service. He never was an enlisted man in U.S. Service and never claimed the war."

Four days later, Woolson read of the death of James M. Lurvey—the last soldier from either side to serve at Gettysburg. There the young drummer boy had silenced his snare and assisted with amputations. "I guess that was the day I became a man," he would say. At his death at 104, Lurvey was living with other ill soldiers from other wars at the Veterans Hospital in Bedford, Massachusetts. "Physically I'm a wreck," he complained. "I'm older now than I ever wished to be." To feel young, he poured a stick of brandy into his morning coffee, stirred it about, and pronounced it his "Oh Be Joyful!" But the toddy could not beat back the pneumonia.

Woolson's mail in September 1951 brought news of Lansing A. Wilcox, the last veteran from Wisconsin. Born to a New York shoemaker, he had served as a corporal and scout and later farmed and taught school in Wisconsin. At 105, after four wives and several broken ribs from a fall, he was near deaf and confined to a wheelchair. He could no longer remember his age. "I feel very weak, and soon my Master will call me home," he wrote to his fellow GAR members. He dreamed of "beautiful eternal camping grounds" and of someday meeting "my comrades who are waiting for me and the great Grand Army." On the night he died, he left a half glass of milk on his bedstand.

Then in March 1953 came the news that made Woolson famous. In Rochester, New York, James A. Hard had died, and that left Albert Woolson the sole survivor of the Union army. In front of his home, reporters already were gathering.

Hard was 111 when he was taken to Rochester's General Hospital. For eleven days he had hung on. Doctors amputated his right leg above the knee and operated on a bungled spinal nerve. Then he slipped into unconsciousness and died fifteen minutes before midnight.

Hard had been working at a saw mill in Jordan, New York, when he enlisted in April 1861, signing on with the 32nd New York Volunteers. They took the train to Washington, he said, and he met Lincoln: "He gave me a handshake that nearly crushed my hand." Bull Run was his first test of fire. His "toughest" moment was along the York River, when a bullet whistled through his coat. He saw action at Chancellorsville, Fredericksburg, and Antietam, and mustered out a month before Gettysburg. He then worked as a civilian construction boss for the Army and on the railroad, and served two terms as commander of New York State's GAR. Each Memorial Day he rode in Rochester's holiday parade. His hearing was gone and he was all but blind, but he smiled at attention.

Rochester's citizens marked Hard's passing in a big way. His body lay in state at the Masonic Temple Auditorium. The bell atop the city hall pealed, and his cortege followed the same downtown route of the Memorial Day parades he had ridden so often. They halted at Mount Hope Cemetery, where mourners heard the formal burial service of the Grand Army of the Republic read aloud.

Woolson did not attend. He was too feeble and distraught, and he knew the burial ritual by heart and could recite it by himself. He had been to his share of both funerals and commemorations. Once city officials had held a ceremony downtown and honored Woolson with the Duluth Hall of Fame Award. They had hung his portrait in City Hall, the money for the painting raised by schoolchildren who saved their pennies—27,652 of them. For Memorial Day 1953 he slipped into his serge suit with brass buttons and shined his GAR cap for a city parade. He laid a wreath at the Soldiers and Sailors Monument in front of the courthouse, and thirty minutes later he was waving from a convertible as the parade's honorary grand marshal. Then it was off to a ceremony at the Duluth Armory, where the Lions Cub presented him with a plaque. Officials from the local posts of the American Legion and the Veterans of Foreign Wars also awarded him special citations.

Now, with James Hard dead, Woolson, the last of the Yankees, could hear the newspapermen outside knocking on his door. He was too troubled to tell them much. But he did acknowledge the "struggle" that Hard had endured, and he said that since he now was the last of the men in blue, he was "ready and willing" to close out the ranks when his time came. "I am proud to be the rearguard of such a gallant group of men," he said.

He settled back into his parlor room chair, lit another cigar, and started writing another letter. This one would be a note of sympathy to Hard's family in Rochester. When he was done, he opened the front door again and told the reporters one thing more. "Moderation in all things," he advised. "And I've got plenty of vim left."

He did. Two months later, in May 1953, the national commander of the American Legion, Lewis K. Gough, tried to hook Woolson up by telephone for a conference call with his counterparts in the South. But things did not go smoothly. Thomas Evans Riddle, 107, was too ill in the Confederate Veterans Home in Austin, Texas, to come to the phone, and he died soon thereafter. William Allen Lundy was impossible to reach in remote Laurel Hill, Florida. In rural Franklin, Texas, Walter Williams still lived in his old cabin, and they could not get a line to him.

So Woolson and a single Confederate survivor, John Salling, a moonshiner from the Virginia Appalachians, agreed to a brief telephone chat. A brief shouting match, really. The line crackled, and both men were hard of hearing, Woolson nearly deaf. Both had to speak up and loudly. Salling had lived his life deep in the hills, and he told Gough that this would be the first time he had ever talked on a phone. He was not quite sure what to say. "But I'll do it," he promised with a laugh, "as long as I can say, 'Hi, you damn Yankee!'"

When the line opened, Woolson waited for some of the static to clear and then he went first. "All you members of the Confederacy," he said, thinking that Riddle, Lundy, and Williams were also on the line, "let us shake hands in peace; let all differences be forgotten by the boys in blue and the boys in gray. God bless you."

Salling was humbled, and he forgot his damn Yankee joke. "God bless you," he told Woolson. "I am mighty proud to be able to speak with you. I hope you can hear."

Gough suggested a joint meeting of the last survivors; hopefully all could attend, Woolson and the four Confederates. Maybe one more time at Gettysburg, he mused, or on Pennsylvania Avenue in Washington. It would be a grand preview for the 1961 centennial year that was approaching.

Salling liked the idea. "I hope we both live long enough to have that meeting," he told Woolson. The Yankee did not respond. Either he did not hear, or the line went dead. Or perhaps he simply put the phone down. There would be no last triumphant reunion of the blue and the gray. But out of that conference call, in part, was born new interest in the Civil War and a Centennial Commission to commemorate a nation broken and a nation healed.

7

....

OLD MEN IN GRAY

His eyesight fading, his hearing impaired, barely able to stand or sometimes to sit up, Walter Williams was shutting down after 114 years. So his family closed the cabin in the Texas woods and drove the old Rebel to Houston, salting him away in that back bedroom. There his daughter Willie Mae Bowles could feed him strained peas and spooned applesauce from a jar, and could help him suck water drip by drip from a baby bottle. Sometimes he was treated to a small taste of barbecued spareribs—just enough to wet his tongue.

The former forage master soldiered on. His family tacked a giant Confederate battle flag on the wall in his room at West Twenty-Third Avenue, and that cheered him immensely. Austin named him an honorary colonel, and Assistant Secretary of the Army Hugh Milton presented him with a new Civil War medal. Entertainers occasionally stopped by to pluck on the guitar and belt out a country and western tune, and that seemed to spark the old man. Once an American Legion band performed outside his window, and his family swore that he kept time with two of his spindly fingers. On his 115th birthday he gathered up his feeble breath and hummed "Dixie."

Doctors were amazed that he made it past 115. Several bouts with pneumonia convinced them he would be gone at 116. Nearing 117, he was briefly hospitalized and then rallied and regained his health. He was discharged, driven home, and put to bed in the back room where the flag covered the wall. He always had said he would hang on just to see what was going to happen next; he always told everyone he would outlive them all.

That alone marked the man's independence. The North had its veterans hospitals for its dwindling number of Yankees, and the South its old soldiers' homes. Williams had no intention of gracing their doors, but many of his comrades ended there.

EACH SOUTHERN STATE'S SYSTEM for assisting veterans was different. In North Carolina, at the war's end, about eighty-five thousand veterans returned home. They were granted paroles as long as they swore a new allegiance to the United States, and for many that seemed fair enough after four years of fighting and surrender.

The Confederate Soldiers' Home in North Carolina sat on the outskirts of the state capital in Raleigh. The government set aside three and a half acres for a row of small structures near the corner of New Bern Avenue and Tarboro Road. They appropriated funds in October 1889, and the doors opened a year later. Within two years, nine Confederate veterans had moved in. Their numbers climbed so fast that by 1913, 986 had crowded through the doors.

Nurses lived on the grounds and cared for the residents' daily needs. Broad porches allowed veterans to dawdle away their afternoons, and dormitories let them sleep at night. Home administrators added a chapel. Stacks of cigar boxes cluttered the porches; one veteran whittled stick figures out of the empties—presents for his great-grandchildren. Nearly all of them read from Bibles on their bedstands. A Confederate flag flew out front; when American doughboys sailed to the Great War in Europe, a U.S. flag was added. Sixty of the old Rebels tried to enlist.

Strict rules were enforced. Inmates could not leave the campus without written permission. Visits downtown were granted just once a week. No loud voices or arguments were tolerated. Food did not leave the cafeteria: drinking was flat-out banned.

By the early 1930s more than half of the residents had died there; one was tossed out. In April 1935, eighty-eight-year-old veteran Joe Carpenter was evicted when the superintendent declared he was "unmanageable." He had enlisted at Raleigh and served as a guard handling Northern prisoners. His two brothers had also joined the Confederate army; one had died at Gettysburg. Carpenter now complained it was unfair to be ousted from the Confederate Soldiers' Home. "I've never seen so much trouble in all my life," he said. Superintendent Wiley T. Mangum said Carpenter was let go on a ten-day furlough for unruly behavior. "He talked bad to the nurses, called another old soldier a liar, and talked rough to me," Mangum said.

Carpenter often drifted in and out of the facility. In 1932 he stormed off and built a shack near Raleigh, using his Confederate pension money. Then he returned but left again, according to Mangum, and showed up on the streets selling his government allotment of tobacco. He left a third time to visit family in nearby Durham but returned to "get some things I left at the Home." That was when Mangum barred the door.

Later the home took Carpenter back, even though six gravely ill inmates in the hospital ward wanted him kept out. "Anyone violating the conventionality of decent and proper behavior should have no place among us," they told Mangum.

The residents also complained when the state assembly in 1937 passed a bill to close the home for good. "The end is in sight for each one of us, and we know that here we will receive tender care and heartfelt sympathy from our attendants," they wrote Raleigh. "Suppose you saw your end approaching, your days were numbered and you were to be kicked out of your home."

In another year all the men were dead. The National Youth Administration began repairing the walls and converting the kitchen and dining area into new dormitories. Where old men had come to die, young men were launching a future.

In Missouri the last to die at the state Confederate Home in Higginsville was John T. Graves. Heart failure claimed him at 108, his teeth gone, his eyes sunken, and his mind lost to senility. He had been born on a Pike County, Missouri, tobacco plantation and enlisted early in the war. He moved to the Higginsville home in 1933. Alone there most of the time, he rocked in his chair and chewed tobacco. Except for four Confederate widows, he had the place to himself. Graves could prove his war record and that he had been discharged near Osceola, Missouri, "on account of sickness." He included in his petition for residency signatures from four Confederates who remembered his military service. He stayed for seventeen years.

Graves reached 108 in 1950. He took a bit of cake and ice cream, but he did not let it spoil his daily round of eight highballs and huge fistfuls of chewing tobacco (which he enjoyed despite his lack of teeth). By then it was costing Missouri about $25,000 a year to feed, house, and clothe the old Rebel. A state legislator in Jefferson City complained that "we could keep him in the best hotel in St. Louis for less money." But that was beyond John Graves's concerns. Mostly he sat, rocked, and listened to a little radio. When he died that spring, they draped his coffin with a Confederate flag and centered it in front of the fireplace in the front parlor of the home. On the red worn-brick mantle stood a smaller Confederate flag. His pallbearers were grandsons of other Confederate veterans, and they carried him out the door and around the corner to the Confederate Memorial Cemetery. They buried him in soft Missouri limestone, already shared by 803 other Confederate veterans, wives, and children.

Walter Williams did not care much for Confederate Homes or military graveyards. Only once did he attend a Confederate reunion. He was not a joiner. He was more like another stoic rocking away his last years in Lincoln, Alabama: Pleasant Crump, who used his porch rocker so much it nearly splintered apart. Deep grooves rutted the floor. His Bible was frayed and thumped, the pages crinkled and finger-stained, some near missing.

Known around his small Alabama town as "Riggs," Crump was the last living soldier to have witnessed the surrender at Appomattox. "I was standing just across the road," he remembered. Then Crump took the train to Atlanta, but at that time, "there wasn't much left of Atlanta." From there sometimes a cart or a wagon picked him up. Mostly he walked the last hundred miles home.

There was no doubting his patriotism. His military file was intact, his pension in good order, and each month he drew a check for $150. He had clocked seven months with Company A of the 10th Alabama Infantry. He had enlisted at sixteen and fought at Petersburg and along the James River in Virginia. After the war he smoked his corncob pipe and rocked in his chair; he read his Bible seven times over, cover to cover. "People who pass the house see me sitting on the porch and think I'm asleep," he said. "But I'm not. I'm just talking with the Lord." For seventy-one years he served as a deacon at the Refugee Baptist Church. His favorite saying came from John 14:1: "Let not your heart be troubled."

Twice he was widowed; he buried three of his five daughters. And Crump never left the thirty-eight acres of horse, mule, and cattle pasture his first wife's father had bequeathed him eighty years ago. He drew water from a well with an old-fashioned windlass. He cut firewood and hauled it in a wheelbarrow. He was thin and short, and he ate sparingly. He liked his dinners without any fuss. "Give me a simple life," he said.

One morning in the spring of 1950, James W. Moore of Selma, Alabama, paid Crump a visit on Confederate Memorial Day. At thirteen Moore had run off to join his father's Confederate outfit in Alabama. He hung around about a year. After the war he gradually became prominent in Confederate veterans' organizations around the South, calling himself "General" Moore. He also took several trips to Hollywood and sometimes helped as a story consultant for Civil War films. Once when a studio greeted him with a wheelchair, he kicked it out of his way.

Moore pulled up to Crump's farm on Route 1 dressed in a fancy Confederate uniform so heavy with medals it would have weighed down Robert E. Lee. He saluted Crump sitting there on his rocker and then bounded up the porch steps. Crump put down his Bible and rose slowly. Dressed in a wool sweater and spring hat, he was not sure what to do next, except to salute back. Moore called him "colonel." The two men walked to the Crump family burial plot, where his wives Mary and Ella lay waiting for him. Flowers and a Confederate flag marked their spots next to the Refugee Baptist Church. The men shared some photographs, and then "the general" was off again.

Moore died the next year. Crump followed him on December 31, 1951. Just a week earlier he had turned 104. At the state capitol in Montgomery they closed out his pension file with the notation, "Last Confederate veteran from Alabama to die."

But the lasting memory of Pleasant R. "Riggs" Crump was of the old man with his Bible in hand, rocking back and forth on the porch. It turned out that during all those years he was doing more than simply praying and reading his Bible; he was watching a tree grow. He had planted a water oak forty years earlier, a tiny seedling when he reached retirement age on the farm. It sprouted roots, branched, and flourished; eventually it towered next to his porch. But in that last winter of Crump's life, the wind and the chill took the leaves, and the tree began to falter. The winter took Pleasant Crump too.

If old Walter Williams in Texas followed the news on the radio, or if someone read him the morning papers, he would have known about several others who died in 1952. Their military legacies were possibly true but highly questionable. The most colorful of these was William J. Bush in Georgia.

A short, gray-whiskered man, Bush once spotted a painting of Union Gen. William Tecumseh Sherman in an Atlanta museum. He jabbed his cane. "Let me at him!" he cried. When his elderly wife, Effie, graduated from the Georgia State College for Women, her husband tried to steal the attention. "I'm getting younger every day," Bush boasted. "My hair is just now fixing to turn black." He could see himself reaching 140; if not, he would settle for 120. That had been good enough for Moses. At public events he flashed around in a $300 Confederate uniform, complete with broad-brimmed hat and braided tassels, presented to him by the Twentieth Century–Fox movie studio. He also took the honorary title of "General" Bush. To best play the part, he scowled.

In 1951 Bush turned up in Norfolk, Virginia, for the final Rebel bash. He arrived in full Confederate regalia, including a crimson sash with gold trim. "I can hear good, I can see good, I can taste good, and I can kiss any damn woman who wants to be kissed," he said when his plane landed. "Now Daddy," shushed wife Effie. "Stop that cussing." Bush then broke into song, an Irish ditty about grog and whiskey. "I want some of it now!" he sang.

He bragged about his uniform, explaining that Hollywood had invited him to the premiere of a new war movie. He joked about his plane ride. They drove to the Monticello Hotel, and Bush held court the entire way.

General Robert E. Lee? "I kinda think I knew him. I was his bodyguard.... He was the best man who ever lived. When he gave a command on the field, it was carried out to the letter. He was a dandy. I love that old Lee."

Longevity? "A man lives as long as he wants to; when he dies he can't help it. Give me plenty of good-looking girls to kiss and I'll keep on living."

War? "I'd fight again if it could be about a good-looking woman."

"General" William J. Bush of Fitzgerald, Georgia, his wife Effie at his side,
arrives in grand style for the opening of the 1951 Confederate reunion in Norfolk,
Virginia. Documents reveal that he was a veteran of his own making.
(Courtesy of the Main Library, Sargeant Memorial Room, Norfolk, Virginia)

Effie lost her patience. "There he goes again," she complained.

At the hotel he leaped from the car and into the arms of a group of white-haired ladies. Some shook his hand. Some patted his hair. One kissed him on the cheek. "I'm from Georgia too," she blushed. "Good old Georgians," beamed "General" Bush. "Never saw one back down on the battlefield yet."

Through the doors he flew and into the hotel lobby. "Where are the cigars?" he barked. "The whisky? The women?"

"Now Daddy," Effie hushed. But she was used to his theatrics. Over the years she had heard it all.

Gettysburg: "I was there. Man, I really fought."

Appomattox: "I watched Lee's surrender."

Gone with the Wind: "Just like it happened."

Four years of war: "I fought to the end."

But the Georgia State Archives had no affidavit of his Confederate army service, no parental consent to let him enlist as a minor, no record of his enlistment oath, and no copy of his discharge papers. Census records showed he was born in 1846, but when he applied for a Confederate pension in 1936 he had backdated his birth date by a year.

In his application, Bush had struggled to answer some basic questions:

How long did you remain in actual military service?

"About six months."

When and where were your company and regiment surrendered or discharged?

"Don't know."

Were you personally present with your command when it was surrendered or discharged?

"No"

Then where were you?

"With state militia at time of surrender."

He added "in Virginia," then scratched that out and wrote, "error."

Why did you leave the army?

"Inability. Too young to serve."

Why did you not return?

"Joined state militia."

Were you prevented from getting back into the Confederate Army?

"Too young."

Did you try to get back into the regular ranks?

"Joined militia. Helped to defend Atlanta."

State officials returned the application. The best they could tell was that William J. Bush had served a short three months, meaning that he would have missed Gettysburg, Lee, and Appomattox. At least six months were required for a pension. But the state in its generosity gave Bush credit for his time in the militia, though they could not at first find those records either and only surmised he "probably" served.

Bush wrote back, insisting that he had soldiered as a Georgia state militiaman until Lee gave up the fight. A state senator from Fitzgerald urged Atlanta to approve the pension: "Get this old man a little to make his last days more comfortable." After "very careful consideration," the state in 1937 reluctantly approved the pension. He died in November 1952, a dozen or so years short of Moses' 120. The Bonnie Blue flag flew at half-staff, and the *Atlanta Journal*, which "covered Dixie like the dew," promised that for heroes like William J. Bush in Confederate gray, "tales of their valor keep them still alive."

Walter Williams did not care for antics, and he did not put on a show. He would not have taken to a man like Bush, who strutted around breathing of whisky. The Texan was content to recall the Chisholm Trail and herding cattle rather than any vainglorious heights in the Civil War. In many ways he was more cowboy than Confederate. As the 1950s rolled toward the Civil War Centennial, he sat quietly on his cabin porch in Franklin and then finally in his daughter's house in Houston.

There he lay one day when a congressman from Washington, D.C., drove up in a big black Cadillac. He came bearing greetings from the president of the United States, the vice president, the two Texas senators, the House majority leader, the governor of Texas, and the mayor of Houston. He also brought a sealed, framed proclamation and a five-page speech.

The old Rebel's daughter, Willie Mae Bowles, attempted to wake her father, wrapped in bed covers and asleep in striped pajamas. "Daddy, honey, ..." she whispered. They waited until the old man's fingers began to stir. Then she pressed a microphone hearing aid next to her father's ear. The congressman, who also served as a member of the Civil War Centennial Commission, leaned in and began to read the tributes honoring Walter Washington Williams as the "oldest of the two living survivors of the millions of soldiers of the Civil War."

8

CENTENNIAL

Nearly everywhere he went, Maj. Gen. Ulysses S. Grant III was asked the same question. He heard it the summer of 1955 in Cincinnati during an annual encampment of the Sons of Union Veterans of the Civil War. He heard it the following January in Manhattan, where he addressed the Civil War Round Table of New York City.

"Why all this interest in the Civil War?"

As the grandson of the Union army hero, Grant could speak from authority. He could reach back to his own youth at West Point and his long career with the Army in the Philippines, Cuba, and the Mexican border war. After World War I he helped the Supreme War Council draft terms for peace at Versailles. In the Second World War Grant headed up the protection branch of the Office of Civilian Defense. Soon he would be elected chairman of the newly created Civil War Centennial Commission.

He also could speak from the high advantage of family. He could recall standing next to his famous grandfather at a window in midtown Manhattan seventy summers ago, as together they reviewed a marching parade of Union army veterans from Brooklyn. He could remember his grandfather in upstate New York, too, in a cottage at Mount McGregor, as the family shuffled around the deathbed of the savior of the Republic. The old general and former president was racing against throat cancer to complete his Civil War memoirs. Outside, where he always stood, was Sam Willett, a private in an artillery company of New York State Volunteers.

He was now a proud member of the state Grand Army of the Republic (GAR), standing a lone watch over the failing Union hero. Before he died, Grant sent a message to GAR veterans in Maine. "Tell the boys that they probably will never look into my face again, nor hear my voic[e]," he wrote in his weakening hand. "But they are en[g]raved on my heart and I love them as my children." A few days later, another honor guard of GAR regulars carried the general's casket.

The grandson knew all this. He understood not just what the war had done but also what the 100 years that followed had meant to America. Speaking in January 1956 to the Civil War Round Table of New York City, he told the armchair history buffs exactly what they wanted to hear.

"The Civil War was *our* war," he said. "It all took place right here, where we can visit the battlefields and the countryside in which it occurred. It is a little like the hometown of the man who, in singing its praises and pointing out its importance, concluded with the statement, 'and most important of all, it contains my home!'"

American GIs had returned from World War II eager to learn more of the struggles of their forefathers. Civil War Round Tables discussed generals on horseback, boots on the ground, and complicated battle strategies. The study groups sprang up all around the country" north, south, east, and west.

Another war hero—Dwight Eisenhower—was ensconced for eight years in the White House, and he had hung a portrait of his hero, Confederate leader Robert E. Lee, in the Oval Office. From his earliest childhood memories in Abilene, Kansas, Eisenhower could remember the faces of old veterans who had fought both for and against the Confederate general.

"If, in Abilene, I never became as involved in the Civil War, this was because it was relatively recent," Eisenhower wrote in his post–White House memoirs after retiring to his farm in Gettysburg. "After all, when Abilene's men and women, and boys for that matter, talked about 'the war,' they meant the struggle between North and South that had ended only twenty-five years before I was born. There were hundreds in the town who remembered the war's beginning; its major campaigns and crises and figures; the ebb and flow of battle that reached from the Atlantic into our state; the downfall of the Confederacy; the assassination of Lincoln. For them, these events were not yet history.

"In Abilene, as in other American towns of that time, scores of men still in their fifties and early sixties who ran local businesses, worked nearby farms, or practiced the professions were veterans of the war," he recalled. "Closeness to it in time made that war appear commonplace to me."

The old veterans tottering along Abilene's Main Street, he wrote, could never envision their neighbor boy Dwight in the years ahead visiting Gettysburg to study tactics as a West Point graduate, and then in 1950 purchasing farm property "next to the fields where Pickett's men had assembled for the assault on Cemetery Ridge."

Indeed, by the mid-1950s what had once been a mighty force of Civil War warriors had dwindled to less than a handful of aged, sick, and dying veterans. Yet, incredibly, a few still lived. Maybe some would last until April 1961 and help the nation consecrate the 100th anniversary of the firing on Fort Sumter. It would be a rare privilege to honor one or two of them 100 years after the war.

In June 1952 the journalist William D. Workman Jr. visited the South Carolina home of a man claiming to be 106 years old and a former Confederate fighter. Workman hoped to record the sound of the infamous Rebel yell. Instead he found a man too ill to offer up anything more than a feeble hello. The Library of Congress also tried to record the South Carolina Confederate in full yell. But the old man's wife stopped them. "He might drop dead on the spot," she warned.

In 1953 a group of Round Table devotees and Civil War historians created the Civil War Centennial Association in New York. Four years later, President Eisenhower signed a joint congressional resolution establishing the national Civil War Centennial Commission. Its aim was to commemorate four years of war that had bloodied America, and also to give new emphasis to a reunited United States.

The history and romance of the Civil War were suddenly and freshly abloom in America. Battlefield parks in Gettysburg and Vicksburg pulled in record numbers of tourists, and government funds to support the Centennial Commission were funneled through the Interior Department not only to spruce up the battle site parks but also to return them as close as possible to their authentic period. Historians such as Bruce Catton and Allan Nevins produced best sellers about the old war.

"This is a matter of national history," the historian Robert Henry told a congressional committee marking up the bill to fund the centennial. "After all, it was an American war. It was a war in which we are entitled to glory in the valor and achievements of the men on both sides." He called it "probably the greatest event and the greatest crisis in the history of our nation."

Congress, its heart touched by patriotism, appropriated the maximum amount of $100,000 a year for the commission to carry out the centennial between 1961 and 1965. Eisenhower announced the appointment of commission members, including historians, congressmen, and local dignitaries.

After their first meeting in December 1957, the commissioners elected Major General Grant III their chairman. Silver-haired and retired but still bayonet straight from his days on the drill field, Grant seemed the perfect choice. He could bring the Civil War home to the American public through his family's link to the great general and his own military career. Speaking to that Civil War Round Table in New York, he called the war the first of its kind in the modern age: "the first in which a nation as a whole was engaged, in which everyone had some part or connection."

He noted that it was the first war fought after the invention of the telegraph, which quickened and enhanced headquarters-to-field communications, and the first to transport large numbers of soldiers and supplies by railroad and over great distances. It was the first to see major improvements in small arms and cannon, and the first in ironclads and submarine mines. Also, Grant said, "it was probably the last in which a general could command his army personally on the field of battle, and the last in which official records were sufficiently few and so scattered that you and I can in our busy days cover the records of an event or operation more or less comprehensively."

He warned of a tailwind of bitterness fanned by some—Southerners fearing that the North would use the centennial to lord its great victory over them, and Northerners concerned that the South, still smarting from defeat, would distance itself further from the rest of the nation. Some worried that the centennial would propel or sabotage the civil rights movement, which by the mid-1950s was garnering support in the North and resistance in the South.

Grant hoped that the centennial commemorations would instead bury the old hatreds. "One general tendency that I cannot understand," he had told the New York Round Table, "is the manifest effort to belittle some men or even their side, in order to make the opponent or other side seem more heroic, and which to my mind has just the contrary result. Neither Grant nor Lee gains anything by belittling his opponent. On the contrary each gains by an appreciation of the genius of the other."

He specifically castigated those in the South who continued to revere Lee and spurn his grandfather. "I cannot help a certain indignation at this unjust vilification of my grandfather and of the man who, after all, did win the war and bring about the reuniting of our country, not only by his victories in the field but also by the magnanimous terms he granted at Appomattox and by his later administration as president."

Many Southerners wanted no part in remembering the humiliation of their great-grandfathers. A Dallas couple urged their Texas senator, Lyndon Johnson, to "stop this effort to cause further internal hate and disruption between sections and races." In the North, a Delaware woman wrote to Grant, arguing that "at this crucial time we should be united in our beliefs" and that to revisit the tragedy of the Civil War and a nation divided would "cause nothing but harm and hard feelings."

Even in the nation's capital, uncertainty hung over what good a nationwide Civil War remembrance would bring. Virginia Livingston Hunt, a well-to-do Washington society doyenne, dashed off a letter to a New York congressman decrying plans for the centennial. Her grandfather had lost his left arm in the U.S.–Mexican War. As a major general in the Union army during the Civil War, he fell during Virginia's Battle of Chantilly in 1862.

"I have no desire to help celebrate a tragic war in which my grandfather Philip Kearny of New Jersey lost his life when my mother was just six months old," she wrote. "The South is only just recovering from northern devastation after ninety years. Congress is struggling with the problems of States' Rights. That was exactly the same in 1861. The Negro will just be further inflamed. What is the purpose; what is to be gained?"

Others strongly defended the centennial effort. They said it would help bandage the last festering wounds from a war a century old. "There was glory and honor for all who fought in the war," argued Karl S. Betts, the commission's executive director. In a January 1959 interview in the *Nation* magazine, he tried to allay Southern fears that the centennial would promote the Union's cause to end slavery over the South's desire to preserve states' rights. "There's a bigger theme," he said: "the beginning of a new America."

Historian Bruce Catton told a Round Table in Washington, D.C., that "in a strange and mystic way, the Civil War united us," because those who fought and the generations that followed shared "a great and unique experience."

After their first meeting to elect Grant, the Civil War Centennial Commission sat down to business in the spring of 1958. In the years ahead, they recorded their activities in a monthly newsletter, "100 Years After," mailed to thousands of state and local officials, donors and fund-raisers, historians and Round Table members, and an American public growing fascinated with the coming anniversary. That May they asked people to search their attics, basements, and garages for any diaries, photographs, newspapers, and books dealing with the war: "The commission recommends that these historical documents be sent to state archives or local museums and libraries for display."

By June thirty states had appointed local Civil War centennial organizations. In July Grant urged vacationers to visit some twenty-eight major battlefields in ten states in advance of the anniversary. In the North, Maine opened a museum that included relics ranging from musket balls to a razor used by President Lincoln. In the South on the Fourth of July, in the first sanctioned event of the coming centennial, "Taps" was played at a ceremony on a James River plantation in Virginia. ("Taps" reportedly first sounded there during the Union's Peninsula Campaign of 1862.) In August the federal government began microfilming Civil War records in Washington. In the South, V. C. Jones, the commission's liaison officer, completed a 3,000-mile automobile swing through the region to drum up interest.

In October Grant received a letter from Florence Sillers Ogden of Rosedale, Mississippi, thanking him for her appointment to the commission's advisory council and signaling that some of the sectional harsh feelings might be on the mend. "I am deeply interested in the Centennial and feel sure it will be a great success under your chairmanship," she wrote. "That is, if you are anything like as good at centennials as your grandfather was running a war."

She added that "since your grandfather shelled my grandmother's plantation as he steamed down the Mississippi on his way to Vicksburg, I know a lot about your family. You may be interested to know that I still operate that plantation, raise cotton on it. It is located one hundred miles south of Memphis. My father, a ten-year-old boy, was on the levee on his pony when your grandfather's fleet rounded a bend in the river, and he saw and heard Confederate sniper fire on the gunboats and the boats then let loose their works. I did not think I would ever receive an appointment from General U. S. Grant, but time and the river have run a long span since that August day in 1862 and the bitterness of those days is long spent. I consider it an honor to serve on your commission."

By the six-month point in the fall of 1958, the commission had created a speakers' bureau, printed a centennial guide, compiled a war chronology, and published a booklet answering that overarching question presented to Grant over and over: "Why study the Civil War?" In December the commission led a drive to help restore the battlefield at Antietam, Maryland. The National Park Service, working closely with the commission, announced a $690,000 facelift for Fort Sumter. A 1911 painting of an old Yankee and an old Rebel enjoying cigars together under a canopy of drooping moss was reprinted. Its title: "Bygones."

Five ex-presidents or former First Ladies were appointed honorary commission members. In Georgia the state historical commission set up a Confederate museum to honor where Confederate President Jefferson Davis held his last meeting and, with defeat at its doorstep, the Confederate Treasury buried its gold reserves. By spring 1959 commission volunteers were "more carefully marking" the graves of Civil War soldiers, including a cemetery in Warrenton, Virginia, where Col. John Singleton Mosby, the "Gray Ghost" of the Confederacy, lay buried.

Plans for reenactments were announced at Antietam, Gettysburg, and up and down the great swath of Virginia. A drive was launched to locate descendants of Union soldiers awarded the Congressional Medal of Honor. Baseball slugger Harmon Killebrew, leading the major leagues in home runs for the Washington Senators, stepped forward as the grandson of the "Union Army's finest physical specimen from the state of Illinois." In the South organizers raised money for a memorial to Stonewall Jackson and to restore some of the battle sites where his name became a legend.

"I am very interested in the Civil War," Richard Moore of Connecticut wrote to the commission. "I am a Confederate fan.... I have my own library books and I have just finished reading Robert E. Lee and young Stonewall Jackson. I have my own Civil War collection of bullets and other things. My mother is very interested in the Civil War, too. I have gathered newspapers and rags. I sold them to the junk man and got a dollar. I hear that you need money to buy the battlefields which Stonewall Jackson fought on. So I am enclosing my dollar. Sometime later I will send another one for the cause. Because right now I haven't any." He closed with "I am eight years old and in the third grade."

Centennial headquarters opened its doors at 700 Jackson Place, NW, across from the White House and next door to Blair House, where Soviet Premier Nikita Khrushchev was staying during a September 1959 visit. Washington police and Secret Service agents closely watched things out front, and one day they noticed a car pull up in front of the centennial offices. A man began unloading guns and sabers on a grassy plot by the sidewalk. Hands on their weapons, security officials surrounded him. "What's going on here?" they demanded.

"Nothing," replied Harry B. Elkins, the commission's administrative assistant. "General Grant is going on television, and these are his props."

"But guns?"

"Sure," Elkins said. "All this is Civil War vintage."

Thirty-seven states now had created their own centennial committees. The national Sons of Union Veterans, in a bow to the South, adopted resolutions stating that the centennial should be referred to as a commemoration and not as a celebration of one side's victory over the other. But fences were not repaired so easily. The *South Atlantic Quarterly*, published by Duke University in Durham, North Carolina, announced that it was "tired of the Civil War" and would not be printing a commemorative issue. The Richmond, Virginia, *Times-Dispatch* warned against a "centennial orgy of sectionalism" and suggested that the 100th anniversary of the American Civil War should only be used to observe that "out of that titanic struggle a nation was forged, a nation which has emerged stronger than ever from two world conflicts."

But in Yadkinville, North Carolina, the descendants of Theophilus C. Hauser and his African American slaves gathered together at the old homestead for an outdoor picnic. Souvenir napkins were passed around, embossed with a message from the ancestors of the former white overseers: "Welcome back to the old plantation. Many of you were born here where your parents remained faithful and true after the War Between the States. Your fathers and mothers are buried here. It is as dear to your hearts as it is to ours. Come again."

By spring 1960 the new theme was "A Centennial for All Americans." New York became the forty-first state to establish its own local committee, and in Washington, D.C., the national commission boasted six hundred members from all fifty states on its advisory council. Thirty commemorative postage stamps were soon to be issued, and a 16 mm, thirty-five-minute film on the centennial was in production. In Alabama, women sewed antebellum hoopskirts for upcoming balls and reenactments. Arkansas license plates were painted in Confederate gray and red. Students in Rockland County, New York, competed in Civil War essay contests; gold, silver, and bronze medals were awarded to the winners, much like the Army Civil War Campaign Medals that suddenly were all the rage. The Gimbels Department Store on Market Street in Philadelphia announced that it would turn over many of its display windows and prime shopping space to a centennial exhibit.

Karl Betts, the commission's executive director, could feel the momentum cresting. "We have nothing to sell," he said in the fall of 1960. "We just want Americans to read their history books and to take note and understand better some of the important events connected with the Civil War. We want as dignified and as reverential an observance of this era of our past as possible. We frown on the term 'celebration'; to us it is commemoration."

Then at last the nation awoke on Sunday morning, January 8, 1961, to the tolling of church bells—exactly 100 years after Southern guns had fired on the Northern steamer *Star of the West* in a prelude to four years of civil war. Giving a rare radio and television address, President Eisenhower formally announced that the Civil War Centennial would soon be upon America and stressed that the greatness of the nation did not lie so much in its bounty of natural resources as in the devotion of its citizens to duty and honor.

"No event in our history ever tested that devotion, that understanding, and that determination more profoundly than did the American Civil War," the president told the nation. "The memory of that event is shadowed with its story of sacrifice, of loss, of dark tragedy long endured. Yet somehow, today, it is the magnificent unity of spirit that came out of it, and the realization that every man is made for freedom and accountable for the freedom of his neighbor, that should be most clearly remembered. … Let us join in the forthcoming centennial observances with pride. The tragedy is passed, but the way in which Americans of North and South met and eventually overcame that tragedy is a living memory forever."

Dignitaries in New York City laid four wreaths at Grant's Tomb on the Upper West Side, the first placed by the general's grandson. Above them was inscribed Grant's statement upon accepting the nomination for president: "Let Us Have Peace." Church bells pealed on Riverside Drive. "We humbly repent the bitterness that turned brother against brother," the Reverend William R. Robbins said in benediction at the tomb overlooking the Hudson River. "We recall those who fell in battle." Light snow melted on the shoulders of 1,500 troops assembled in front of the granite steps. A battalion of West Point cadets in long blue coats and white belts stood in tight formation. Another row lined the front steps in old Union blue jackets and kepi caps.

In Midtown Manhattan a fifth wreath was placed at the statue of Abraham Lincoln in Union Square. Army troops stood rock still; a volley of rifle shots rolled overhead. The Sons of Union Veterans of the Civil War directed the observance. Some from the 79th New York Volunteers, the "Cameron Highlanders," wore kilts. A Boy Scout drum and bugle corps played somberly. Lincoln's Gettysburg Address was read aloud, the 272 words carried aloft in the chill winter air. Speaking as the former New York state commander of the Sons of Union Veterans, Maj. William F. Bruckel concluded the ceremony with "we reverently bow our heads at this time to all who made the supreme sacrifice."

In Lexington, Virginia, at Gen. Robert E. Lee's burial site, the sons of the South gathered to pay their homage. Virginia Military Institute cadets and visiting dignitaries crowded into the white pews of the campus chapel at Washington and Lee University, on the grounds where Stonewall Jackson taught philosophy and artillery before the war and Lee afterward ran the school. The United Daughters of the Confederacy set a wreath next to Lee's crypt, where his remains lie in the basement of the chapel he built.

Grant's grandson sent a telegram praising Lee as "a great and knightly American soldier and citizen." William M. Tuck, a former Virginia governor and now a congressman, read Grant's telegram honoring Lee's humility, which helped to fashion "the reunited country." Then Tuck had words of his own. "A large part of the concord and harmony which we as a nation enjoy today is due to the righteousness of spirit and the nobility of character of the great Southern chieftain at whose tomb we stand now," he said. "He sought to inculcate these priceless principles into the hearts and minds of those whom he led on the battlefield, as well as those whom he taught here."

The school chancellor, Francis Pendleton Gaines, said Lee should be remembered for looking beyond defeat in the South, an accomplishment particularly difficult for a man who in the war lost his home in Arlington, Virginia, and his citizenship upon his surrender. But, Gaines observed, Lee "closed resolutely every door of yesterday" and "busied himself about opening doors of tomorrow for a reunited country."

If Robert E. Lee had had a slogan for all the veterans after the Civil War—blue and gray, North and South—the chancellor said, it would have been: "We are all Americans now."

9

LAST IN BLUE

In April 1953 a group of young veterans from World War II mailed a letter to President Eisenhower. A year earlier they had formed a small fraternity called the Florence Guards "to preserve our friendships and particularly study American history." Now they met every third Tuesday in a small hotel clubroom in Chicago.

They wrote to the White House after discussing an "item from the passing scene" that one of them had spotted and clipped from a newspaper. "In Duluth, Minnesota, there lives an elderly gentleman of 106 years old," they told the president. "He is the last survivor of the nation's Northern Army of 2,675,000 in the Civil War. He lives with his daughter and son-in law, Mr. and Mrs. John Kobus, at 215 East Fifth Street. His name is Albert Woolson, and today he is the nation's senior war veteran."

The veterans noted that Memorial Day was approaching. "If God spares his life," they wrote, "Albert Woolson will be the only veteran left of the cause that gave us the grand tradition of Memorial Day." The men did not ask for anything special for Woolson, but they did hope that Eisenhower would "take steps to call the eyes of this nation to Duluth, Minnesota" during the coming holiday. In closing, they noted that "this request comes from five young men who served under your command in Europe in the last war."

Weeks passed, and the veterans heard nothing. Then, in early May, Frederic Gilbert Bauer, national counselor of the Sons of Union Veterans of the Civil War, happened to be in Washington. He sought a meeting with top White House officials about the Chicago letter, but he also wanted something a little more. He asked the Eisenhower administration to bestow upon Woolson a special brevet general rank to honor him as the last of the brave men in blue.

Bauer was unable to get an invitation inside the White House, so he mailed the administration a letter from his home in Ridgewood, New Jersey, stating that he "saw no reason why the sole survivor of the Grand Army of the Republic could not be commissioned in the Officers Reserve Corps." He told White House Chief of Staff Sherman Adams that "I could have presented it more cogently orally than in writing, but I enclose a formal request to you and ask as a favor that you will take the matter up with the president."

Woolson was more than worthy, Bauer wrote, as "there is now surviving only one of the more than two million men who answered President Lincoln's call to defend the Union in 1861–65." He noted that Woolson had served as a drummer boy in the Tennessee campaigns of 1864–65, and that his father had died from an injury during the war. The honor of a commemorative brevet rank for Woolson, Bauer argued, "would cost the United States nothing except the piece of paper for the commission."

"Such actions by the president," he added, "would, I am sure, be popular with citizens as a whole as well as with members of our organization. As Comrade Woolson was a drummer boy, the Army Band might consider it an honor if he were commissioned in their organization, though only on paper."

Then Bauer quoted Shakespeare, stressing the need for a speedy reply: "As Macbeth says, 'If it were done, when 'tis done, 'twere well it were done quickly,' for Comrade Woolson passed his 106th birthday in February and from the nature of things cannot be expected to live much longer."

In the White House, Adams, a former Republican governor from New Hampshire, sought advice from Army Lt. Col. Robert L. Schulz, the president's military aide. Schulz had worked closely with Eisenhower for years. He served as aide-de-camp to the general's chief of staff after the war, as his immediate assistant when Eisenhower presided over Columbia University in New York, and also when Eisenhower headed up international military security for NATO in Europe. Just four months ago, in January 1953, Eisenhower had brought Schulz with him to the White House, and there Schulz remained through the two-term presidency. Later he would support Eisenhower as his right-hand man and executive assistant in the former president's retirement in Gettysburg.

Unfortunately for Woolson, the Sons of Union Veterans of the Civil War, and the World War II veterans in Chicago, Schulz denied the request. It fell to Adams to break the bad news to Bauer. It came just a week before Memorial Day.

Adams told Bauer that, in establishing the Reserve Corps, the intention of Congress was to create a ready force of soldiers, sailors, and airmen "for the defense of the United States in case of need, and not for the purpose of honoring our heroes for past deeds.... I am sure you can understand why the Department of the Army must adhere to the policies established to govern appointment in the Reserve Corps. An exception, no matter how meritorious, would lay the department open to criticism from rejectees better qualified to be officers. To make an exception in Mr. Woolson's case would be unfair to the many deserving individuals who have been denied such a privilege. Also, criticism would be directed toward the Department by the active reserves who take pride in belonging to a force which is established to defend the country, and who look forward to belonging to the Retired Reserve after a number of years of active participation and expenditure of time and effort to make the organization effective."

The White House also sent a short, two-paragraph letter to the Florence Guards of World War II. The news was not pleasant for them, either. The president did not think it advisable to single out Woolson for a Memorial Day tribute. "I am very sorry that the decision in this matter has taken so long, and that it must be negative," the Chicago men were told five days before the holiday. "I am sure, however, that you will understand that were we to honor Mr. Woolson, it should likewise be done for the few surviving veterans of the Confederate Army. The president asked me to express to each of you his regrets."

In the White House, internal files on the matter were attached with a crisp, single-line note, putting an end to the requests: "Sorry—the

Pres. said NO." But Eisenhower and official Washington did not completely ignore the vestiges of the Civil War. In February 1954, to commemorate
the 145th birthday of Lincoln, the president laid a wreath of blue iris and
red and white carnations at the Lincoln Memorial. He was joined by a
phalanx of the Sons of Confederate Veterans, as well as Maj. Gen. Ulysses
S. Grant III. It marked the first time that Confederate descendants had
joined Union representatives in rites honoring the martyred Lincoln.

Two years later, three southern congressmen pushed for legislation
granting free medical care for the last Confederate veterans, much like
Woolson enjoyed as a U.S. Army veteran. Congress also authorized new
gold medals for veterans in blue or gray. The Civil War Centennial Commission would soon be under way.

In Duluth, Woolson began that Memorial Day 1953 much as he did
every morning. He dressed in shirt, tie, and vest and carefully climbed
down the stairs. After his eggs and bacon, he awaited the morning mail.
Outside the air was still brisk and chilly, even at the end of May, and
he snuggled into a woolen greatcoat and his GAR hat before stepping
outside. With cane in hand he greeted students from the neighborhood
Nettleton Elementary School. They cheered and waved tiny American
flags; Woolson snapped his heels under a larger American flag flying over
his front lawn and saluted the youngsters.

The day would not warm up much. Overcast skies and biting winds
whipped the city. But Woolson ventured out nevertheless. Today he was the
honorary grand marshal in the city's Memorial Day parade. He opened the
program by laying a wreath at the Soldiers and Sailors Monument. Inside
the local armory, he accepted tributes from the Lions Club, the American
Legion, and the Veterans of Foreign Wars. Shouting so all could hear him
above the racket of the armory's furnace, Woolson bellowed, "My heart
goes out to all you people who gave sons in past wars. God bless you all."

Ben P. Constantine, judge of the probate court, addressed the gathering next. He spoke of the coming Civil War Centennial and the current
Cold War between the United States and the Soviet Union. "Today," he
told them, "nearly 100 years later, our nation is threatened both from
without and within. We still find bullets, not ballots, are being called on
by some to decide issues."

Nodding to Woolson on the dais, Constantine continued: "The presence of Albert Woolson, the lone survivor of the Grand Army of the Republic, here gives us a link with the days of the Civil War. In the years between the Civil War and today, man, it seems, has not learned his lesson." The judge alluded to sharp differences between North and South that still troubled the nation. "We must learn to live together and remember to be tolerant," he warned. "If we do this, we will be doing what those men whom we honor here today fought for and died for."

Woolson went home to his daily regimen. In December he briefly was taken to a Duluth hospital, struggling against bronchitis and pneumonia. Nurses reported him as in "fairly good condition." Dr. C. H. Christensen could hear him in his room, his voice carrying out into the hall because he was hard of hearing. "If I ever marry again, it will be just for companionship," Woolson joked, his spirits still high.

Soon he was home again, formally attired in his old GAR uniform to entertain the neighbor kids by tapping on his drums on his front porch. When he turned 107 in February 1954, a team of two mailmen could not manage all the cards and greetings to his front door, so the Post Office dispatched a truck to East Fifth Street to deliver the bundles. One of them was a birthday wish from President Eisenhower.

"Don't count me out yet," Woolson said with a sparkle and a grin. "I'm going to be around for at least three or four more of these nice birthdays." For his visitors the drummer boy of 1864 tapped out a roll on his snare. He recited parts of "The Battle Hymn of the Republic," and he kissed some of the women who came by to wish him a happy birthday. "I'm feeling all right," he assured everyone.

Three months later, on Memorial Day 1954, more friends, neighbors, and local officials called or visited. His daughter Mrs. Kobus complained that their house had been turned into "Grand Central Station." Woolson wanted to join in the holiday events around town, but she urged him to stay home. Finally she let him ride in one of the parade cars, but there she drew the line. "For the first time we're turning thumbs down on several things he's done for years," she said. "Things like giving speeches, taking part in school programs and cemetery services, and going to special church services."

Albert Woolson, the last in blue in the twilight of his old age,
still could hit the drums like a boy sounding the march to war.
(Courtesy of Whitman College and Northwest Archives,
Walla Walla, Washington)

The old Yankee came home from the parade and disappeared through the front door. He did not have much to say. "Feeling as good as always," was about all he managed.

But he could not escape the press of the crowds. In August the Sons of Union Veterans of the Civil War honored his war service, and Woolson sent them his thanks. "As the last survivor of the Union Army, I have seen these United States grow into the greatest nation in the history of man," he told them. "Our sacrifices were not in vain."

The Sons displayed a new bust of the old man at a ceremony at the Hotel Duluth. The governor and the mayor were on hand in the hotel ballroom, and a chorus of nurses from St. Luke's Hospital entertained the 600 guests. Prominent among them was Maj. Gen. Ulysses S. Grant III.

Woolson dressed smartly in his double-breasted GAR jacket and cap. Holding firmly onto his cane, he stood between the mayor and the major general and watched as his young granddaughter Frances Ann unveiled the bust that soon would be on permanent exhibit at the city hall. The GAR motto was etched into its base, words first heard during the Gettysburg campaign: "To the Last Man."

"It's a good likeness," Woolson said. He thanked the sculptor, Avard Fairbanks of Salt Lake City, whose works had included Abraham Lincoln and four sculptures in the Capitol building in Washington. "We are all here for a grand purpose," Woolson said. "Thank you for this splendid assembly."

Gov. C. Elmer Anderson proclaimed that Minnesota was "proud of Albert Woolson, one of the few men who remembers that terrible struggle" of almost a century ago. "In fighting to preserve this nation, the men of the Union forces made one of the greatest contributions in the history of this country, as well in the history of western civilization."

Major General Grant read greetings from Vice President Richard Nixon. Gen. Douglas MacArthur wired that the "tradition that Woolson represents is perhaps the finest in the history of the republic." (Woolson had sent MacArthur a birthday greeting a month earlier, in January, and MacArthur, in thanking the Yankee veteran, twice misspelled his name as "Wootson.")

Fairbanks spoke too; he had just been commissioned for another sculpture of Woolson, this one to be a life-size work commemorating both Woolson and the legacy of the Grand Army of the Republic. It was to be placed at Gettysburg, the watershed spot in the war.

Woolson did not hear the speeches or tributes. By this time he was almost completely deaf. Even at his home that morning, his daughter had to write a note in large block letters telling him that Major General Grant was at the door to pay a short visit. Woolson read the note and then looked up sharply. His eyes beamed.

"I've always had nothing but the greatest of admiration for your grandfather," he blurted out. "General Grant was my man. I loved and respected him." His voice boomed loudly across the parlor. The first General Grant, he said, was "one of the greatest military men that ever lived."

The Civil War general's grandson looked down and smiled at the old man who strained to hear him. Before he left, he scribbled a note telling Woolson that he had brought him a box of cigars.

Next to arrive were reporters, and Woolson leaned back in his chair. Despite his deafness and his failing eyesight, despite how difficult it was to climb out of bed and down the stairs each morning, to read the morning papers and the mail, despite the exhaustion of honors and parades and the chill off Lake Superior, he aimed to show them his mind was still as sharp as ever, and his constitution too.

He could not hear their questions but assumed they wanted his take on world affairs in these dark days of the Cold War. What would an old man from a distant war think of today's problems? He gathered up his strength and gave them the best he had.

"Old Uncle Sam needs to be cool and calculating these days," he said. "You have got to work your way carefully in world affairs. I think our President Eisenhower is doing that right now. He's a cautious man going very carefully…. I don't think there's any danger of war at the present time. We are too well equipped. I don't think the Russians will venture into a war now. I think the Russian masses would be opposed to it."

Force, he said, "is wicked. If we want to keep peace, the best way we can do it is to be strong." He meant "tough," as in what he had seen in his war. "All of our young men should learn strict military discipline and to obey orders. They should learn to work together in unison. A brief period of military training is good for the boy."

February 1955 brought another avalanche of cards and letters. President Eisenhower wrote to Woolson that "people throughout America regard with honor the brave men on either side of the conflict in which you served nearly a century ago."

The old soldier was 108, and the years were showing on his brittle frame. He mostly shunned the crowds now. He could no longer shovel the sidewalk. Instead he spent many an afternoon on the front porch. "Checking the weather," he said, bundled up against the cold. For a while he alternated between cigars and a pipe. He watched television a bit but could only guess at what the actors and newsmen might be saying. He no longer had any words of wisdom for a modern world. "I'm no authority," he said.

But he did venture to city hall and the rotunda for the installation of the new Woolson bust. He offered only a few words in thanks, spoken slowly to the 300 gathered around his chair up front. "I hope my career has been an example for the younger generation," he said.

For several days he posed at home for Fairbanks the sculptor, busy at work on the Gettysburg statue. Sometimes Woolson spoke to the artist, often in a loud voice, about Lincoln and Grant and the grand old days when the Union won the war. Sometimes he asked questions, and the artist jotted down answers with his heavy grease pencil on a large tablet. Other times Woolson just sang to himself, often the sentimental 1840s ballad "Ben Bolt."

Grass grows on the master's grave, Ben Bolt,
The spring of the brook is dry,
And of all the boys who were schoolmates then
There are only you and I.

Two weeks after his birthday, he was hospitalized with lung congestion. Doctors frowned that he still smoked eight cigars and enjoyed his half ounce of brandy each day, and believed this new flare-up was similar to his earlier attack of bronchitis. But Woolson rallied, and they sent him home within two weeks.

There he remained as Memorial Day 1955 arrived, and he decided to sit out the fuss of parades and tributes. He did send greetings to the three living Confederate soldiers in the South—in Florida, Virginia, and Texas. "They fought for what they believed in and I fought for what I believed in," he said. "God bless you all, from a Yankee."

But Woolson was not completely housebound. On Saturdays he rose early with his family and rode out to a lake cottage an hour away. His appetite remained strong, his attitude stronger. The area schools sent large bouquets of flowers, and he delighted in their beauty. All in all, reported his daughter, "he's feeling very good."

In June he was back at St. Luke's. He was placed under an oxygen tent to ease the congestion, and eventually he came home again and returned to his cigars.

Woolson sent a birthday greeting in November to the Confederate veteran in Texas—Walter Williams. "Happy birthday and a good year to come!" he wished him. In February 1956, Williams returned the favor with a telegram to Woolson in Duluth. "Happy birthday greetings from Colonel Walter Williams, now 113."

More cards and letters bombarded the Woolson household. Charles Edison, son of Thomas Alva Edison, told Woolson that his father was also born on February 11, 1847, and that while Woolson was playing the marching drum the future inventor, "as a young telegraph operator ... helped to relay the reports of battle." The First Lady sent birthday wishes from the White House. "May enduring peace and abiding happiness be yours in abundance," wrote Mamie Eisenhower. Her husband added his greetings: "I am delighted to join once again in saluting you."

Albert Henry Woolson was now 109 years old and declining. In early March the doctors put him back in St. Luke's Hospital. Sen. Estes Kefauver, a Tennessee Democrat running for president, stopped to visit. Maybe that cheered Woolson up or helped him rally, because after two weeks under oxygen tents he was discharged and driven home. His first evening back he fired up several cigars and cleaned his plate at dinner.

In the days that followed, a special nurse visited the home as a precautionary measure should his lungs accumulate fluid again. A neighbor boy, Tim Johnson, recalled how one day the caregiver invited him and his siblings in to meet Mr. Woolson. "He was in bed and looked as old as anyone I had ever seen," Johnson said. "He spoke loud. He told us he was a drummer boy in the Union army, a long time ago. He was hard to understand and had the biggest ears I had ever seen." The old man was pleasant, but soon he wearied. "The caregiver told us he was tired and we should go now."

In mid-July Woolson was returned to St. Luke's and the oxygen tents. They gave him air through a nasal tube and fed him intravenously. For days and nights he struggled with congestion, and yet, between his horrendous coughing spells and gasps for breath, he soldiered on. Lying in his hospital bed, he recited from memory poems and other bits of verse from the Civil War, plus snatches of Lincoln's Gettysburg Address.

Each morning he requested the same breakfast. "We just couldn't seem to get the bacon crisp enough for him," reported his nurse, Myrtle Solberg. "But he was always polite, modest, clean, and cooperative. When he rumpled his bed a bit he always said he was sorry that we had to fix it up for him." For lunch they brought him vegetable soup. "I always saw that there was a bowl of broth on his tray," Solberg said. His preferred dinner was corned beef and cabbage.

And he always asked for cigars. "The doctor didn't want him to smoke because of his lung congestion," Solberg said. "But there wasn't much anyone could do about it. Mr. Woolson wanted his cigars, so we lit them for him." Mostly she remembered her patient as a gentleman. "Whenever he wanted something, it was 'please,' and whenever anyone did anything for him, it was always 'thank you.'"

Then on a Saturday he lapsed into a coma, and doctors downgraded his condition to critical. Yet even then as he lay unconscious in bed, the hospital staff detected a "strong, indomitable will to live." Dr. Charles Bagley marveled that Woolson already had defeated death several times, had long ago beaten the odds against a long life, and had always pulled through. Where the source of his inner strength lay, the doctor could not say. So they just watched, the doctor and the Woolson family, as the days wore on and he lay silent in his sleep. Dr. Bagley warned the family on August 1 that death was imminent. "There's nothing to be optimistic about," replied his daughter, Mrs. Kobus. "We're resigned that he won't recover.... It's just a matter of time."

Woolson died in his sleep the next day, August 2, 1956. Chronic heart disease and lung failure took him at a quarter before ten in the morning.

"The American people have lost the last personal link with the Union Army," President Eisenhower said in a statement. "His passing brings sorrow to the hearts of all of us who cherish the memory of the brave men on both sides of the War Between the States."

Gen. Maxwell Taylor, the Army's chief of staff, said that Woolson's passing saddened the ranks of the military, having lost someone so "distinguished as a volunteer and respected as a soldier." Congressman John A. Blatnik of Duluth remarked, "He was our number one citizen, the last of his army and an era." In upstate New York, Major General Grant said the death "marks the end of a great epic in our history. May he rest in peace and rejoin the happy comradeship of the boys in blue who preceded him."

Flags were lowered in Duluth and around the country. One hundred and nine Army guardsmen, one to represent each of Woolson's 109 years, marched alongside his cortege. His eight surviving children, twelve grandchildren, fifteen great-grandchildren and four great-great-grandchildren mourned as his body lay in state, dressed in Yankee blue. Secretary of the Army Wilber M. Brucker headed a delegation that flew in from Washington, and he presented Mrs. Kobus with the flag from atop her father's bronze coffin. "This is no ordinary flag, nor ordinary day," he told her. "This is the last flag that shrouded the remains of the last veteran of the Union army."

Twenty-five hundred people attended the funeral at the Duluth Armory, the site of so many of Woolson's past honors and tributes. A military cordon lined the entryway; an army band performed as six army sergeants carried him inside. The Carillon Chorus Club of Duluth sang "The Battle Hymn of the Republic," the song that, even in his old age, Woolson could recite by heart.

An Army chaplain, Col. Augustine P. Donnelly, spoke of a long life lived well: "To few men are given such length of days as were given to Mr. Woolson. To few men has it been granted to see the realization and the goal of the war in which he fought, the preservation of the Union and so many boys of the North and South joining hands to fight in later wars for their nation." Woolson, the chaplain said, saw America transformed from "a young struggling people to a world power, from sectionalism to a national unit." Then he quoted from Lincoln at Gettysburg, more words that Woolson had committed to memory: "Let us resolve that these dead shall not have died in vain."

The Sons of Union Veterans placed a wreath and a single rose, plus a miniature American flag, on top of the casket. Six military pallbearers hoisted their comrade up and into the hearse. The funeral proceeded down Superior Street, and then the four miles to Park Hill Cemetery. Children and grandparents, young and old, filled the lawns and sidewalks, some with cameras, some with flags, many in tears. Boy Scouts held toy rifles; some of them saluted. An Indiana fife and drum corps played slowly.

At the cemetery, three volleys of rifle fire crackled in the air. An Army bugler from Texas played "Taps" as ten F-94 Starfire jets roared above in a cross formation. Then they lowered Albert Woolson into the earth. One of the last to leave the gravesite was a teenage drummer.

In Washington that fall, U.S. District Court Judge Burnita S. Matthews, born in Mississippi as the niece of two Confederate soldiers, declared the Grand Army of the Republic officially no more; the last of their members was gone. The few GAR furnishings that remained—two flags and a box of badges—were donated to the Smithsonian Institution.

In Gettysburg the Woolson statue was formally dedicated that September. It shows the old warrior holding his cane, his hat by his side, sitting on a tree stump and surveying the battlefield. Speaking at the ceremonies was Frederic Bauer, national counselor for the Sons of Union Veterans of the Civil War, who three years earlier had failed to persuade the White House to honor the old man with a Memorial Day tribute. Bauer noted that the statue's front base did not bear Woolson's name because he had not fought at Gettysburg (that battle raged the year before Woolson had enlisted). Rather it said, simply, "In Memory of the Grand Army of the Republic."

Civil War historian Bruce Catton penned an epitaph for the once mighty fraternal organization of Yankee legions. "When the final handful of dust drifted down on Albert Woolson's casket, and the last notes of the bugle hung against the sky, the door swung shut" on the GAR, he wrote. "It cannot be reopened." Woolson, he wrote, was at the end "one incredibly old man who stood alone without comrades.... We have lost something we can never regain. One very old man died, and all of us are made a little more lonely."

Long ago in his youth, Woolson had hurried off to war to seize his "share of the glory," as he himself once remembered. But in his failing years, the old Yankee came to see his experience in a remarkably different light. Like the nation itself, he had grown and matured; he had learned to set aside his harsh feelings and to reject the old hates. "We were fighting our brothers," he once said in lament. "In that there was no glory."

Now his Southern brethren, the three Confederate veterans still living, wondered who among them would be next and who would be last.

William Lundy, 108, limped around his Florida farm with a wooden sawhorse for support. He claimed he had served in an Alabama Home Guard. "I regret very much the passing of Mr. Woolson," he said.

At 110, John Salling of the Virginia Appalachians continued to delight visitors with his booming baritone, his kaleidoscope of Confederate medals, and a fancy new Army blouse. His family at first did not tell him about the death in Duluth, worried that he might be too "greatly disturbed." But eventually a friend gave him the news. "Albert has gone to his rest," said "General" Salling. "I hope someday to meet him across the great river."

Down in Texas, Walter Williams was 113. "I am right sorry to hear about it," he said. "But this just goes to prove what I said before: the South is going to outlive the North."

10

....

DEBUNKED?

he day Albert Woolson died in Duluth, a man few had ever heard of stepped forward in a small town in Oklahoma and announced that he now was the last surviving Union soldier in America. Louis Nicholas Baker said he was a year older than Woolson, had enlisted with a Missouri company of Yankee volunteers, and, just like Woolson, had been a drummer boy in the Civil War, if only for three months. His claim in Guthrie, Oklahoma, touched off an investigation that spread to the Pentagon in Arlington, Virginia.

Until then, Baker had mostly been known around town simply as "Grampa." For years he sat quietly alone on the stone steps of a Division Street office building in downtown Guthrie. Occasionally he was spotted at the local recreation parlor, where he liked to play Pitch, but he did not say much there either. For years he had seemed spry and healthy, and he hurried out each day for a two-and-a-half-mile walk. But mostly he loafed around the streets and bragged about his Pitch playing. "I have the championship touch," he boasted. He never wore a tie and rarely dressed up. "I don't want all the fussin' around," he said.

He still smoked—a pipe and cigar—and though his eyesight was almost gone, he managed to get through the morning newspaper with help from a large magnifying glass. For hours he sat on the steps in front of the office building, reading every item in the paper until the sun slid behind the building and it was time to walk home.

Baker said he had been born in France and brought to this country by his parents when he was eight. They farmed around St. Louis, then pushed west to Kansas, and in 1889 he hitched up a covered wagon and dropped down into Indian Territory in the years before Oklahoma became a state. He settled in the Pleasant Valley region north of Guthrie and claimed to be the only surviving original homesteader of Pleasant Valley.

He claimed he was the last of a lot of things. He said he was one of the few living members of the Anti–Horse Thief Association, first organized in Clark County, Missouri, in 1854, and thirty-five years later in Oklahoma Territory. He could show a few delegate ribbons presented by the local lodge. He said he had served with the Union Protective and Detective Association and that he once holstered a revolver and patrolled Payne County as a deputy sheriff. He had joined other fraternal organizations as well, like the Modern Woodmen and the Owl Lodge. But in 1918 he had given up homesteading, farming, and chasing horse rustlers and retired. He moved to a thirty-six-acre lot on the west end of Guthrie, where he kept a cow and planted a vegetable garden.

Baker said he had seen four wars but could name only three. He complained that "civilization is gettin' worse all the time." In September 1945, at the close of World War II, he had twenty grandchildren, but only one was in uniform. That fall a seventy-nine-year-old sister, twenty-one years younger than Baker, visited from Illinois to mark his 100th birthday. The family managed to coax the old man off his downtown stoop and to a granddaughter's home for a small open house. The next morning he returned to his perch at Division and Oklahoma streets.

At 103 he sold the cow, plowed over the garden, and moved in with a daughter. He gave his seven children a couple of farm plots and other property he said was worth $40,000. "What would I want with it?" he asked. "I kept enough money in the bank to buy everything I want." He said he was the last living person in town to have started a savings account at the Guthrie Bank the day it opened. "I've never borrowed a penny," he swore. "I paid cash, or I did without."

Another year and another birthday later, when the few remaining Union veterans were meeting for their final Grand Army of the Republic (GAR) convention in Indianapolis in 1949, Guthrie townspeople and reporters were surprised to find Baker still sitting on his stoop. Shouldn't he have been in Indianapolis? "I come to town just like I do every day," he replied. He never took part in any GAR events and had never applied for a Civil War pension. He said no one would find his name on the GAR rolls, either.

Where did he serve? What battles did he fight? "Ohio volunteers," Baker answered, but he could not remember the name of the company or its unit number. (Missouri must have slipped his mind.)

He was more interested about turning 104. "I heard them talking something about a party," he said with a grin.

On the morning of August 2, 1956, Albert Woolson died in Minnesota. By then Baker, by his own count, was a month shy of 111. And that afternoon news from the radio started buzzing around the town square. But Baker was no longer on his stoop; now he was confined to a bed in a Guthrie nursing home. There he told anyone who asked that he had never wanted to make a "hullabaloo" out of his three months in the war. Why did he pass on seeking a Civil War pension? "I didn't need it," he said.

His relatives said his Union army discharge papers had been lost long ago; in fact they had never even seen them. His daughter, Mrs. J. A. Yeager, doubted the family could come up with any proof. The old man in the nursing home could not be of much help. "He's doing pretty well," she said. "They sit him up for brief periods during the day, but they can't leave him up too long because his arteries are hardening. The doctor said there is nothing the matter with him, other than hardening of the arteries. He looks good."

The newspaper in the state capital started looking into Baker's story. The *Daily Oklahoman* checked with Washington, D.C., sources and found the record of a Louis I. Baker of Illinois, a similarly named Civil War veteran listed in the National Archives. He had been part of Company E of the 6th regiment of the Missouri infantry. The records gave no exact birth date for this Baker, and other documents did not match with the Louis Baker in Guthrie. The Louis Baker of Illinois had been born in Luxembourg and was twenty-nine when he enlisted in June 1861. He entered the Union army at St. Louis and spent three years—not three months—until he was honorably discharged out of Chattanooga.

The newspaper asked the Haskin Service, a document research

company in Washington, to dig deeper. In November 1956 the Haskin researchers issued their final report, "Another Union Veteran?" They had located the other Louis I. Baker—different from Guthrie's Louis Nicholas Baker—who was "a carpenter by trade" in Illinois. They found that he had applied for and started earning a $20-a-month Civil War pension in 1879, based in part on several Civil War wounds, unlike the Oklahoma Baker, who had boasted he never bothered to seek a pension because "I didn't need it." The Illinois Baker had married and fathered two children; the Oklahoma Baker had seven. And the Illinois Baker had died in 1909. "If still living," the report noted, the Illinois "Louis Baker would now be 124 years old."

So Louis Nicholas Baker, whiling away his afternoons in downtown Guthrie, somehow had heard of the Louis I. Baker in Illinois and tried to steal his identity, or perhaps he had innocently confused himself in his old age. But none of it mattered much longer. In January 1957 the Oklahoma pioneer died at the Resthaven nursing home in Guthrie—five months after Woolson in Minnesota. His obituary gave him some of the recognition he had sought late in life. It noted that he had "claimed" to be the last Yankee soldier of the Civil War. And it left it at that.

ONLY THREE CONFEDERATES now remained.

William Allen Lundy hobbled around Crestview, Florida, with a wooden sawhorse rigged to his waist for support. He put his age at 108 when Woolson died. When asked for his secret, he had no answer. "I eat anything," he said, his chin grizzled in whiskers, a brushed suede hat atop his head. "Anything I can get to eat."

Frail and wrinkled, he no longer was as alert as in years past. "I used to have a big time and get around but I don't do no more rambling," he said. "I walk around the house a little. That's all I can do. I ain't strong enough, somehow." Most of his life "Uncle Bill" had stayed off tobacco, and he looked down at those who chewed.

Liquor? "When I can get it," he said.

How much? "Many and many a gallon." Liquor store prices were too high, he said. But Lundy had long ago developed a homemade recipe. "I'd still make it if I could."

How is it he had lived so long? "Keep away from them doctors, and take a little nip all along." And, of course, "living right."

After suffering a stroke, Lundy moved in with a son and his family in Crestview on the Florida Panhandle. Winters he spent inside, with the venetian blinds lowered just enough to cut the glare from the sun. When the phone rang, he seldom answered. "Women on it," he complained. "Yak, yak, yak! All the time." In the summers he sat outside, partly to avoid the phone.

He was immensely proud of his Confederate heritage. In April 1952, at 104, he told the *United Daughters of the Confederacy* magazine that he had but one regret: "I just wish I could have had one of those fast jet planes when I served in the Confederate Guard. I bet I would have scared hell out of every one of those Yankees." Asked if he approved of Southern slaves winning their freedom after the Civil War, Lundy said, "Yes, I'm glad. Sometimes they were abused, and besides, it's not the wish of the Lord for any man to be a slave."

He said he was born in Alabama in January 1848 and served in the Coffee County Home Guard when he was fifteen. He moved to Florida around 1890, settling on a farm in the Murder Creek community near Laurel Hill. In old age one of his ten children would sometimes drive him into town, but Lundy insisted, "I can drive a car as good as anybody." He said he was still a remarkable shot with a rifle and could knock a squirrel out of the highest tree in Yellow River Swamp. He could catch any sort of fish too, pulling them right out of the water. He especially enjoyed picnics, and always won a trophy for being the oldest one there.

Life magazine photographed Lundy in 1953 at his son's farm. They found the old man in big thick boots, dark denim overalls, and a gray coat. He sat on a rickety old stool next to a broken fence board, a cane in each fist, the suede hat crowning his silver hair. They shot him hobbling around with his sawhorse too. "You are here to take my picture," he told the photographer. "But you will go away, and I will forget that you were ever here."

Another photographer, Bruce Roberts, drove up from Tampa the following year and took pictures of Lundy around the farmhouse, playing checkers, breezing himself with a church fan, and wrapping the Stars and Bars around his legs on the porch. "He wasn't boastful. He was polite and cooperative, and I was really impressed," Roberts recalled. "He wasn't claiming to have been in any great battles or shooting people off of horses, and he said very clearly it was just a Home Guard. And he certainly was accepted by the local people. He played the part well."

In November Lundy bagged one of the first deer of the fall season on the sprawling Eglin Air Force Base hunting reserve. He measured the buck at six points and 140 pounds. He said the deer "ran right out in front of me and lifted up his head in the right position for me to paste him right between the eyes.... I'll be back next week and get another one." He said he loved hunting: "It makes me feel good, just like I do after taking a good swig of homemade skeeter juice." *Sports Illustrated* gave him a one-paragraph mention in its "Pat on the Back" column, noting that for a man who once "hunted Yankees in the Civil War, Lundy can still handle a gun pretty well at 106." Lundy had his picture taken with the buck's carcass strapped on the hood of his black sedan. He stood ramrod straight, rifle in hand; on this occasion, he did not need any sawhorse to hold him up.

He reached 107 in January 1955 and celebrated by digging into his favorite meal: corn pone, fresh pork, ham, turnip greens, baked hens with dressing, and "tater" pie. A television crew from Pensacola put him on the news. He remembered that he once guarded a bridge near Elba, Alabama, as part of the state's Home Guard, and they were under strict orders not to fire unless Union soldiers tried to take the bridge. Luckily, he said, "they did not." "I have always been sorry I didn't shoot one or two of them," he added, and yet, "I'm not mad at anybody." Not anymore, not after all this time. "'Not even [at] a Yankee."

In the spring he lined up in cap and gown with fifty-eight Crestview students and was awarded a high school diploma. It was just an honorary degree, and he had been invited because two of his grandnieces were graduating. He sat in the front row and thought the whole thing a lark. He kept staring at his diploma, although it was doubtful he could read. "I'm going to have it framed," he said. "Hang it on the wall. And I might start teaching school."

Two weeks after Woolson passed on, a writer visited Crestview and asked Lundy about his exploits in the Civil War. Lundy said he would grant the interview, but only if first he could hold the writer's two small daughters in his arms. "Someday," he said, "they can say that a Confederate soldier held them and kissed their rosy cheeks."

He then gave quite a different account from what he had told before, especially about his age and what had happened on that bridge. In the past he had said he was fifteen and only served with the Home Guard, not the Confederate army; he also said he had strict orders never to fire his rifle. This time he told another story.

"I was conscripted into the Confederate army in March 1865 when I was boy of only fourteen years of age," he said. "The entire country was at war! We were hearing of the intention of General James Harrison Wilson to burn the city of Selma, Alabama. On April 2, I was stationed at the entrance to a bridge on the main road into town. I saw the first horse troops as they headed toward my bridge. I aimed my gun on the leader and would have killed him for sure, but something told me not to fire my gun. For that brief moment, as I hesitated, the Union officer passed by and did not see me. If it had not been for that small voice saying, 'Don't fire your gun,' I could have killed my first and only Yankee."

Plenty of people believed him. Gen. Nathan Farragut Twining, the Air Force chief of staff, presented him with a special gold medallion. Lundy gazed at the prize for a long time and then held it aloft. "It's real gold!" he beamed.

On his last birthday he reached 109. Two thousand people attended a party in the Crestview High gymnasium. He wore a faded Confederate hat and climbed the stage while hanging onto a blueberry-root cane. Two pretty girls helped him up. A chorus sang "Way Down upon the Swanee River." "We've done all the hating we ought to do," Lundy told everyone. Then he commenced to kissing the girls. They paid little mind, and gave him 109 silver dollars and a birthday cake. He said he would rather kiss girls than eat cake.

In March 1957 he underwent a gallbladder operation in Pensacola. He had prostate trouble too, and his kidneys were distressed. A doctor from Wisconsin performed the surgery, and said Lundy pulled through "much like a younger man might have." Once past the danger point, the old man lay around the hospital waiting to go home, telling nurses and the staff

"Uncle Bill" Lundy found his way into a pile
of national magazines as one of the last living
Confederates, despite a stack of birth, census, and
pension records that documented otherwise.
(Courtesy of *Progressive Farmer* magazine)

how he once had fired several "potshots" at Yankees on that bridge—offering yet another version of the encounter near Elba.

He eventually went home to Crestview. For the Fourth of July, he was named an honorary member of the Ground Observer Corps at the air base, just in case any Soviet fighter pilots might slip through the Florida cloud cover. A winsome brunette pinned the silver wings on his chest. It was hot that afternoon, nearly 100 degrees, but Lundy looked perfectly pleased. "I can whip 'em, I'll protect 'em," he said of his new assignment. "I joined up to spot Russian planes. It's getting so I can't walk much anymore, so I thought I'd take to flying." A colonel handed him a certificate to go with the honorary wings but Lundy was not impressed. "The colonel ain't as pretty as a gal," he quipped. When the ceremony came to a close, he glanced around and asked, "Anyone got a nip?"

Progressive Farmer magazine put Lundy on their cover in August 1957. "Fought With Lee," read the caption. He wore his suede hat, a string tie, and a broad grin. "Indestructible," the editors proudly said of their cover boy. "Have you ever seen a more expressive twinkle in any eye?" They caught up with him at home, where he had hung a massive five-foot Confederate flag on the wall beside his bed. He spent most of his time there now, relaxing. The Crestview Chamber of Commerce suggested he fly the flag outside for everyone to enjoy. No, Lundy said. "I want it where I can see it."

He talked about the war but did not mention any bridge. This time he said he had protected the Coffee County Courthouse. He said he never fired any potshots, either. But mostly Lundy wanted to chat about women. "The ladies are just as pretty as they were when I was young," he declared. "I think they look better."

A few days later he was driven to the hospital with a high fever, never having recovered fully from the gallbladder surgery. There he died. They shaved his beard and cut his long hair. His family could not find his old Confederate uniform. It must have crumbled away years ago, they guessed. A local sewing circle had been making a new Confederate general's uniform for Lundy when he took sick, but he died before they could finish. So his family dressed him in a simple gray suit, white shirt, and gray tie. They took the flag off the wall and spread it over his casket. That was his wish; he had asked them repeatedly to remember to cover him in his Stars and Bars. After his burial in Laurel Hill, Florida, his son Charles brought the flag home and tacked it back up.

Was a Confederate flag–draped casket the proper final salute for William Lundy?

Census records show he actually was born in May 1860. When soldiers marched off to the war, Lundy had not yet learned to walk. According to the records, he was about twelve years younger than he claimed. In the federal censuses for 1910 and 1930, he did not even mention that he had served in the Civil War. He also had problems securing a Civil War pension and only was approved when the Florida state legislature took the extraordinary step of passing a special act to pay him the money.

Like many veterans, he first filed a pension claim in the bottom years of the Great Depression. He said he had served in 1864 in something called "Company Brown" in Alabama's Home Guard. He was discharged, he claimed, at the "close of war." Two comrades, one named Adams, the other Mason, filed affidavits on his behalf.

For two years his application lingered in Tallahassee, so he filed it again in October 1933, this time writing that he had served with Company D of the Fourth Alabama Cavalry. Gen. James McKinley, the adjutant general in the War Department in Washington, searched the records and came up empty. "The name William A. Lundy has not been found on the muster rolls on file in this office of Company D," he wrote to the Florida state comptroller. Nor, for that matter, did Lundy appear with "any Confederate States Army organization numerically designated 4th."

Lundy filed another claim. Now eighty-five (he claimed), he insisted that he had worn Confederate gray from March 1864 through May 1865.

He was turned down again. So he bypassed the bureaucrats and appealed directly to the politicians. In 1939 the state legislature rose to his defense. The lawmakers fudged his age a bit and then rammed his pension through:

WHEREAS W. A. LUNDY, of Okaloosa County, Florida, is now Ninety-one (91) years of age and in feeble and weakened physical condition so as to incapacitate him for work to support himself, and he is in destitute circumstances and greatly in need of a pension;

AND WHEREAS W. A. LUNDY has resided in the County of Okaloosa for more than fifty (50) years and is one of its oldest citizens;

AND WHEREAS W. A. LUNDY at the age of sixteen (16) years enlisted in the Confederate services in the Home Guards in Coffee County, Alabama, and rendered valuable services therein to the Confederate Cause.

The state awarded him $40 a month for "the remainder of his natural life or until otherwise provided by law."

Lundy wanted more: a bump up to at least $75 a month. He said the Home Guards were as tough as any Confederate fighting outfit. He appealed to the state for an increase. In August 1941 the secretary of the Florida Board of Pensions declined to raise his pay. But over the years other cost-of-living increases came through; by 1953 his monthly pension stipend had risen to $150.

By then Florida and Alabama were each claiming Lundy as their own last Confederate rebel; both states touted him as their own. His Florida hometown planted a sign on the city outskirts: "Welcome to Crestview, Home of Uncle Bill Lundy." In the city park they flew a Confederate flag in his honor. When he died, they carried him to a small hilltop rise in a cemetery just a few miles south of the Alabama-Florida line. In death, though buried clean shaven and minus a Confederate uniform, everyone wanted a piece of Uncle Bill.

THAT LEFT TWO. FROM WHAT WAS once a mighty Confederate war machine of hundreds of thousands, the ranks had thinned to two wizened veterans. The Civil War Centennial was just a few years away. Could either of them hang on?

John Salling was a tall, thin, wiry man. He did not march with any Confederate regiment or serve with any Home Guard. His task during the war, as he described it, was a short stint digging saltpeter for the Confederacy near his cabin on a slope of the Appalachian Mountains. He was about thirteen or fourteen then, he guessed. Now he seldom left his flyspeck of a town along the Clinch River at Slant, Virginia, but he crowded his last years promoting himself as one of the last Civil War veterans. He did it with a wide, infectious grin.

It was difficult not to like the old man. A saltpeter miner, a moonshiner, a logger, a railroader, a mountain farmer, he was full of cornball wisdom and hillbilly humor—a regular knee-slapping sort of feller. He lived so deep in the hills and hollows of southwestern Virginia, it nearly was Tennessee. When fame and celebrity rousted him out of the mountains in the 1950s, he relished every precious moment.

"I'm not a scholar," Salling said during the final Confederate reunion in Norfolk, Virginia. "I've never had a fight. I've never been locked up in jail. I've been a great hand to visit the sick. I've given more than I've got, and I always tried to treat everybody right."

He missed the Saturday nights of his youth, when "everybody got together for a square dance and there was plenty of good, hard cider to pep you up." Sometimes he played the fiddle, his mouth free to puff cigars. Once he told that story to a doctor, and the physician looked him straight in the face and said, "John, you've been a hellcat, haven't you?"

Like Lundy, Salling wrapped himself in the Confederate flag, and he loved the ladies: "I never met one I didn't like." Unlike Lundy, Salling had his own Confederate general's uniform and the honorary title too. He wore both with gusto.

His early years had been remarkably tough, even for a mountain boy. He could recall backbreaking days carving a life out of those hills: "Many a day I've split one hundred or more fence rails out of cedar logs for ten cents a day and then went home and plowed my land with oxen." Yet when he grew old, unhitched the oxen, and stopped cooking the cider, Salling still cut quite a youthful figure. Well into his 100s, his hair remained jet black, his appetite as hearty as ever. He drank a half-gallon of milk every day. His teeth might be gone, but he could see for miles, he said, and his hearing had held up, though sometimes when a storm blew through he would squiggle a hearing aid into place. "Can't hear thunder without it," he said.

Reporters would ask him to explain his thick, dark hair. "Always wearing a hat and never washing my hair. Maybe every five years or so."

What did he have for breakfast? "Three or four eggs, coffee, plenty of sausage and fatback, puffed wheat, and plenty of bread."

Dinner? "Fat meat when possible, fried chicken, soup beans, and corn-bread."

Did he take vitamins? "They ain't much, I'm telling you. We had plenty of good food back in the old days that had more of them things in it than all the pills you can get today. And we were never sick with colds and such, either."

What about the moonshine? "I've made a sight of brandy. Good likker never did hurt no man, if he knew how to drink it.... I found more excite-ment making illegal whisky than in the Civil War."

The country life? "I've kept my nose out of other people's business and have tried to get along with everybody."

Big cities? "I don't like to be about big towns. I'm plain about that."

Religion? "The Lord has been merciful on me a great deal more than I have been on Him."

And the central question: Why do men fight, why do men go to war? Salling lifted his long, thin finger and tapped it twice on his forehead. "They're touched!" he said.

He was born, he said, in May 1846, and that is the date engraved on his six-foot-tall memorial stone on a hillside just down the road from the Salling family cemetery. Erected by the Virginia division of the United Daughters of the Confederacy, it honors him as "General" John Salling, "Virginia's Last Confederate Veteran."

According to family lore, Salling was one of four children born in Scott County, Virginia, to his fourteen-year-old mother, a slave named Caroline Matilda Salling. They raised him up in the hills; hardly had he learned to talk than he picked up the English lilt that had arrived with his father's ancestors from Britain. Not long after the Civil War, he married Mary Flanary of Stony Creek, Virginia; their life together spanned seventy years and seven children. She died in 1939 and Salling started to push past 100, but still he rose each morning and walked the mile into town to pick up the mail, trade barbs with the locals, and walk home.

What no one knew around town was that the 1860 federal census showed that Salling had been born in 1856, ten years later than he claimed. The records indicate that he was born in Scott County to Caro-line M. Salling, and that she was twenty-six years old at the time, not fourteen. The 1880 census puts his birth year in 1859, making Salling even younger, and it notes the African American blood on his mother's side. The records describe him as a "mulatto." His wife is listed simply as "Mary." The 1910 census put him younger still: born in 1860, the year before the war guns sounded and the Confederacy needed any saltpeter.

In the Depression year of 1933, however, Salling went looking for a pension. He filed his papers in March. "I was in the branch that made salt-peter," he wrote to state officials in Richmond. For his disability, Salling listed "old age." He reported that he earned only $50 a year from a little farming. Asked whether there was a group of Confederate veterans in his community, he replied, "no, there is not." Asked to name any wartime comrades, he came up with only one: a James Salling. Unable to read or write, he signed the papers with his X.

Gen. James McKinley, the War Department adjutant general, wrote that "the name John Salling has not been found on the rolls on file in this office of any Confederate States army organization. The records show that one John Salling served as an expressman in the Quartermaster Confederate Army at Fort Smith, during the month of November 1862, but the date of commencement and termination of his service has not been found." Nor could McKinley find any record of a James Salling in the Confederate services.

James K. Johnson, the Virginia state pension clerk, searched the state archives in Richmond for a James Salling, but the closest match was a James R. Collings or Collins from Scott County, who had served as a captain of Company D of the 25th Virginia Regiment. Johnson wrote back to John Salling and mentioned the expressman named John Salling at Fort Smith. But, he added, "We do not imagine this applies to your service, as in 1862 you were merely a boy."

Johnson noted that the state required a sworn statement that Salling truly had "enlisted in the Confederate army before entering the salt-peter works, or during this time you were employed in the salt-peter work, and detailed as an enlisted Confederate soldier." He continued: "It is rather a peculiar coincidence we have two applications from Scott County recently, one from James Salling, who claims to be 84 years of age, and worked in salt-peter works, also one in the name of John Salling, received this month, who claims to be the same age and to have been in the same works. Is it possible that James Salling and John Salling are one and the same person? Please let us hear from you."

John Salling replied that he served under a James R. Collins (as a friend spelled it) "to work in salt-peter mines." He signed his X.

State officials moved cautiously, concerned that these two Sallings in the mountains might be brothers or cousins who were trying to fool them. They asked for more proof, telling the pair to sort it out. The Sallings told Richmond they were not related; they just happened to have the same last name and had worked together digging saltpeter.

The state ultimately granted James Salling a pension, and in 1934 his wife, Lydia Salling, filed for a widow's pension when her husband of nearly sixty years died. But she had no idea which branch of the army he had served in, and could not name any of his superior officers. "I don't know," she wrote on the application. She signed her X, and the widow pension came through.

As for John Salling the Appalachian moonshiner, he did not respond to the discrepancies in his pension application. Once challenged about his service, he backed off. According to the records, he never was awarded a Civil War pension. But through the subsequent years he stuck to his story about digging saltpeter. At the start of the war, many young men volunteered for that duty to keep from being drawn into a Confederate combat unit. This was particularly true in the mountain regions, where people often were less willing to embrace the Southern cause and many remained loyal to the Union.

Salling said he spent a year in Lawson's Saltpeter Cave on Copper Ridge. It was dirty, backbreaking work. Called "peter boys," they wore caps and suspenders, sliding their small bodies into the mouths of caves at sunrise and slithering out at dusk. Often they crawled on all fours, with candles or burning splinters to light the way. By the time they reached manhood, their bodies carried the ravages of the mines—chronic back pain from the heavy bags heaved through the narrow passages, and lungs scarred from the dust and dirty air. Many died young.

"Yes, I dug saltpeter during the time of the war," Salling said in a January 1959 interview. "I helped from under floors; I never worked in no mine. I helped get it out from under floors and they put it in sacks and hauled it off from there. And Captain Collins was the peter man."

He did not remember any fighting around Slant, he said. "Not that I can remember. I couldn't remember that." But he did recall seeing "lots" of soldiers. "They wore gray, gray stuff," he said; many carried "old army guns."

Did he ever shoot a Yankee? "No."

Did he meet Robert E. Lee or any other high officers in the Confederacy? "No, no, I didn't.... But I do recollect that Stonewall Jackson got killed, and General Lee fell down."

Did he remember the day news drifted into the hills that the war was over? "No, I can't remember.... I couldn't tell what year it was."

How old was he when the war ended? "I just couldn't tell exactly. I couldn't tell you exactly."

The war he could not remember became his life; it defined him in old age, it brought fame, medals, and a fancy gray general's uniform that he wore for special occasions. Sometimes it turned his mountain humor into little nuggets of wisdom. "Wars are uncalled for," he told the *Washington Post*. "Wars are all part of some scheme or for a man who wants himself put on a monument."

But mostly he kept up the cornball humor, as in the story he told the *Richmond News Leader* about two U.S. revenue agents who showed up in Slant to arrest him for cooking whiskey and take him to jail in nearby Abingdon, Virginia. "The way to go into the moonshining business is first to make friends with the revenuers," Salling said. "Then everything should be lean and pure to make good likker. One night, I was up there in the holler alone. It was drizzling rain. I thought I saw a flash of light, and then somebody knocked at the door. I just had my hand over the still cap to test the singlings when they called for me to open up. It was two local revenuers, federal men, and I knew 'em both."

Salling asked, "Want a drink of likker, boys?" "Yes, bad," one agent said. So, Salling continued, "both of 'em took a drink. I told 'em I had a leak in my cap, and one of 'em fixed the leak while the other one shoveled the fire. Well, I says to 'em, 'Boys, we'll all go to Abingdon now.'"

One of the agents went home with a keg of whiskey, the other a quart.

Now there was no way they could haul Salling in for what they had just done. But they did not leave without a word of warning against mountain hooch. Salling replied, "I says to 'em, 'I ought to caution you. Don't you fellers say nothing about finding this still.'" One of the agents assured him that his secret was safe: "This is the best place to make likker I ever saw."

Salling loved to show off his still and explain his recipe: six bushels of finely ground cornmeal, a bushel of rye meal, a half bushel of corn sprouts ground down for malt, and three or four gallons of molasses. But most visitors did not want to learn about whiskey; they wanted to hear about the war.

So Salling would tell them he had attended the seventy-fifth blue and gray reunion at Gettysburg in 1938, one of his rare trips off the mountain, and had watched the president light the eternal flame. An amazing feat, he thought.

"Me and a couple of Yankees set together and listened to President Roosevelt speak. He didn't have nothin' to start from much, but he said he was going to set a light up there that would burn forever. I set up close to one of them Yankee fellers and I said, 'Now, ain't that a mystery?' This here Yankee took a drink of likker and said, 'Well, he won't never do it.'"

Old Salling would slap his knee at that one, grinning with a mouthful of gums. Other times he would let his family turn the tables on him. "Course he still likes a pretty girl," said his daughter, Nancy Thompson. "You ought to see the shines he cuts when he sees one coming up the road. And when he gets a spoonful of likker in 'im, he's equal to a Holston preacher. He can preach a sermon then!"

Wife Mary died in 1939, and John carried on. Many afternoons he went fishing, a pastime he learned skipping school when he tired of "larnin'." Once during World War II he felt a knot on his face and visited a hospital in Johnson City, Tennessee. He refused to be X-rayed because he did not trust pictures. Because it was a veterans' hospital, the staff first wanted to make sure he was entitled to treatment.

"The doctor asked me what war I was in," Salling recalled. "And I said, 'Hell, I was a Rebel.' 'Hell fire,' he says. 'You can't stay here. Uncle Sam had rather see a German or a Jap in here than a Rebel.'"

In 1951 he left the mountains for his first airplane ride. He flew across the state to Norfolk, Virginia, for the last Confederate reunion. He dressed in his general's uniform with medals ablaze. When they landed, he asked for a drink; at the Gettysburg reunion, he had taken his share of spirits with the rest of them. "I might do a little preaching, too," he hinted.

He was 104, he said, his hair still jet black and—miraculously—his hearing suddenly improved. It must have been the plane flight, he thought: "I feel that I can hear better way up in the sky."

He almost did not make the event. He had been down with a cold and in bed at home and felt it best to stay put. But then he thought he should make an appearance for the sake of the Old Dominion. To get him to Norfolk, the Pentagon sent the plane. So he waved in the parades, reviewed the bands, and crossed his heart at "Dixie." He had himself a barrel of fun. "Whiskey won't hurt you if you know how to drink," he assured everyone. "You just tip it up and pour it down."

He flew again to Richmond two years later, climbing unassisted out of the plane at Byrd Field. It was a stopover on his way to West Virginia, where he would be honored by the Patriotic Sons of America. He wore a new Confederate uniform donated by the Women's Army Corps at Fort Myer, Virginia. He covered his chest in medals again. He hoped to live as old as Methuselah. "I want to set a new record," he said.

Reporters on the tarmac wanted his thoughts about U.S. involvement in Korea. "They shouldn't be over there," he replied. "There shouldn't be any war. I've lived all this time and have never been in jail and never had a fight. If I can get along with other people that well for 107 years, I don't see why nations can't get along as well."

Salling traveled up to Washington to "confer" with his congressman, again in full Confederate splendor. In Richmond the General Assembly granted him a special $500 soldier's bonus, and he snagged an honorary military pension of $135.45 a month as well. By 1955 everyone was calling him "General" Salling or "Uncle John." Back home he sat in his mountain cabin with the embroidered picture of Jesus on the wall and waved from the window. Sometimes he made hay: "There's a woman flirting with me now," he teased once. "But she's eighty-two. Who wants a woman that old?"

In February 1956 he caught a cold that turned into pneumonia. Doctors made him quit his daily snort. Some thought this might be the end,

A trio of dubious Confederate veterans hobnob at the 1951 Confederate reunion in Norfolk, Virginia. Left to right: William "Billy-Dan" Townsend of Olla, Louisiana, John Salling of Slant, Virginia, and William J. Bush of Fitzgerald, Georgia. (Courtesy of the Main Library, Sargeant Memorial Room, Norfolk, Virginia)

and neighbors and newsmen started gathering around the cabin. Salling sent out a note: "I'm not dead yet."

At 109 he was loaded up with gifts. The Army gave him a gold medallion: on one side pictures of Grant and Lee, with the Union and Confederate crests on the other. The governor in Richmond presented him with a Confederate gray shirt; the Texas Rangers gave him a ten-gallon hat. Old John Salling poured on the country charm. "I might even take a bath," he cracked.

But time was closing in. At 111 he said he felt "like a two-year-old egg—rotten." To cheer him up, a local city club bought him a new leather recliner. At 112 the Civil War Centennial Commission visited Slant and awarded him an honorary membership "in recognition of your distinction as a veteran of the Civil War." A hundred-car motorcade rolled through the tiny mountain hamlet and up the hillside to present him with a framed, hand-inscribed, water-colored certificate. In his wheelchair out on the porch, wrapped in a thick blanket even though it was May, he just squinted at the crowd. They filled up the four-room cabin and a good part of his thirty acres, where most days his harness and team of mules stood around doing nothing.

In January 1959 an oral historian came to the mountains. They talked about home and the Appalachians and how the farthest north Salling had ever been was Gettysburg. But the old man seemed confused and distracted, lost in his cave of memories. To keep him focused, the interviewer buttered him up.

"Uncle John, I think you're the most favorite, famous citizen."

"Well," Salling said, "I'll have to tell you a little joke." He rambled on with a story about a knife and a plug of tobacco, but it made little sense. The interviewer tried to bring him back to the topic of the Civil War.

"We had good men on both sides," Salling said. But he wandered off some more, telling of his grandmother Tildy and how the Indians had scalped her father. He talked some about hair and moonshine too.

The interviewer tried again to refocus him on the war. He pressed him about the mines and the Confederacy, about Stonewall Jackson and Robert E. Lee. Did he have a part in the war or not?

Old John Salling, 112 years old (if he was to be believed), leaned back in his wheelchair. He paused a good long while. "I aim to tell a man the truth," he said, "or nothing at all."

He died of pneumonia six weeks later. They brought his body back from the hospital in Kingsport, Tennessee, and to his home in Slant. They lowered the flags, and a bugler played the long sorrowful notes due a fallen soldier. They dressed him in Confederate gray and covered his copper casket with the Stars and Bars. Thousands turned out for his funeral. Full military honors were awarded the man who said he had dug saltpeter.

Of the many wreaths, flowers, and floral arrangements that decorated the funeral, one came pinned with a short sympathy note from Walter Williams, the Confederate veteran scrunched up in bed in his daughter's extra bedroom in Houston.

"Am I the last one?" Williams asked, his words barely a whisper, his breathing faint and shallow. "Well, I always wanted to stay here until they were all gone, to see what happened."

11

....

IN HIS MEMORY-CLOUDED MIND

When "Uncle Bill" Lundy died in Florida in 1957, Walter Williams was 114 and in bed in Houston with a 103-degree fever. He had been ill since the night before, the fever coming on around three in the morning. At daylight they helped him up, thinking that some fresh scenery might do him good, and gingerly lowered him into a rocking chair in the front room of the small white frame house.

His daughter, Willie Mae Bowles, told him that Lundy, the last Confederate in Florida, had just died. He managed to lift his head. "I am sorry to hear it," he rasped. She said there was one more Confederate still to beat, a "General" Salling in Virginia. Williams seemed confused at first. "One more," she said. Then he understood. "I'll still outlive the other one," he insisted.

And he did, though it took nearly another two years of Williams lying in that bed, receiving baby bottles and spooned applesauce, before Salling passed on in the winter of 1959. Then Williams and his family sent the wreath and sympathy card to the hills of southwestern Virginia.

The family always trusted the old man had the strength to outlast them all, though his doctor, Russell Wolfe of Houston, cautioned that Williams could be gone with little warning. "Anything can happen to a man that age," the doctor said.

But the old Confederate persevered—and with as much flair as he could muster. For Veterans Day in November 1957 he rode in the Houston parade, flat on his back on a stretcher in the rear of an ambulance.

Alongside him, younger men who had fought in Europe, the Pacific, and more recently Korea marched on foot. Williams could not see much, and hear less, so his daughter described the cheers from the crowd. When the ambulance circled past the reviewing stand, she pointed out the window. He lifted a frail hand in salute.

They returned home, and Willie Mae put him back to bed. She wondered if these kinds of public outings were good for her father anymore. "The parade didn't hurt him," she said. "And it didn't help him."

A few days later he turned 115, and they plopped a ten-gallon hat on his head and wheeled him into the front room of the house on West Twenty-Third Avenue. Everyone sang a chorus of "Dixie." Four-year-old Sydney Kay Boyd asked, "Granddaddy, can I have some cake?" Told Hollywood might cast him in the part of an unreconstructed Rebel, they all laughed, but Williams rather liked the idea. "It's about time I was doing something," he barked. "Laying in bed all the time has just made me lazy." When everyone stood to leave, he invited them back next year. "I'll be here to meet you all on my 116th birthday," he promised.

In late March 1958 a lawyer in the Commerce Building in downtown Houston wrote to the Civil War Centennial Commission in Washington, D.C. Cooper K. Ragan had served as a lieutenant commander in the South Pacific. He was an author, historian, and president of the Houston Civil War Round Table, and soon to be chairman of the Texas Civil War Committee and secretary-treasurer of the Jefferson Davis Association. Now he was championing Walter Williams, just as the national Centennial Commission in Washington was outlining plans to honor the last Confederate.

"Mr. Williams is under the care of Dr. Russell S. Wolfe," Ragan wrote. "Dr. Wolfe was formerly head of the Veterans Hospital here in Houston. He tells me that Mr. Williams is growing weaker and that he thinks the ceremony which you outlined should take place within the next month if possible. Mr. Williams spends most of the time in bed, but on occasions he is able to walk around a bit and does have lucid moments. It is necessary to have nurses with him around the clock."

Ragan recounted that Williams had been born in Mississippi and served as a forage master in Hood's Brigade. "He was in charge of the beeves and provisions for his unit," Ragan wrote. But, he added, "his daughter said she did not think he was an active participant in any of the many battles that this brigade was in during its service in Virginia and Tennessee." He said that the daughter, Willie Mae Bowles, had set aside a room to care for her father, and that "his sole means of income is from a Confederate pension from the state of Texas."

To verify Williams's Confederate service, Ragan advised that "undoubtedly there is a file on Mr. Williams in the office of the Secretary of War.... Dr. Wolfe also tells me that a report is made monthly concerning Mr. Williams' condition to the Fourth Army in San Antonio."

Ragan explained that the planned ceremony to honor the Confederate "of necessity will have to be had at Mr. Williams' residence. I gather that it is a small place and perhaps can accommodate only a small group, although the weather being generally good at that time of year there will be room outside of the house for the overflow. Dr. Wolfe thinks this would be a fine thing for his patient because he says that within certain limits the more outside contacts Mr. Williams has the better it is for him. He finds that when he is interviewed or has news stories written about him or takes part in parades that it seems to improve his general health and outlook."

Three days later, after Ragan visited West Twenty-Third Avenue and met Williams, he sent a follow-up letter to the Centennial Commission. Mostly he wrote a biographical sketch, filling in details from Williams's long life. Of his nineteen children, only one of the seven with his first wife was still living, as were only nine of the twelve from the second marriage, including Willie Mae, the youngest. He had sixty grandchildren, seventy-three great-grandchildren and "numerous" great-great-grandchildren. Ragan told how, after the war, Williams moved to Texas and spent most of his life around Franklin: "He was a farmer and stock raiser. In the early days when cattle were sent over the trail to railheads in Kansas and other states, I understand that Mr. Williams made several trips as a cattle driver. He became a resident of Houston about two years ago, after he became bedridden."

But Ragan could not state with certainty much about Williams's Civil War record. "I do not have available any of the state of Texas pension records, but Mr. Williams has been on the pension rolls many years," he wrote. "In fact, the last legislature (1957) passed a special act to increase his pension to $300 per month." Nevertheless, Ragan continued, doubts still remained. "In J. B. Polley's 'History of Hood's Texas Brigade' there appears the muster roll of Company C, 5th Texas Regiment, which does not show Walter W. Williams as having been a member. There are three men by the name of Williams listed, namely, F. M., James, and W. K. However, the Confederate muster rolls in most instances are highly inaccurate due generally to their having been lost or misplaced following the surrender."

Ragan also confided that "no information" existed regarding any "battles or actions" that Williams may have fought. Nevertheless, he wrote, "members of the Houston Civil War Round Table are most anxious to cooperate in bestowing this honor on Mr. Williams." He added that, despite the discrepancies, in the last ten years Williams had received a good deal of publicity and other honors. Now his health was slipping. "Mr. Williams is not able to walk and has to be fed by his nurses," Ragan told the commission. "But his pulse is strong and on occasions he is talkative and has lucid intervals. He understood enough Saturday morning to raise his hand to grasp mine when I was introduced. However, the end cannot be too far off, so it is suggested you make your date as soon as possible."

Within the week, Maj. Gen. Ulysses S. Grant III, the Civil War Centennial Commission chairman, wrote to President Eisenhower reporting that the group planned to honor Williams soon with "a brief, simple and dignified ceremony" at the daughter's home in Houston. "We can think of no more fitting and effective way of symbolizing the spirit that binds our nation together and at the same time of setting the tone that the commission seeks to import to all that it does—the tone of a common patriotism and heritage that transcend sectional memories," he told the president.

Edmund C. Cass, acting secretary of the Centennial Commission, wrote to Willie Mae Bowles, announcing that they would like to visit in late April. "We would take all precautions to protect your father from fatigue or undue excitement," he assured her. "We certainly do not want to jeopardize his welfare."

Cass also wrote to Dr. Wolfe, seeking his medical opinion on whether the ceremony would prove too much for the fragile Williams. He promised the dignitaries would "minimize any strain on Mr. Williams."

The doctor responded on April 1. "Your plan has my wholehearted

support," he said. "Although Mr. Williams is growing weaker, such pre-
sentations and the celebration you have outlined seem to add materially
to his longevity rather than detract from his welfare. He at times is quite
aware of his surroundings and likes nothing better than to participate in
a show of some kind." The physician hoped the ceremony would change
the minds of some in the Houston community and around Texas who
were unconvinced that Williams was a genuine Confederate veteran.
"I have been a little discouraged at times at the apathy manifested by
some local and state groups in respect to our senior surviving veteran of
national and world renown. He is almost like a prophet without honor in
his own country."

Doctor Wolfe closed his letter by referring to Williams as "Uncle Walt"
and added, "Walter Williams is known as and is referred to as Colonel
Williams. Some of us like to call him General Williams, and indeed he
was designated a general of the Confederate Armies by the Sons of the
Confederacy at their convention of last year."

On Saturday, April 26, a black Cadillac stopped in front of the home,
with its cottonwood trees and neatly trimmed lawn. Out stepped Rep.
Fred Schwengel of Iowa, a member of the national Civil War Centennial
Commission, and Capt. Evan P. Aurand, the president's naval aide. They
carried greetings, tributes, and scrolled certificates from dignitaries in
Washington, Austin, and the mayor's office in Houston. One was signed
by the president himself. It stated that Williams was being awarded an
"honorary membership" with the Civil War Centennial Commission as
it prepared "for a most meaningful observance of the tragic war which
once divided our land. Your presence in this commission symbolizes the
living bonds which unite our beloved country. Together we shall move
forward, confident of unlimited opportunities open to our Union and to
free men around the world." President Eisenhower added a special note
for Williams: "It is a privilege to send personal greetings to you."

The honoree never opened his eyes. His daughter had dressed him in
a wide-brimmed black hat and a gray Confederate tunic, and she pulled
the bed covers up to his chest. His hearing was so poor that they had to
use the hearing-aid microphone, practically shouting into the device in
the small, crowded bedroom. Someone held a Confederate flag behind the

headboard; someone else bent over a fiddle. Outside, neighborhood kids pressed against the window screen for a peek.

"Daddy, honey," said his daughter, leaning into the microphone. "This man has a letter for you from President Eisenhower." When Schwengel and Aurand spoke loud enough, Williams seemed to tap his fingers. But when flashbulbs from news cameras lit up the room, he did not blink; when movie cameras clicked, he did not flinch. The youngsters pressed harder against the screen and nearly fell into the room, but Williams did not notice.

Doctor Wolfe stood outside with the children. "The old rascal's doing fine," the physician said. "Look how he's enjoying it."

Schwengel droned on, talking about war at Fort Sumter and peace at Appomattox. The commission, he shouted into the microphone, was created by Congress to "furnish leadership and prepare our country for an adequate, proper, and worthwhile observance and commemoration of a conflict that was entirely our own affair and was our war."

The congressman quoted from a poem about the dwindling ranks of patriots from another American war—the American Revolution: "Hardly a man is now alive / Who remembers that famous day and year." Looking down on the crumpled body in bedsheets, Schwengel shouted that Williams remained "very much alive! We are glad! All Americans are glad! Long may you remain so!" He hailed him as the "gallant gray host of nearly a century ago" and proclaimed, "to you, Mr. Williams, valiant upholder still of the honor and spirit of a most gallant, most American, army, we offer our hearty congratulations on this most auspicious occasion. We salute the memories which hover ever about you. And we pray to God that many happy days and years still await you in the land which gave you birth."

The dignitaries departed, the Cadillac headed for the airport, and the neighbor kids walked home. In the bedroom, Willie Mae slid the tunic off her father's shoulders and left him in bed in his striped pajamas.

The tributes kept coming. President Eisenhower signed a bill providing additional pension money for the old Confederate, and Williams said he had no qualms about spending Yankee dollars. "Money is money," he said. At his birthday in November—number 116 by his reckoning—they allowed him one puff from a cigar and a nibble of cake. His teeth were all missing, his hair but a wisp, his pajamas too large for his small frame. He hardly perked up when *Life* magazine came to feature him in their May edition. "The Last Survivor of the Civil War," read the headline, with two pages of photographs. On the wall of the bedroom hung the U.S. flag and the Stars and Bars, with a Confederate formal dress uniform in between. Williams lay quietly in the uptilted bed. For the camera, someone stuck an unlit cigar in his mouth.

The magazine also reprinted a grainy photograph of a younger Williams and his brother in civilian clothes sometime after the war. They ran another shot of a Confederate forage party during the war, "of the type Williams served in." A gaggle of daughters and grandchildren crushed around the old man's bed for a group shot, including Willie Mae, who was born when her father said he was sixty-four. A brass band from the Houston American Legion serenaded outside the window screen; they played "Old Soldiers Never Die." Someone swore Williams drummed his fingers.

On Memorial Day 1959 they lifted him into another ambulance for another ride in the Houston parade. In June a group calling itself the Confederate High Command promoted him to five-star general. Though an honorary title, it meant he outranked Robert E. Lee. "We are a semi-military organization" said Donald A. Ramsey, the group's executive commissioner. "We can create our own ranks."

Williams slept through the ceremony. His doctor said he had been suffering from a slight chill, so he approved giving his patient "a slight pip of scotch" to keep his temperature down.

Later in June Williams suffered a mild stroke. "This bout has hit him pretty hard, harder than anything he has ever had. He is still very weak," reported Willie Mae. "But he returned to his regular diet on Tuesday. He also asked for some chewing tobacco, and we knew then he was feeling better." As a precaution, they hung an oxygen tent over his bed. Dr. Wolfe told him, "I'd like to let you have a cigar, general, but you can't smoke in that."

The next day he sank further. "He answers me when I speak to him, but I haven't been talking to him today—saving his strength," his daughter said. Some family visited, thinking this might be the end. Among them was Thomas M. (Bud) Williams, at eighty-two his oldest surviving child, a retired Brazos County farmer. But then the old man started to call for his cowboy boots, a sign to Willie Mae that her father was gaining strength. Doctor Russell stopped by. Amazed at the old man's will to live, he put Williams in "precarious but not critical condition." His temperature was a bit high at 100. "But his pulse is good," the doctor announced. "Strong and slow."

The scare prompted Bill Elliott, a Harris County judge in Houston, to write to President Eisenhower that many in Houston feared the end was upon Williams. Elliott hoped the White House was prepared to properly mark his death. "His personal physicians advise that the general's passing is imminent, perhaps a few weeks at the most," Elliott wrote. "The purpose of this letter is to advise you in confidence of the situation, so that any arrangements with respect to your attendance at his funeral can be made in advance. Funeral plans have been finalized for an Official State Funeral. The general's passing will mark the end of a sorrowful era in American History which began just under 100 years ago under President Lincoln. His eyes have truly seen the glory of a century of progress of this Republic, and this impending event, sad as it may be, particularly to those of us in the South, has important significance to every American as we approach the time of closing this final chapter of the War Between the States."

Thomas E. Stephens, secretary to the president, answered Elliott. "While it will not be possible for the President personally to come to Houston," Stephens wrote, "he will be glad to have you get in touch with him about this at the appropriate time."

Another White House aide, Brig. Gen. Andrew Jackson Goodpaster, instructed the commanding general of the Fourth Army at Fort Sam Houston in San Antonio to serve as the president's representative once Williams died. Maj. Alfred Kitts at Fort Sam Houston told White House staff that preparations were well under way for a funeral, noting that the fort "was in receipt of voluminous correspondence on this subject, and that elaborate plans were in readiness to be put into effect at any time."

Again Williams relapsed, this time with pneumonia. Another oxygen tent was draped over his bed. That helped some. When the newspapers reported he was fighting for his life, Dr. Wolfe waved them off. "I wouldn't call it critical yet," he said. "But any time he gets ill, he is in a precarious condition at his age." The patient's fever broke, he continued to improve, "and we thought he was out of it until yesterday," the doctor said. "Suddenly he became worse."

Three days later, Williams appeared back on the mend, close to beating the pneumonia. "It looks pretty good," the doctor announced. "He is much weaker than last week, but we've pulled down his fever and he may pull through." They kept him in bed under the oxygen anyway.

Much of the nation followed his progress in the newspapers; many thought he would not last the summer. In July the Senate Judiciary Committee approved a bill authorizing the president to lower the nation's flags when Williams passed away.

By August 10 he was failing again. He had not eaten much in several days, except for a creamy bottled mixture of milk, eggs, and water. Dr. Wolfe now listed his patient as critical, saying "it's only a matter of days." Another night and another morning, and Williams appeared worse. "It's just up to the Lord," said Willie Mae.

Frank E. Vandiver, a Civil War historian at Rice University who also served as an advisory council member to the Centennial Commission, wired Major General Grant III in Washington: "General Williams sinking fast. Have you any special instructions?" Grant wired back, asking Vandiver and Cooper Ragan to act as the commission's official representatives at the funeral, which seemed likely any day now. "No specific instructions," Grant wired. "Hope you and Cooper Ragan will express sympathy of commission and present wreath to be ordered from here. Your help greatly appreciated."

The White House and the Army began final preparations. "The situation with the man is evidently critical now," warned an internal White House memo, laying out options once Williams died:

1. If the president comes, would he desire military honors?
2. Identification of the Presidential Aircraft?
3. Would there be a Presidential Wreath?

It was decided that if Eisenhower did attend the funeral of the final Civil War soldier, the president "would not expect military honors." But it was highly unlikely, they agreed, that "the president would be able to appear in person" anyway, and instead a presidential representative should be designated in his place. The plane carrying the presidential stand-in would be *The Columbine*, flown by the Air Force for special events. The representative would bring a White House wreath.

The administration also thought it smart not to favor one side of the Civil War over the other. They decided it best to accord Williams the same honor bestowed the last Yankee, Albert Woolson, when he had died in Minnesota. Flags were lowered for Woolson and the White House issued an official statement of sorrow, but Eisenhower did not attend the funeral in Duluth. So a joint resolution marking Williams's passing was approved by Congress and sent to the president's home office in Gettysburg. There they would "hold it so that it will be available for submission to the President in the event of the passing of the last surviving veteran of the War Between the States."

A presidential proclamation was drawn up as well, and kept at the ready at the Gettysburg office. The Civil War Centennial Commission drafted a similar note of sympathy, not only for the Williams family but also for the nation as a whole on the eve of the war's anniversary. At Fort Sam Houston, the Army was advised that the funeral service would be conducted in Houston but that Williams would be buried a hundred miles away in Franklin, Texas, where he had spent those long years growing old on his cabin porch. Should the White House change its mind and decide the president would fly to Texas, the army did not think a 100-mile motorcade was advisable.

Then, on the morning of September 3, 1959, the nation's readers unfolded their newspapers and found an expose from Lowell K. Bridwell, a young Washington correspondent for the Scripps-Howard newspaper chain. His father had been active in the long-gone Anti-Saloon League, he wife was a physician, and his brother an FBI agent assigned to the Ohio field office. For some years Bridwell had reported the news out of the statehouse in Columbus, Ohio. During that time the FBI had pegged him as a "liberal writer," and it was said that J. Edgar Hoover had placed him on a "watch list" of suspicious subjects during the anticommunist fervor of the 1950s. It was also said that the bureau had asked his brother, agent Charles Bridwell, to "spy" on Lowell, but that he had refused. A year earlier, in 1958, Lowell was transferred to the Scripps-Howard bureau in Washington. He later would move to the Kennedy administration and in less than a decade was appointed head of the Federal Highway Administration.

But it was this story on this morning that made his name.

"Walter Williams of Houston, Tex., accepted by the nation as the 'last living link with the Civil War,' is a Confederate veteran only in his memory-clouded mind." Thus went the first paragraph.

It continued:

The Texan, ill and under the constant care of a daughter, is looking forward to Nov. 14, happily anticipating the attention bestowed upon a man on what he figures must be his 117th birthday. It probably matters little to him that old census records indicate he's really only 103.

Just when and where the aged Texan became universally and sentimentally accepted as a member of the famed Confederate Hood's Texas Brigade isn't known. Maybe it resulted from the tales of elderly men passing the time on county courthouse steps.

Apparently no one bothered to check, or no one really cared. Nevertheless, the meticulously kept Confederate records in the National Archives fail to disclose Williams' association with the most lionized of all Texan fighting outfits.

Perhaps after years of clouding memories, Williams has forgotten that he was a mere lad of eight on his father's Mississippi farm when the unit he now believes he fought with was making its final stand in Virginia.

Bridwell was correct. The 1860 federal census for the Williams family in Mississippi listed little Walter as too small for kindergarten, and far too young for war.

The tip for the story had come from Mrs. Opal Beckett of Miamitown, Ohio. She telephoned the *Post and Times-Star* newspaper in Cincinnati, telling editors that she had grown up on a farm about ten miles from the Williams place near Franklin, Texas. She recalled that many of the locals knew him as "Uncle Walt," and that sometimes she had attended dances at his farm on Rural Route 5. She also told them that Williams had never served in the Civil War and that many of his friends and neighbors had known for years he was an imposter. It was quite a topic around town, she said. But most everyone put up with his charade. They listened "tolerantly but skeptically," she said, because the man was old and feeble, and his stories seemed harmless.

But why would she reveal the truth now, after having moved away from Franklin twenty years ago? "I didn't mind him getting the veteran's pension," she explained. "But when I heard he was going to get a military funeral and he was never in the Army, it just wasn't justice." And anyone left around Franklin who remembered the old man would feel the same way, she said. "It's the biggest joke on the American people I ever heard of."

Cincinnati passed the tip to Bridwell in Washington, and he pursued the story. He noted that the White House, Congress, and the state of Texas were making plans for an elaborate military funeral, and that Congress had passed and Eisenhower signed the directive to lower the flags to half-staff for a day of national mourning. He noted as well that Williams was being paid a special federal pension approved a year earlier, in addition to his Civil War pension in Texas, and that in 1957 he had been presented with a gold medal by yet another act of Congress.

But Bridwell struggled to explain why Walter Williams would have moved to Texas and passed himself off as a Confederate veteran. To reinvent himself, it would have seemed a lot easier to claim he was just another nameless soldier among hundreds of thousands of Confederate Rebels, rather than someone as conspicuous as a member of Hood's legendary brigade.

Maybe, Bridwell wrote,

Williams was merely reflecting the pride of his adopted state when he filed a sworn affidavit that he was a member of Company C, Fifth Regiment, Hood's Brigade, eleven months before the war closed. The men of Hood even today are looked upon with respect and awe because of their bravery and key parts in Confederate victories over Union forces in 1861 and 1862.

Williams and thousands of others undoubtedly have forgotten that Hood's famed unit was broken up and lost its historic designation long before Williams believes he enlisted. Those cold records preserved in the National Archives, much more complete than is generally accepted, fail to turn up any evidence of Williams' proclaimed service.

The reporter quoted Gerald Turner, assistant director of the Texas Veterans Affairs Commission. "No official records from any source are available which would verify the statements made by Mr. Williams," Turner said. In the early 1930s, state officials relied on a man's word in his pension application, he added. Little investigation was done before a pension was approved.

But census records do not lie. The data are collected from the families themselves, and in 1860—the year before the war—his parents George and Nancy Williams reported that little Walter was a child on the family farm in Itawamba County, Mississippi. By 1870—five years after the guns silenced—the Williams family had moved to Brazos County, Texas, and Walter, living with his parents, was not yet a teenager. The 1880 census revealed that Walter had married and brought his wife, Florence, to live with him and his parents. Later came a series of children: eventually nineteen from two wives, as verified in the census tracts. The youngest was Willie Mae Bowles.

Bridwell's story caught fire; all the national papers picked it up, along with radio and television. In Houston Willie Mae was floored. "We have forty or fifty letters from people who said their fathers served in the Confederate Army with my daddy and they knew him personally," she protested. But she did not provide those letters. Instead she said she wished there were family records, maybe a Bible or photographs of her father in uniform, that would prove the newspapers wrong and restore her father's integrity.

"I wish so much that we had written things down and kept records over the years," said a flustered Willie Mae. "But we didn't, and it is too late now to talk to him about such things." She pointed out that if her father was only 103 years old and not about to turn 117 in two months, then he would have fathered his first son when he was only thirteen, and that made little sense. Overwhelmed, she added: "It's the most ridiculous thing that ever happened—to bring up something like this when the old man has only a short time left to live."

The *Dallas Morning News* rushed their central Texas reporter over to Franklin to interview longtime residents. "I've knowed Uncle Walt all my life," said eighty-three-year-old L. D. O'Neal, who once ran a grocery a few miles from the Williams cabin. "He used to come to my store often and we'd talk. He never did mention anything about the war until later years after he was on the government payroll. Personally, I never did believe he was in the war. But it was none of my business and I didn't do anything to help or hurt him. I don't know if the government ever checked it close or not. I've heard lots of talk that people, now dead, used to tell of being a barefooted boy with Walt."

John Rutherford, who published a small paper in Franklin, said many never took Williams seriously. But, he said, "I don't see how he could have fooled the state and federal governments this long. It isn't easy to get money out of them."

Others believed Williams. Horace Hamilton carried the rural mail, and he had seen Williams nearly every day. "Seems to me, the government and Uncle Walt should know more about it than some woman who wasn't there," the postman said, referring to the tipster, Opal Beckett in Ohio. "Why didn't they bring it all up before now?"

Some were not sure. "Oh, I've heard stories a long time that Uncle Walt was using one of his older brother's war records," said Justice of the Peace Lee Farmer, a longtime county resident. "But I'm inclined to believe him. I don't know why, I just am. This is a town of old people, 60 to 85, and anytime you mention an old one somebody will argue he isn't that old."

In his research, Bridwell reviewed only Williams's original Confederate pension application in Washington, D.C. He apparently did not retrieve a copy of the entire file in Austin. Had he dug deeper, he would have uncovered more evidence that Walter Williams was a Rebel fraud. The file in Austin shows that Williams did not seek a veteran's pension until the Depression year of 1932, though if he truly had been a Confederate soldier he could have been collecting money for more than thirty years previously. The state first started authorizing pensions for "bona fide" applicants back in 1899.

In 1932 Williams told state officials in his application that times were hard and he was eighty-six and far too old to farm anymore. His request was supported by two "witnesses" willing to swear that Williams had indeed served as a forage master in Hood's Brigade. A third was a county judge in Franklin, who said that, from what he heard around town, "Mr. Williams is a very deserving old Confederate soldier." Based on those testimonials—and those alone—the pension was granted, and Williams began receiving $200 a month.

There were other curiosities. In 1947 Willie Mae had asked the state comptroller, George H. Sheppard, for more money. "He has been very ill for the past 6 weeks and staying at home here in Houston," she wrote. "Two doctors have said he will not get well because of his age of 104 years. He holds a statement from you to the effect that a mortuary warrant for $100 will be paid upon proof of his death by affidavit from his doctor or undertaker. I would like to know if there is any possible way of getting this increased to more than $100. As you know, that amount will not go anywhere with prices as they are today. We are unable to get any insurance on him because of his age, so are making this appeal to you."

Sheppard responded promptly. "You are advised that $100 is the maximum amount which can, under our present law, be issued on account of the death of a pensioner," he told her.

In March 1953 a man named Robert E. Swayne of Malvern, Pennsylvania, wrote the Texas comptroller's office asking for details about this "oldest Confederate veteran." Swayne explained that in recent years he had been "collecting data" about the last Confederates, and he specifically wanted to know whether Williams had fought in any battles. Sheppard answered him the same day. Williams, he wrote, did "not show what battles he fought in during the War Between the States."

In Franklin, however, Williams sometimes had boasted to neighbors and others that he was more than just a forager under Hood. He claimed that he also had ridden with Quantrill's Raiders, another revered detachment of Rebel fighters. At his 111th birthday party, he told a thrilling story of how he and his fellow Confederates ambushed a group of Union soldiers and "killed a hundred of them." Yet whenever someone started asking questions or trying to pin him down on his Civil War adventures, Williams often changed the subject.

Swayne read Sheppard's response and sent another letter to the comptroller. "I note you did not give the *exact date* Mr. Williams *enlisted*," he wrote. "Also I note the record states Mr. Williams was born on Nov. 14, 1846, which makes him 106 years old. I note the papers and his claims that he is 110 years of age. I do not understand why the reporters insist he is 110 when he is only 106.... I guess you cannot take the word of an aged man."

The following year, 1954, Dr. Wolfe mailed a request to the new Texas comptroller in Austin, Robert S. Calvert. The doctor asked for more state assistance for his increasingly famous patient. He said the extra money was urgent, as Williams could be gone at any moment. "Our medical staff has displayed a very keen interest in the condition of this 111- (soon to be 112-) year-old Confederate veteran, and we are doing all that we can, unofficially, to make his last weeks or months comfortable and pleasant," the doctor wrote. "It is our fond hope to preserve his remarkably good general health until he at least passes his 112th birthday, and as far beyond that as we humanly can. In this connection, we are wondering if it is at all possible to have his pension payment substantially increased by $100 a month or so, for the increasing cost of care of his 83-year-old wife and himself."

Doctor Wolfe noted that specially prescribed food for the old Confederate was expensive, as were costs for homogenized milk, one of his favorites, and in-home nursing visits. He wrote that Willie Mae often found it too much to care for even the "simple needs" of this "old gentleman." The doctor appealed directly to the comptroller's patriotism: "The nation at large is very much aware now of Uncle Walter's existence and keenly interested in his longevity. We should very much like to see the State of Texas acquit itself favorably in this respect."

Calvert said no. Williams and his wife already received the maximum allowed for a married couple—$200 a month. "Any increase in pension payments must be an act of the Texas Legislature," he replied. He did, however, offer Willie Mae another option. He said the old patriarch could transfer to the Men's Confederate Home in Austin. The couple's monthly pension allotment would drop in half, to $100. But, the comptroller pointed out, "he will receive board, room, hospitalization, medical care, and everything necessary for his comfort free of cost."

Instead Willie Mae moved him in with her.

For a while rumors spread that Williams had died, and several people sent inquiries to Austin. "I am happy to inform you that Walter Williams is still living," Calvert told them. "But he is very feeble, I understand, and at one time they thought he would not survive a severe spell of sickness but he did."

Willie Mae wrote to Calvert in November 1957. She told him her mother, Ella Mae Williams, had died and left her father a widower. The elderly couple's monthly pension by then had been increased to $300, and Willie Mae worried it would be reduced now that he was single. Calvert sent bad news: the pension indeed would be reduced to $200.

She wrote again in early 1959, around the time "General" Salling had died and the nation recognized her father as the last living soul from the Civil War. She asked about a burial fund of $300 for when her father died. "Please send me some kind of certificate or paper showing that he does have that amount towards burial." Calvert told her they were entitled to only $200.

In May Dr. Wolfe wrote to state officials. He said the family wanted more information about Williams's Confederate service. "None of our records and certificates concerning Walter W. Williams, last surviving Confederate soldier, can give us the dates of his service," the doctor explained. "We know that he served under General Hood in Company C of the 5th Regiment as a forage master." But, the physician said, "now that he is such a newsworthy subject, we are often called upon to furnish the dates of his service. Will you please supply them for us? This request is from members of his immediate family."

State comptroller Calvert sent them what little information Williams had given them—that he had applied for a pension more than thirty years after he would have been eligible, that he claimed eleven months with Hood's Brigade, and that he said he served until "Gen. Lee surrendered." Then, looking closer at the file, state officials spotted something else. "The date of Mr. Williams' enlistment is not given in the application," they told the family. He never had told the state exactly when he supposedly joined the Confederate army, other than that he served for about eleven months until the surrender.

Asked later by another concerned citizen whether Williams really was 116 and about to turn 117, state officials threw up their hands. They admitted they truly could not answer that fundamental question about the man they had been paying a taxpayer-funded pension all these years. "I do not know," Calvert confessed. "Other than the statement of some members of his family."

Now in September 1959 the nation was confronted with the same question: Confederate or counterfeit? Who exactly was Walter Williams?

"Personally, I have doubted Williams' claim for a long time," announced Robert S. Harper of Washington Court House, Ohio, a Civil War scholar and fellow at the American Association of Historians of Princeton University, after reading Bridwell's newspaper revelations. "It seems that this is just one more misunderstanding about the Civil War that has failed to stand up under examination." But, he said, "I am not fully sold on the idea that Williams is a fraud. It is open to question and should lead to an official investigation to verify his status."

In Bryan, Texas, Vick Lindley, managing editor of the *Daily Eagle*, unearthed a copy of a special edition his newspaper had printed thirty-five years previously, giving the names of all those who had served in Hood's Brigade. He said the list was compiled by the secretary of the Hood's Brigade Association, which had met regularly in Bryan. Lindley scanned the list but could not find Williams. Lindley wondered whether Williams, in his old age, had confused himself with a brother back in Mississippi who did serve with Hood.

Others defended Walter Williams. "I think General Williams is the last living Confederate soldier and last veteran of the war," said Margaret Crocker of Columbus, Ohio, past state president of the United Daughters of the Confederacy and the organization's honorary national president. "Confederate records in Washington and the states are incomplete, and it's too late to bring up the question now. I've seen many cases where it was difficult to prove service of veterans where, eventually, their claims were shown to be correct." Had his pension application and other statements over the years been a lie, she argued, experts would have unmasked him by now: "He's been accepted as the last veteran, and I think Texas will bury him that way."

The Sons of Confederate Veterans rode to his defense too. "There is no doubt in our minds that Williams is a veteran," proclaimed national president Tom Crigler Jr. of Macon, Mississippi.

Even from the Union side, Williams had his supporters. "I take no stock in the stories saying Williams isn't the last Civil War veteran," said Col. Warfield W. Dorsey, commandant of the Mount Vernon, Ohio, Sons of Union Veterans Fife and Drum Corps. His band had played at Albert Woolson's funeral in Duluth; it now was rehearsing for a state and military funeral in Texas, should Williams succumb.

Dorsey recalled that on the day Woolson died in Minnesota, Louis Baker of Oklahoma had claimed he was the last Union veteran, and yet regardless of that assertion, Woolson's record remained intact. As for the Confederate in Texas, Dorsey said, "Williams was a forager—a soldier who went out after food for the troops, rounding up cattle, turnips, and whatever could be found. Often these men wore no uniforms. Many walked home from both armies without their discharges ever being recorded.... We have been invited to a state funeral for Williams, and if it is held, we will go—representing the Blue in tribute to the last man in Gray."

Copies of newspaper stories and other materials circulated through the White House, but the administration thought it best to withhold comment about the inconsistencies and doubts over Williams's past. At the National Archives, officials said the truth might never be known, citing the incomplete records and nearly a century of elapsed time since the Civil War.

But up on Capitol Hill, Sen. James O. Eastland, a Mississippi Democrat who had sponsored the resolution for a period of national mourning upon Williams's death, said the country would stick to the plan to pay him proper homage. Only "overwhelming evidence" discrediting Williams would change things at this point, he stated.

In Texas, officials rallied around their hero. "They'll have an awfully hard time trying to prove he wasn't a Confederate veteran," said Charles Morris, the state Veterans Affairs commissioner. "Those Yankees just think they've killed all us Confederates off," said Ethel Everitt, head of the Confederate Pension Fund in Austin. She said she could remember when Williams applied for a pension in 1932 and that his paperwork had been examined closely by her predecessor and the state comptroller. "They went up to the State Library and checked to see whether Williams had served," she said. "They were satisfied he had."

Finally, Texas officials announced that they had investigated the allegations and reviewed the records and were pronouncing themselves satisfied that Williams was indeed genuine. "All the evidence available in state offices and Confederate records indicates that Walter Williams is the last surviving Confederate veteran," proclaimed Gov. Price Daniel. "In this matter, we shall respect and follow the records of the state and the Confederacy rather than the archives of the federal government, which have always been recognized as incomplete with respect to members of the Confederate Armies."

Robert Calvert, the state comptroller, said that, at least for now, the state records would speak for themselves. "We are not going to take him off the pension rolls," he said. "We consider him a Confederate pensioner until it is legally shown otherwise."

In Dallas a woman whose father had been a Confederate veteran said that he could have vouched for Williams—if he were still alive. Mrs. G. W. Chambers said she was the oldest living daughter of G. M. Burkhart, who had passed away at the age of ninety in 1932, the year Williams had applied for his pension. "Many's the time my father used to tell me stories about the Civil War," she told the Associated Press. "He had a tintype picture and would show it to us children and say, "That's old Walter Williams. I wonder if he is still alive and what he's doing."" She told reporters that her father, like Williams, had been born on a farm in Mississippi and that he later moved to Tennessee. She said her father and Williams had definitely served together in Hood's Brigade. "From the way he talked, he and Williams must have been very close friends," she said. "I just can't let him die without telling somebody I know he served in Hood's Brigade during the Civil War."

Lester N. Fitzhugh, an assistant district attorney in Lancaster, Texas, came up with an old history of Hood's Brigade and a listing of Company C of the 5th Regiment that included a "W. Williams." "This gives him some backing to the claim," Fitzhugh stated. "But positive proof would be almost impossible, since all of the muster rolls of the brigade were lost after the capture of Richmond."

At the capital in Austin, Mrs. Fisher Osborn, an assistant state archivist, dusted off an old muster roll of Hood's Brigade that included a "W. W. Williams" attached to Company D of the 1st Regiment. But it also carried a notation that this soldier had been "discharged, underage." The roster had been compiled in 1911 by William R. Handy of Austin. Handy had served with Company B of the 4th Regiment of Hood's Brigade; it was not known what sources he used to draw up his list.

Also discovered was yet another "W. W. Williams" with an infantry company of the 11th Brigade of Texas volunteers. But the card file in the state archives stated he had enlisted in July 1861 in Houston County, Texas, and did not come from Mississippi or sign up toward the end of the war, like Walter Williams.

Nothing seemed officially settled for certain, and yet Washington leaders quietly backed up Texas and the rest of the old South. Senator Eastland said his resolution for a national day of mourning was based on the "full faith and credit" gleaned from Texas records, and that the resolution also carried the blessings of the American Legion and the White House. When Walter Williams dies, the senator repeated, the nation will mourn.

In her little home in Houston, Willie Mae Bowles was relieved. She thanked all those who had rushed to her father's defense. "My daddy is the type of person that never lied about anything in his life," she insisted. But she never told him about the controversy or warned him that many in the country doubted his authenticity. The news did not matter anymore, not to her or to her dying father. She decided it was just better to leave it alone. "He doesn't understand anything these days," she said.

12

LAST IN GRAY

Remarkably, Walter Williams recovered from the colds and pneumonia of July and August 1959. Three weeks after all the furor, Willie Mae Bowles raised the volume extra high on his radio in the back bedroom, hoping that her father might be able to hear a bit of the old-time hillbilly tunes.

The Armed Forces newspaper *Stars and Stripes*, in a feature story headlined "We're Catching up with Methuselah," devoted a couple of pages to the Texas Rebel and the phenomenon of old age. "Medicine now is helping the longevity climb of bedridden Walter Williams of Houston, Texas, last Civil War survivor," it noted. "Perhaps he could live even longer than he will if he had had the benefits of medical knowledge all his life. Again, perhaps not."

By his account, Williams was about to turn 117. His family was planning another party, and he signaled that he wanted spareribs. But he looked far too weak for hearty fare, given the pneumonia that now had settled in his chest again. Dr. Wolfe said that Williams would probably be too frail to join in the festivities but that "he wants lots of people to come see him."

On his birthday, Saturday, November 14, Willie Mae woke him at five in the morning. "When are all the people coming, and where's the music?" he rasped. He wanted scrambled eggs and coffee. To calm him down, she cranked up the radio some more and fed him a drop of coffee on a spoon.

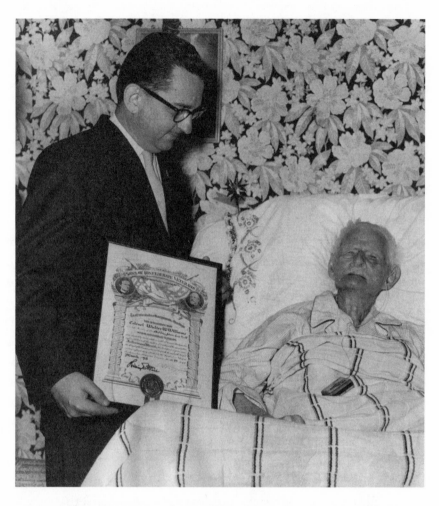

Death approaching, soon to usher out the last of the Civil War era, Walter Williams
lies near comatose in the back room of his daughter's Houston home in December 1958.
Dr. Heyl G. Tebo, commander of the Houston chapter of the Sons of Confederate
Veterans, presents him with a citation proclaiming him an honorary lifetime member
of the organization. (Courtesy of the *Houston Chronicle*)

She waited a half hour, ground up some eggs, and fed him those through a bottle. Thirty minutes later she gave him another spoonful of coffee. Then he was quiet. "Otherwise," she reported, "he didn't have anything to say about his birthday."

It rained most of the day. The mailman arrived with several bundles of letters and birthday cards. The president sent birthday greetings, and so did First Lady Mamie Eisenhower, who shared the same birthday as Williams (though she was fifty-four years younger). The Fourth Army headquarters at Fort Sam Houston in San Antonio, quietly preparing for his eventual military funeral, wired their congratulations.

The next day Willie Mae woke him again before daylight. This time she fed him a few sips of juice and a taste of spareribs. Soon his children, grandchildren, and great-grandchildren began dropping by. "Lots of people are coming," she tried to tell her father, billing it the largest Williams family reunion ever assembled. In all, some three hundred people were on hand, including the twenty-member local Garden Oaks American Legion Band and a group of high school ROTC cadets.

But Williams did not seem to notice much, neither the crowds nor the noise nor the five-tier cake topped with two Confederate flags and his photograph, arrayed in gray, in his Confederate general's uniform. Red, white, and blue candles were embedded in the white icing.

The rain had blown off, so the band performed on the lawn, under the scent of the still dripping cottonwoods, sycamore, and oaks. They played "Dixie," of course, and some other Southern standards. "Waiting for the Robert E. Lee" proved a particular favorite. A group of Houston florists sent 117 red roses. Inside the bedroom, Williams napped most of the afternoon. Once when he was awake, his son B. W. Williams of Houston talked about their old deer-hunting trips. That seemed to perk the old man up. "I'm tired of staying here," he growled in a low whisper. "And I don't feel bad." B. W. looked around at those crowded into the room, scrunched in next to the bed, and at the oxygen tent folded up in the corner. He said his father had still hunted at 101. "He rode a horse until he was 103," he remembered.

Dr. Wolfe was on hand too. He declared it remarkable that Williams kept beating his pneumonia and other illnesses. Birthday parties and other celebrations seemed to give his patient new vigor. "I suppose that the next thing we'll have to work on is Christmas," the doctor quipped.

When the day grew late and the party had thinned out, Ira P. Cox, manager of the American Legion Band, recalled how Williams always had said he would still be around at his 117th birthday, and he was right. Now Cox hoped that Williams would live long enough to see 118. "I want you to promise to be a good boy and be here for next year's celebration so I can bring my band back," he told Williams.

The old man did not answer.

He only worsened. By December 10 he was in critical condition, fighting another assault of pneumonia. Dr. Wolfe visited the next day and ordered the oxygen tent lowered over the bed. "It may be only forty-eight hours," he predicted. "He has no reserve. Respiration is shallow, pulse irregular. He is very weak. He tries to speak but is incoherent."

On Saturday, December 12, Williams was wheezing and gasping under the tent. The doctor feared his patient was dying. Willie Mae thought her father might have slipped into a coma. "But it's hard to tell," she said. "He's so weak." The visiting nurse started an intravenous line with a mixture of sugar and water; he had not taken the bottle or the eye dropper or a tablespoon of liquid since the day before.

On Monday he rallied. Dr. Wolfe noticed a slight improvement but for good measure kept Williams under the oxygen tent.

Still the old man hung on. On Wednesday night he slept little, and on Thursday he barely made a sound. On Friday his temperature hit 105. "He's lost quite a bit of strength and is much weaker," worried Willie Mae. "I don't see how he can rally this time," admitted Dr. Wolfe on Friday. "It's only a matter of hours. I thought he was gone this morning."

The next day he was. Walter Williams died on the afternoon of Saturday, December 19, 1959.

His son-in-law, Ed Bielamowicz, and a grandson, Sydney Boyd, were cradling him in their arms when he passed away. "He just quit breathing," Bielamowicz said. "He had done that before, and we just lifted him up and he'd catch his breath and start breathing again. But this time he didn't start breathing again. There was no struggle, no sound, nothing. He just went to sleep."

Dr. Wolfe had visited Williams only a half hour earlier. He said pneumonia was not what finally killed Williams; it had cleared his lungs two weeks previously. Death was caused by a blood clot in a large vessel leading to the brain. "He just died from the natural complications from old age," the doctor said.

Before he was taken to the Jack Carswell Funeral Home in Houston, Willie Mae asked for one last private moment with her father in the back bedroom. "I'm going to miss you so much," she cried, her face tumbling into grief. "I never did get tired of taking care of you."

Undertaker Jack Carswell had been hoping he would be chosen to conduct the funeral. He was strongly conservative and, more significantly, a local Civil War buff. So here at the cusp of the Civil War Centennial, with the last presumed soldier from that war now fallen, was Carswell's moment.

"He knew Walter Williams' family, and he courted them for the funeral," recalled one of his employees at that time, Stephen Jones, later to practice law in Enid, Oklahoma. "He and his wife would stop by often to see them. He told me when I worked for him that he anticipated he would handle the funeral for Mr. Williams. Certainly he wanted to.... It was a big funeral, and the newspapers ran the pictures of the pallbearers carrying the casket out of the church. At the front of the casket was Mr. Carswell."

Tributes poured in. The White House communications center sent an urgent, "operational immediate" message to presidential aide General Goodpaster: "Word just received of death of Walter Williams, last surviving Civil War veteran ... Press queries being received here regarding proclamation."

Arrangements were finalized to fly a presidential wreath on a commercial airliner to Texas. White House military aide Col. Robert L. Schulz asked Lt. Gen. Guy S. Meloy Jr., the commander at Fort Sam Houston, to place the wreath "at an appropriate time during the rites." He also instructed Meloy against "making any special efforts to promote or avoid publicity."

Then the president issued a statement. Despite the serious questions raised about Williams's authenticity, Eisenhower chose to ignore the public doubts. In saluting Williams, however, someone in the White House (possibly the president, as the handwriting is similar to his) crossed out the title "General" Williams in the proclamation and inserted "Mr."

"With millions of Americans throughout our land, I pause in respectful silence to honor the passing of the last surviving veteran of the War Between the States, Walter W. Williams," Eisenhower's statement read. "The wounds of the deep and bitter dispute which once divided our nation have long since healed, and a united America in a divided world now holds up on a larger canvas the cherished traditions of liberty and justice for all. With Mr. Williams' passing, the hosts of Blue and Gray who were the chief actors in that great and tragic drama a century ago have all passed from the world stage. No longer are they the Blue and the Gray. All rest together as Americans in honored glory. An era has ended."

The president set aside a national day for mourning and ordered the U.S. flag lowered to half-staff "until the body of Walter W. Williams is laid to rest." Such a national tribute was owed Williams, said Eisenhower, because he "served in the Army of the Confederacy for the last eleven months of the War Between the States as a forage master, Company C, 5th Regiment of Hood's Brigade, on active duty in Mississippi and Texas."

Nevertheless, most newspaper and magazine obituaries recalled at some length the controversy of three months earlier, citing the scandal that had touched the dying Williams and questioned his honesty. *Time* magazine's coverage by far was harshest, deriding Williams as all but phony and ridiculing Texas officials for buying into the lies. They summed up the whole affair as "The Unquenchable Legend."

"By the time old Walter Williams passed away at a self-reckoned 117 years," *Time*'s article began, "just about every official in Texas knew that he had spun a tall tale about his days as forage master of Hood's Texas Brigade in the War Between the States. But for a long time they had believed him and showered him with Confederate honors; then, when a too-enterprising reporter proved in the records that Williams could have been only five years old when Hood was marching, they decided to go right on believing just the same." The magazine mocked both Williams and the president: "Recent investigations have indicated that Hero Williams was only five years old when war broke out, but his fame is secure. President Eisenhower, pursuant to a July act of Congress, declared a day of national mourning, and Fourth Army units will lead a parade to Franklin, Texas, where Williams will be buried with full military honors."

Others praised the man who had outlived all other Civil War veterans. Robert D. Price, an Associated Press authority on Civil War history, penned a lengthy elegy. "Now the Civil War belongs to the ages: the last veteran is dead," he wrote. Walter Williams "was the last living of four million men who wore blue or gray in 1861–65. He gave his age as 117 and thus had lived some 94 years since he doffed the uniform that was his badge of honor in history. Thus passes a brave and hardy breed."

More tributes marked not just the death of Williams but the end of the greatest upheaval in American history; his death was viewed as a prelude to the upcoming centennial to commemorate a stronger, united country. Lyndon Johnson of Texas, the Senate majority leader, said Williams's death "seals the door on a great but tragic era." Texas Gov. Price Daniel, borrowing a line from Confederate martyr Stonewall Jackson, said, "General Williams has passed over the river to rest in the shade of the trees with hundreds of thousands of soldiers in blue and gray who went before him." Texas Congressman Albert Thomas declared that Williams would live forever in American history, hailing him as "one of the great historical characters of the nation and the Southern Confederacy." Texas Senator Ralph Yarborough soared in his praise of the final Confederate: "He was the last warrior of a lost cause, the sole remaining soldier of a whole civilization." Houston Mayor Lewis Wesley Cutrer issued a singular honor, declaring that December 19 would be observed as "Walter Williams Civil War Memorial Day."

Best-selling Civil War author Bruce Catton, writing in *Life* magazine, sought to sum up the last of the men in gray, whoever they truly were. "An aged man named Walter Williams died in Houston, insisting in the end that he was the last Confederate soldier. Although his claim has been challenged, one thing is certain: with his death the rebel army has gone forever." Catton's epitaph was written more for the Confederacy than Walter Williams: "There is some question about whether or not he actually served in the Confederate army, but this does not really matter, for, whether it was he or somebody who died earlier, the last veteran has been laid away. What matters now is that the army itself is gone."

Williams's body lay in state for two days, dressed in the gray and gold of a Confederate army general. His specially designed coffin was tinted gray. Five white velvet stars were sewn into the inside lining. A tailor-made Confederate flag draped the lid.

The bier was placed in the rotunda of the Civil Courts Building in Houston; five thousand people paid their respects, twenty-five of them slowly passing the casket every five minutes. Men doffed their hats, children hung onto their parents. An old man in a tattered coat knelt. A young boy asked his mother, "Why is he wearing that gray uniform?"

Willie Mae stood next to the coffin. George W. Hill, director of the Texas Civil War Centennial Commission, told her they hoped to erect a monument at his grave. She reached inside the coffin and patted her father's head. She could not stop crying.

At a separate tribute in the Houston Music Hall, Governor Daniel and officials from ten other Southern states, along with various administrative and military dignitaries, sat quietly to the strains of the old fife and drums. The songs included old favorites such as "When Johnny Comes Marching Home" and the "Yellow Rose of Texas." But "Dixie" stole the evening.

In the late morning of Wednesday, December 23, Williams's body was carried to the South Main Baptist Church downtown. Five hundred mourners attended the hour-long service. At the pulpit, a retired minister, the Reverend S. Stephen McKenney, preached the eulogy. "He has achieved an honor to which each of the millions of veterans of our War Between the States earnestly aspired but never achieved, and never can," McKenney said. He alone in the providence of God has survived in the vast multitude that has gone down to the silent chambers of death before him." The reverend added one final salute to the departed warrior: "It is safe to say that no name among our nation's citizens has come to be better known than that of our distinguished friend whom we honor today. Tens of thousands of our school children have learned to call him reverently by name."

A soloist sang "No Night There." The choir offered "My God and I." Out on the church lawn, dozens of Civil War reenactors from the Confederate 2nd Kentucky Cavalry could hear the organ bass and the lifted chorus. They stacked their rifles and bowed their heads.

Pallbearers, all gray-clad members of the Albert Sidney Johnston Camp of the Sons of Confederate Veterans, carried him out of the church.

A thirty-car motorcade started off shortly after the noon hour, and a crowd estimated at 25,000 pushed the edges of Main Street, straining under the city's hanging Christmas decorations to catch sight of the hearse, the limousines, and an eight-man military honor guard.

The procession turned north out of Houston, and four hours later, late in the afternoon, it reached the outskirts of Franklin. By then it trailed a mile long, with hundreds of Fourth Army troops, police cars, and motorcycles shepherding the old man toward the Mount Pleasant Baptist Church and the parish cemetery. They stopped atop a small hillside, where Williams was to be buried near the grave of a Civil War veteran who had died nearly forty years earlier.

Two bands, one comprising descendants of Yankee veterans, the other from the South, played softly. The Yankee fife and drum corps from Mount Vernon, Ohio, present as promised, performed "Onward Christian Soldiers." Twenty-one rifle shots shattered aloft. "Taps" floated into the coming winter dusk.

The dirt already was turned, the grave awaited, but first they all paused. The family asked that the lid be lifted once more, and they each took one last look. Then the Confederate flag was folded, and the flowers gathered up. The last of the gray was gone. The last of the blue was gone. All the tired soldiers lay peacefully dreaming; all was quiet along the Potomac.

13
....

OF THE DEAD, SPEAK NO EVIL

W alter Williams went to his grave never knowing that he had come under fire as a Confederate imposter. But the Texas State Senate was enraged, and when the part-time body met for the first time a year after his death, it immediately set out to right the wrong done its "distinguished son of Dixie."

In January 1961, just after the Civil War Centennial Commission had held its first commemoration at the tombs of Grant and Lee, the senators in Austin unanimously approved a special resolution titled "In Memory of Walter Washington Williams." Then they signed the document and sent copies to all the governors of the former Confederate states.

They first declared the South's secession from the Union a just and noble act: "With saddened and sorrowful hearts, and with deep humility, the sons and daughters of the South were compelled to defend their honor and to protect themselves and their homes against the further encroachment and imposition of unconstitutional measures and from the divestiture of their guaranteed rights."

They then hailed Williams a hero: "It is a matter of significance, as well as coincidence, that the last soldier of that conflict should reside in the Lone Star State." They insisted that "as a young man, Walter Williams donned the gray of the South," that he had served as a forage master until the war's end, and that he did indeed live to be 117 and "remained so until he was called to rest on 'Fame's eternal camping ground,' and be there consecrated to the 'bivouacs of the dead.'" And when he died, "his casket covered with the Stars and Bars of Dixie, the honors accorded and the tributes bestowed on the mortal remains of General Williams exemplify the love and high esteem in which this warrior, of a century past, was held by an admiring and grieved nation."

The senators attacked the critics and the press, singling out reporter Lowell K. Bridwell, for daring to question Williams as an authentic Confederate veteran: "Unable and helpless to defend himself, he became the victim of one of the foulest and most dastardly assaults which only an evil, diseased and venom-filled mind could conceive, less honorably than a rattlesnake—without warning—as the viperous diatribe—'the foulest whelp of sin.'" They dismissed the press accounts as "venomous slander," stemming directly "from North of the Mason-Dixon Line." They said the press was guilty of "utterly ignoring historical facts" and adopting "the wolfish grin of Fagin." No sin was worse than to "humiliate and embarrass, if not destroy, the record of gallantry and the reputation of an old soldier, soon thereafter to be committed to fadeless and deathless immortality."

The resolution covered a full page of the official Senate journal, and the Senate saved its bitterest vile for *Time* for leveling its harsh attacks upon Williams's credibility. The magazine was "a strumpet of scandal and a harlot of untruth." It should be ashamed that it had "poured its cup of venom on the grieved hearts of those left to mourn his passing."

"De mortuis nil nisi bonum," warned the Senate. (Of the dead, speak no evil.)

The Civil War was 100 years old. The veterans from both sides had all been laid to rest, as were the imposters who sought to steal a piece of fame, a pension check, and their own corner of history. Some were soldiers, some were not. The flags of the Grand Army of the Republic were stored away in museums. The great Confederate picnics and sunlit parades down Canal Street in New Orleans, swords gleaming, drums beating, echoed no more.

The families of the veterans were dwindling too. At the time of Williams's death in 1959, federal pension rolls show that only 3,600 Union widows and 792 children still lived to retell the old tales of battle. In the South, fewer than a thousand widows and only four children survived.

But Civil War veterans, North and South, were honored separately as the heroes they had become. In Washington, D.C., Missouri Rep. Champ Clark remembered visiting retired Union Gen. Daniel Sickles, and how Clark's son would leap upon the old man's lap, the lap missing a right leg since Gettysburg. "Frequently he would go over to the old soldier's seat," Clark recalled, "climb upon his lap and toy with his spectacles, crutches and watch-chain. He generally came back with his pockets bulging with candy, apples, oranges and other gimcracks."

On Memorial Day 1884, Oliver Wendell Holmes Jr., once an officer with the 20th Massachusetts Volunteer Regiment and who still carried the scars of war—he was wounded at Ball's Bluff, Antietam, and the Second Battle of Fredericksburg—spoke before a gathering in Keene, New Hampshire. By then he was an associate judge of the Massachusetts Supreme Judicial Court. In two decades he would be elevated to the U.S. Supreme Court in Washington. Holmes spoke of the "memories of love and grief and heroic youth," and how today "we of the North and our brethren of the South could join in perfect accord." He said they all held just as strong a conviction, and that "every man with a heart must respect those who give all for their belief." Let the reunited America commemorate the war and honor the dead in statues, monuments, and courthouse squares.

"Such hearts—ah me, how many!—were stilled twenty years ago; and to us who remain behind is left this day of memories," Holmes told the Memorial Day crowd. "Every year—in the full tide of spring—at the height of the symphony of flowers and love and life—there comes a pause, and through the silence we hear the lonely pipe of death." It falls to the living, then, to remember the dead and teach those who were not there the lessons of "honor and grief." The veterans, he said, were "us who stand almost alone, and have seen the noblest of our generation pass away."

Yet when the next conflict came—the Spanish–American War of 1898—Northerners fretted over transporting U.S. troops through the cities of the South to bases in Tampa for shipment to Cuba. In fact they bypassed Richmond, Virginia, altogether. Emotions and confusion were flying in every direction. Maj. Gen. "Fighting Joe" Wheeler, a decorated former Confederate officer now helping lead the U.S. forces in Cuba, was overcome with emotion when the Spaniards turned in retreat on the

Caribbean island. Lost in the moment, suddenly transported back to an earlier war, he shouted, "We've got the Yankees on the run!"

A dozen years later, in August 1910, former President Theodore Roosevelt, a veteran of that Cuban campaign, was surrounded by an audience of thirty thousand for an address in tiny Osawatomie, Kansas. The event was to dedicate a new John Brown Memorial Park, at the site of some of the Bleeding Kansas border warfare that had foreshadowed the four years of national slaughter to come. The air was hot and steamy, yet the audience poured in on foot, bicycles, autos, buggies, and wagons. Women opened their parasols to deflect the harsh sun. Roosevelt, in shirt, tie, coat, and vest, waved from the back of a train as it huffed into the Missouri Pacific depot. By the time he moved to the center of a grove and climbed atop a large kitchen table to be seen and heard, the skies opened and torrents of rain fell.

Roosevelt was out of office but soon to campaign again for the White House. His theme that day was a "New Nationalism." And he repeatedly spotted old men in the waves of the hot, drenched crowd who fifty years earlier had gone to war as soldiers, most of them from the Yankee North. "You men of the Grand Army," he said, "you men who fought through the Civil War, not only did you justify your generation, not only did you render life worth living for our generation, but you justified the wisdom of Washington."

Roosevelt had been a boy leaning from a window of his family's New York brownstone when in 1865 the funeral cortege carrying Lincoln's body passed by on its return to Springfield, Illinois. "It was you who crowned Washington's work," he told the veterans, "as you carried to achievement the high purpose of Abraham Lincoln." He said it was all those from the Civil War who had made the nation not just whole again, but stronger. "We can admire the heroic valor, the sincerity, the self-devotion shown alike by the men who wore the blue and the men who wore the gray."

Five years later, Army officials announced that the last Union soldier from 1861 would be retiring. Maj. Gen. John Lincoln Clem, a drummer boy at Chickamauga and Shiloh, whose drum was smashed by Confederate artillery, retired fifty years after the end of the war. As a young orphan, he had snuck off from Newark, Ohio, to join the Union army.

After the war he was promoted from first lieutenant to captain, major, and colonel. Upon his departure from military service, a special act of Congress elevated him one last time to major general. He also had married the daughter of a Confederate veteran. That alone, he often said, made him the most "united American" in the United States.

The old fire, anger, and sectional hatreds slowly burned off. Not long after the end of the war, a Union veteran who had lost a leg spoke at a United Confederate Veterans reunion in Richmond; he was roundly applauded. In Washington, the North's Grand Army of the Republic escorted a parade of United Confederate Veterans down Pennsylvania Avenue.

But mostly these relics of a long-ago war spent their afternoons on park benches or under the shade of town squares. They often were sad, lonely figures. Nothing in their long lives could surpass what they had accomplished in their youth. As the world changed so dramatically—a world becoming louder, faster, and uproariously egocentric—they replayed in their thoughts perhaps a night standing guard in a lone wood or the rush of fear with bayonets fixed, none of it ever undertaken for individual glory.

Henry Adams recalled how he and his friend John Hay often looked out of their windows above Lafayette Square in Washington, D.C., "to notice an old corps commander or admiral of the Civil War, tottering along to the club for his cards or his cocktails. There is old Dash who broke the Rebel lines at Blankburg. Think of his having been a thunderbolt of war!" Now these brittle, stooped, and uncertain characters were carefully maneuvering through the park. Yet, "there they went! Men who had swayed the course of empire."

They could also be seen in small towns such as Bedford, Virginia, where, years earlier, William Henry Lafayette Wells had gone off to join the Old Dominion Rifles and a light artillery battery at Bull Run and Gettysburg, and saw some fifteen skirmishes. He attended the great Gettysburg reunion in 1938 as a skinny invalid in a wheelchair, wearing a broad-brimmed hat, his chest in appropriate gray and slathered in Confederate medals. That was the final highlight of his long life. If the Civil War had a second act, it was that reunion. It plucked him off the park bench and carried him back not under the flare of cannon but into the limelight of history. He died a year later, two years short of 100.

The splendid reunions at Manassas and Gettysburg were difficult to stage, and as the national centennial approached, many in the South still worried that the North would use the anniversary to laud their victory over them and stress the divide between the two regions. States in the South chose to celebrate the creation of the Confederacy rather than to remember a bloody struggle that had ended in their defeat. In many ways, both sides initially ignored the efforts of the Centennial Commission to bridge their differences and bury the old hates.

In early January 1961, just as the Texas Senate was signing its resolution condemning Walter Williams's detractors, Montgomery, Alabama, began preparing for a parade, a ball, and a reenactment of Jefferson Davis's taking the oath of office as president of the Confederate States of America in 1861. The city established its own Centennial Commission and urged women to sew hoopskirts and merchants to encourage employees to dress in antebellum costumes. Werth Roberts, chairman of the Confederate Colonel Council chapter, promised that every man who grew a beard would be addressed as "honorary colonel." Young women competed in a "Belle of the Confederacy" sweepstakes. The top prize was a new car; other awards included a mink stole, new luggage, and transistor radios.

W. J. Mahoney Jr., the "As I See It" columnist in the *Montgomery Advertiser-Journal*, wrote that, while the Civil War Centennial Commission in Washington hoped for a new national unity, most of the celebrations "for geographic and historic reasons were centered almost entirely in the South" because most of the war was fought in the South. With this focus on Dixie, he feared that the South would once again be branded as traitorous and portrayed as the "nation's whipping boy." "So what are we about to celebrate?" he asked. "The centennial of the Confederacy's birth or the start of a war we lost and are still paying for?"

Grover C. Hall, the newspaper's editor, contributed a front-page column saluting his fellow sons of the South, stressing a new era for Alabama. "Southerners are reconciled to the result of the war, and they are too busy marching to prosperity in their gracious land to brood over the crime of Reconstruction," he wrote. "The South had the highest standard of living in the country before the war and has it in mind to regain that status."

Many, however, could not let go of the old bitterness. In a pubic letter to the editor in February, William Martin of Pike Road, Alabama, complained that Southerners confronted the same harsh conditions their great-grandfathers faced a hundred years ago. "Federal dictatorship is literally being stuffed down our throats," he wrote. "Integration is now a major issue, not just a rumor. The battle is not solely one of segregation versus integration, anymore than the Civil War was one of slavery versus freedom of slaves."

Meanwhile, Montgomery mounted its show glorifying the Confederacy. An attorney, T. B. Hill Jr., was chosen to portray President Davis. He was escorted from the railroad station by horse and carriage through a rainstorm, passing seven thousand waving, shouting, drenched spectators. He climbed up Dexter Avenue and the statehouse steps, recited the oath, and read part of Davis's 1861 inaugural address.

Bobbie Gorman, a twenty-two-year-old housewife and secretary in the state's Alcoholic Beverage Control Board office, garnered enough votes to be crowned "Belle of the Confederacy" and given the new car. "I'm so happy I don't know what to do," she said. At a "Man of the Hour" celebration that ran for five nights in the State Coliseum, she was escorted by Hill playing Davis to the sounds of more cheers.

In another procession, Hill led hundreds of people from the Exchange Hotel through the streets of downtown, carrying torches provided by the fire department. He repeatedly doffed his stovepipe hat to the well-wishers. Women twirled their umbrellas in response. Smoke from artillery cannon powdered the air. In all, fifty thousand people took part in the festivities; the Centennial Ball alone drew five thousand. Said Paul B. Fuller, general manager of the city's Chamber of Commerce, "I have never seen the people of Montgomery join in anything so wholeheartedly."

Jackson, Mississippi, went next. A lead editorial in the *Clarion-Ledger* newspaper, next to a drawing of a smiling Confederate soldier marching with the Dixie flag, warned that the South had been "healing" just fine until the North became jealous that the region was strong and prosperous again. "Once again," the paper opined, "South-hating image makers started to work. It has become just about a full-time job of loyal Southerners to hold the ugly-picture takers in check."

In a spirit of goodwill, however, the people of Jackson invited Northern representatives to Mississippi to help honor all the men who fell at Vicksburg, now a national military park. The editors of the *Union Leader* in Manchester, New Hampshire, readily accepted, hoping it would ease tensions from the "Brothers' War" that continued to fester. "It is always fitting, of course, to pay tribute to brave men who gave their lives for a cause," the New Hampshire paper noted. "The men of the North and the South who died at Vicksburg cannot be held responsible for the actions of those who precipitated this bloody and unnecessary war."

Jackson had its own cast of reenactors, and they focused on the secession. They mounted a gallant parade on Capitol Street before thousands of people flashing carnival-like smiles, munching on peanuts and candied apples. The largest Confederate flag ever woven was carried for two hours by Central High School students down the center of the parade route, winding past a giant reviewing stand at the Governor's Mansion. Three thousand men flashed by in Confederate uniforms. Belles from Delta State College at Cleveland, Mississippi, waltzed along in yellow-checked gingham dresses and matching parasols.

Another march, though smaller, was under way that day too. Some fifty African American students decided to protest the arrest of nine black youths for staging Mississippi's first civil rights sit-in. Marching to the city jail, the protesters were met with tear gas canisters, police dogs, and scores of deputy sheriffs who chased them off Pearl Street.

The issue of segregation nearly ruined the next Confederate celebration, this one in April in Charleston, South Carolina. The plan called for a reenactment of the firing on Fort Sumter to commemorate the opening volley of the Civil War, and officials from the national Civil War Centennial Commission and state centennial groups were invited to attend.

Madaline A. Williams was a member of the state commission in New Jersey; more significantly, she was the first African American woman elected to the New Jersey state legislature. Her husband served on the national board of the National Association for the Advancement of Colored People (NAACP). After her invitation to Charleston, she unexpectedly received word that she could not stay at the Francis Marion Hotel, the elegant, waterfront location where most of the meetings, meals, and festivities were to be held.

The manager of the hotel, J. William Cole, said he had never received a specific reservation request for accommodations for a black woman. But, he argued, the hotel would have to deny anyone of color because that was the law in South Carolina. If Williams had asked for a room, Cole said, she would have been told there were no more vacancies. She could attend luncheons and a banquet at the hotel, and the business meetings too. She just could not spend the night.

So Williams and New Jersey balked at attending; so did Massachusetts, Illinois, New York, Missouri, and California. Then President Kennedy intervened, announcing at a Washington press conference that the official events would be moved to the U.S. naval base near Charleston harbor. "The Centennial is an official body of the United States government," Kennedy said. "Federal funds are contributed to sustaining it. There have been appointments made by the federal government to the commission, and it is my strong belief that any program of this kind in which the United States is engaged should provide facilities and meeting places which do not discriminate on the grounds of race or color."

His words inflamed South Carolina officials. "Neither the president nor the governor can dictate to a hotel who it may or may not receive as guests," said Gov. Ernest Hollings. Sen. Strom Thurmond called Kennedy's decision "high-handed interference." The president, he complained, had no authority "to enforce a policy of racial integration in connection with" the Fort Sumter commemoration.

Maj. Gen. Ulysses S. Grant III attended the Charleston observances at the naval base, telling local critics that he could not disobey the White House and stay at the Francis Marion. "I'm sure you realize we cannot just pay no attention to the president," he said.

At a dinner during the commemoration, Ashley Halsey, a Charleston native and associate editor of the *Saturday Evening Post*, blasted the New Jersey delegation for making a public fuss over the hotel incident and marring the festivities. He said those from the New Jersey delegation were two-faced, and that New Jersey had its own hotels "where members of one race find it impossible to register.... Racial prejudice and discrimination in New Jersey are such that it takes amazing effrontery for its politicians to rebuke any other state or community upon any circumstance or pretext."

Delegates from the North and South held separate meetings and com-memorations, not coming together until the final day for the Fort Sumter reenactment. In a show of defiance, the Southern states assembled for meetings at the Francis Marion. They covered the ballroom dais with Confederate flags. Thurmond told the all-white delegates that integration was a communist plot to weaken America. "It is the surest method for the destruction of free governments," he warned.

The most outspoken firebrand that day was state Sen. John D. Long, who sponsored resolutions to fly the Stars and Bars over the statehouse in Columbia. "Out of the dust and ashes of war," he thundered, "with its attendant destruction and woe, came Reconstruction more insidious than war and equally evil in consequences, until the prostrate South staggered to her knees assisted by the original Ku Klux Klan and the Red Shirts, who redeemed the South and restored her to her own."

When the commemoration week ended and the two sides separately headed home, Joseph Dempsey, vice chairman of the New Jersey Centen-nial Commission, accused the national commission of "pathetic misman-agement." He pressed for the removal of Grant and his top assistant, Karl Betts. "There is ample evidence that these two people should not participate in this centennial," Dempsey said. "They are guilty of gross incompetence."

Both men eventually resigned, though Grant said he left for personal reasons; his wife was ill. The underlying truth was that the national Civil War Centennial Commission and its planned commemorations had come square up against the civil rights movement and the Freedom Riders in the South. Among the critics was Lawrence D. Reddick, an African American author and educator who spoke before two thousand at the Waldorf-Astoria Hotel in New York. He said the centennial celebrations were polarizing the opposing sides of the civil rights debate. The centennial was promoting a rash of Confederate flags and other symbols that blanketed the South and were viewed by the North as racially insensitive. They should be "gathered and burned," Reddick said. The truth should be told, and not "the Confed-erate myth for the unhistorical romance much of it is."

The national commission also confronted criticism that summer for its commercialization of a reenactment of the First Battle of Bull Run. All these disputes led Grant and Betts to an early departure, and President

Kennedy appointed two historians in their place. Allan Nevins took the top spot and immediately called for an end to any more reenactments. "Above all," he stressed, "our central theme will be unity, not division. We shall allow the just pride of no national group to be belittled or besmirched." He said future commemorations would be "instructive and constructive," honoring "the heroism of the 600,000 men who gave their lives."

Under Nevins's leadership the commission held two national programs in Washington, the first to observe the signing of the Emancipation Proclamation at the Lincoln Memorial. United Nations Ambassador Adlai Stevenson spoke, saying "once more we feel as men did in Lincoln's day, that the future of mankind itself depends upon the outcome of the struggle in which we are engaged." Nevins addressed the other major Washington event, highlighting Lincoln's Gettysburg Address. He was joined by a panel of American writers and philosophers.

Around the country, the states acknowledged the Civil War's anniversary in their separate ways. Connecticut printed copies of all of Lincoln's speeches and distributed them to schools and libraries. On Capital Square in Richmond, Virginians held a centennial reenactment of their beloved Robert E. Lee's resignation from the Union army to head the forces that would defend his homeland. New Jersey sent aloft a human-driven balloon, similar to those used by observation scouts in the war. Arkansas opened a new park at the Pea Ridge battlefield. Ohio saved 400 bullet-shredded flags. Missouri served up a Civil War regiment meal that included mess items such as "hardtack and cornpone, buggy rut water and roof drippings." Two desserts were offered: "Soggy pie or souffléd wild onions."

In Albert Woolson's Minnesota, state officials commemorated the Sioux uprising that had erupted in the midst of the Civil War. As a young man Woolson had witnessed the execution of some of those Indian warriors. In Walter Williams's Texas, they built a $2.5 million archives to microfilm and store all of the state's Civil War service records. Among the documents saved was Williams's Civil War pension file, which to this day casts doubt on whether he ever actually served.

And then in Gettysburg, in July 1963, 100 years after the turning point in the Civil War, 50,000 turned out to watch a symbolic reenactment of Pickett's Charge. Four months later, many returned to Gettysburg to commemorate Lincoln's address. Former President Eisenhower, in retirement on his farm near the battlefield, offered brief remarks. President Kennedy sent a specially recorded message. "Let us rededicate ourselves to the perpetuation of those ideals of which Lincoln spoke so luminously," he said. "As Americans, we can do no less."

His vice president did him one better. On Memorial Day that year, Lyndon Johnson spoke at the battlefield, delivering a very short speech, barely two typed pages, much like Lincoln's in its brevity. His audience included a number of World War I veterans, looking much like the Civil War veterans they had replaced. He recalled the sacrifices of the Civil War, and he defended civil rights. "Our nation found its soul in honor on these fields of Gettysburg," Johnson said. "We must not lose that soul in dishonor now on the fields of hate."

The final assembly of the Civil War Centennial Commission convened in May 1965 in Springfield, Illinois, Lincoln's home and final resting place. Historians and dignitaries, 800 in all, attended from around the country for five days of readings and programs. Among them was Lincoln's great-grandson and last living namesake, Robert Todd Lincoln Beckwith of Hartfield, Virginia. It was his first trip to Springfield.

Glenn H. Seymour, a history professor at Eastern Illinois University, spoke about how different Lincoln's Illinois had been a century ago. "Very little of the land was still owned by the federal government," he related. "The telegraph was in use, the railroad system had been built, but none of the state's ten incorporated cities had paved streets or a sewage system, and livestock ran loose."

Speaking from the vantage point of Dixie, Sen. Ralph Yarborough of Texas offered an image of "Abraham Lincoln as a Southerner," noting that he had been born in Kentucky, that he surrounded himself with Kentucky law partners, and that many of his wife's brothers and brothers-in-law fought for the Confederacy. "For too long," Yarborough said, "the South has shortchanged itself by not claiming Lincoln."

Nevins delivered the keynote at a Saturday afternoon luncheon. He said the Civil War lived on because "more than has been told remains to be told." Other speakers read Civil War speeches and Civil War fiction. Author Shelby Foote said the best of American literature falls "before" and "after" the Civil War. He singled out Stephen Crane's *The Red Badge of Courage*. Still others read poetry. All agreed that Walt Whitman, who had tended the wounded and dying, remained the poet laureate of the Civil War.

"We shall not be the last throng to stand here at this venerated place," said Adlai E. Stevenson III, an Illinois state representative and son of the UN ambassador, as he delivered the last address of the final program at Lincoln's tomb. "Countless men and women will, like Walt Whitman, mourn him 'with every returning spring.'"

A month later in tiny Fitzgerald, Georgia, a town founded by an equal number of Confederate and Union veterans, residents held their own "Blue and Gray Days." Seven local streets were named for Union generals; seven more for Confederate generals. Four more were named for Civil War battleships. Even the sidewalks were painted blue and gray. The town's roots had been embedded a generation after the war, when Yankee veterans started moving there to show their gratitude to Georgians who had donated food and supplies to Northern cities hit by drought. Beverly M. Dubose Jr., chairman of the Georgia Civil War Centennial Commission, thought it appropriate that the final centennial commemoration should be held in Fitzgerald, honoring those who had fought on both sides. "Their story of peace," he said of the veterans from both colors, "stands as a living symbol of unity to every American."

Peace was hard won in the 1860s, and it would be long in coming in the struggles over civil rights in the 1960s. Reconciliation and sacrifice were the overriding themes in a speech by Nevins included in the Centennial Commission's official final report. He described Henry A. Wise, the governor of Virginia, "kneeling in the moonlight as his boy's coffin is opened, after the battle of Roanoke Island, kissing the cold brow and crying in anguish, 'Oh my son, you have died for me!'" He spoke of Rebecca Harding Davis, "a poor, thin mountain girl waiting on a train platform in the Pennsylvania Alleghenies." When the brakeman stopped briefly to unload a pine box, she threw her arms around the coffin "in utter desolation as the train steamed away." Nevins then mentioned four African American girls recently killed by white racists in a Birmingham, Alabama, church bombing. "The fight still rages, and the line of fire still stretches across the entire American map, North and South," he said. "A hundred years after Cold Harbor and the Wilderness, the trumpet yet summons all of us urgently."

What was the centennial all about, after all the speeches and hoopla and fundraising endeavors, if not a tragic hunt for honor in the country's darkest hour? Foote completed the second of his three-volume Civil War narrative halfway through the centennial period, in 1963, and posed that question. He noted that the writer Edmund White had suggested that, rather than hold a national celebration, "a day of mourning would be more appropriate." Southern novelist Robert Penn Warren thought the whole thing was like "picking the scab of our fate."

One hundred years earlier, the Army of the Potomac and the Army of Northern Virginia had disassembled; the soldiers went home, and the veterans grew old. For years their ghosts haunted the ever-changing land, and they still do today—in statues in courthouse squares and in the mouths of rusting cannon in city parks, where spiders spin webs and boys poke their heads. Many of the ancient warriors met at fraternal encampments and marched down confetti-filled city streets; after long lifetimes they put away their swords and their differences and sought to embrace one another before the last of them passed on.

That, Nevins maintained in the commission's final report, was what the centennial had hoped to demonstrate—that the struggle for peace can be just as challenging and difficult as the necessity for war. "Peace has its battles no less than war," he wrote, "and its demands upon valor no less than the field of exploding shells."

There was no word spoken about the imposters, of course—those who had acted for money or fame, or from the confusion of old age or senility. Not until another Civil War historian, William Marvel, a Virginian who had moved to New Hampshire, began studying the old pension records and census data some years later. He concluded that the last authentic Confederate had been Pleasant Crump, the Alabama veteran and preacher who spent his postwar years rocking on his porch, reading and rereading his Bible and watching a water oak grow tall. Marvel determined that Albert Woolson of Duluth was not only the last Yankee but the last of either side when he died in 1956. Marvel suggested that Gettysburg should modify the plaque on Woolson's statue and honor him as the last of them all.

The records debunked most of the "great imposters," Marvel wrote, although "the trail of deceit seems never to end." While acknowledging that many continued to insist that Walter Williams of Texas was the last Civil War soldier, Marvel argued otherwise in a brief 1991 article for *Blue and Gray* magazine. "Williams was a fake," he declared. "The only records lacking are those proving he participated in the Civil War. There are plenty to prove he did not."

Then why the lies? Why the charades in a land where truth and honesty were presumably as cherished as God and country?

Some of the deceivers loved the pageantry, the adulation, and the gallant uniforms that sparkled at formal dinners and fraternal reunions. Some were desperate for money to pay the rent on the farm, to purchase new clothes, or, in one case, to buy a new cow. Some perpetuated their myths for so long that, in the twilight of their lives, they could not possibly own up to the lies and admit they had disgraced their family, their country, and themselves. Most of them lied because they could.

And few if any challenged them. While some snickered at the impossibility of someone this old and this heroic, and others shook their heads, most never questioned the old tales of the Civil War. Why would they? America has always loved a myth and adored a hero. Even today, many of the descendants of the dubious heroes insist that their stories were true. No one dares speak ill of the dead.

Mark Twain tried to figure it out. America's premier humorist took a stab at explaining the phenomenon of clouded memory and outright deception. In his 1924 autobiography, published before the lean years of the Great Depression that prompted many of the imposters to step forward for Civil War pensions, Twain wrote, "When I was younger I could remember anything, whether it had happened or not; but my faculties are decaying, now, and soon I shall be so I cannot remember any but the latter." Twain's hero Huck Finn called them "stretchers." "I never seen anybody but lied, one time or another," Huck said.

Down in Texas, Willie Mae Bowles did not care what anyone said. She was not upset by the critics, the records in Washington, or the United Daughters of the Confederacy, whose members still doubt that her father was the last of the men in gray. But even the state of Texas had second thoughts. In 1963 the Texas Civil War Centennial Commission began reviewing census records and other material and could not tell whether Williams was who he said he was. The state debated placing a Texas Historical Marker in front of the Franklin cemetery and finally went ahead despite the objections of one family that did not want their ancestors dishonored by sharing the same plot of ground as Williams. The state planted the black-and-white marker with one significant caveat. The inscription begins by stating that Williams was only "reputed" to have been the last surviving soldier of the Civil War. "There would be historical value in the marking, for future generations will seek the grave, authentic or not be the last survivor's claim," the commission's research director, Mrs. D. M. Parmelee, advised local officials in Franklin. "That is the way of the world."

The *Guinness Book of World Records* also changed its mind. In 1968, after reviewing census records and researching other material, it formally withdrew Williams's claim as the last living survivor of the American Civil War. He was "too young" for the war, it concluded.

None of it ever bothered Willie Mae. She had cared for her father all those years as he lay dying in her small home in Houston. She loved him dearly; her devotion was endless. And when she followed him in death, they buried her in Texas too. "Willie Mae Bowles," reads her light brown, granite-and-bronze headstone, "Confederate Daughter."

POSTSCRIPT

In 1971, twelve years after Walter Williams died, Sylvester Magee lay dying in a hospital in Columbia, Mississippi. A onetime slave, he used to tell about being forced into both the Confederate and Union armies, and he claimed that twice he had been wounded during the siege of Vicksburg. He sported white whiskers but only three teeth, and he had lived for years in a $12.45-a-month shack with no electricity, no bathroom, and not much of a roof. He could not read; he could not write. He gummed tobacco, and he sipped wine. A family Bible that he said had listed his birth date had been destroyed by fire, and records of slaves mustered into military service were dubious at best. Once he had appeared on national television and told war stories. He also had applied for a soldier's pension but was turned down.

Civil War historians could not agree on whether he was genuine or not. Some people called him "Slave," some called him "Mack," some called him "Lick Skillet." He said of himself, "I'm an old man. I could go any minute." He was, he said, 130.

SOURCES

1. TWO OLD SOLDIERS

Albert Woolson's final days were widely reported at the time, particularly in the *Duluth (Minn.) News-Tribune*, Mar. 13 and Aug. 3, 1956; the *St. Paul Pioneer-Press*, Aug. 2, 1956; and *Stars and Stripes*, July 31 and Aug. 1, 1956.

Likewise, Walter Williams's last days were given wide news coverage, especially in the *Houston Post*, Dec. 20, 1959; the *Sacramento Bee*, Dec. 20, 1959; *Stars and Stripes*, Dec. 11, 12, 15, and 18, 1959; and the *Chicago Tribune*, Dec. 13, 1959.

The *Life* magazine feature on Williams can be found in its May 11, 1959, issue.

The story of the Georgia veteran (William J. Bush) who disrupted the Civil War museum has been richly told, and it can be traced from various sources, including the *Norfolk Virginian-Pilot*, May 30, 1951; the *Florida State News*, Nov. 12, 1952; the *Milledgeville (Ga.) Union-Recorder*, Aug 23 and 30, 1951; and the *United Daughters of the Confederacy* magazine, Feb. 1989. More material on Bush and the anecdote is available at the Blue and Gray Museum in Fitzgerald, Ga. The novelist Flannery O'Connor saw these articles, which inspired her to write her short story, "A Late Encounter with the Enemy."

Bruce Catton's recollections of meeting Yankees as a child come from his memoir, *Waiting for the Morning Train: An American Boyhood* (New York: Doubleday, 1972), and *Mr. Lincoln's Army*, from his Civil War series The Army of the Potomac (New York: Doubleday, 1962).

2. REUNION

The story of President Taft's harrowing motor car drive to Manassas, Va., is recounted in Michael L. Bromley, *William Howard Taft and the First Motoring Presidency* (Jefferson, N.C.: McFarland, 2003), which also includes a good profile of Maj. Archibald Willingham Butt. The major's writings are compiled in *Taft and Roosevelt: The Intimate Letters of Archie Butt, Military Aide*, 2 vols. (Garden City, N.Y.: Doubleday, Doran, 1930). Another source on Butt is a profile in the *Potomac (Md.) News*, June 6, 1991.

The *Manassas Journal* and the *Manassas Democrat*, as well as the *Washington Post* and the *New York Times*, gave lengthy treatments to the reunion, beginning on July 20, 1911. The Manassas Museum published a commemorative edition on the Jubilee in June/July 1986, and copies of the work are available at the museum. Other works include Catherine T. Simmons, *Manassas, Virginia, 1873–1973: One Hundred Years of a*

Virginian Town (Manassas: Manassas City Museum, 1986), and R. Jackson Ratcliffe, comp., *This Was Manassas* (1973), both retrievable at the museum.

Walt Whitman's account of the Union retreat from Manassas is taken from *The Sacrificial Years: A Chronicle of Walt Whitman's Experiences in the Civil War*, edited and with an introduction by John Harmon McElroy (Boston: David B. Godine, 1999).

Details about the life of George Carr Round and his leadership of the Jubilee reunion at Manassas are included in his obituary, papers, and other records housed at the Manassas Museum. The museum also has many of Round's letters, including those he wrote home during the war as well as other correspondence and reports detailing his work on the Jubilee effort. A worthwhile profile of Round ran in the *Potomac (Md.) News*, Aug. 10, 1988.

The *Washington Post* of July 19, 1911, reported the protest by Brooklyn GAR members against the Confederate flag being flown at the Manassas reunion.

James Redmond's interview with the *Washington Post* was published July 21, 1911.

The odd story of James E. Maddox first surfaced in the *Washington Post*, July 23, 1911. Further details were reported in the *Manassas Democrat*, July 27, 1911; the *Manassas Journal*, July 28, 1911; and the *Washington Post*, July 29, 1911. H. A. Strong's report to Round is part of the records on file at the Manassas National Battlefield Park.

The fiftieth reunion at Gettysburg was covered in great detail by the *New York Times* beginning June 29, 1913. *Civil War Times* magazine printed a retrospective called "Gettysburg: The 50th Anniversary Encampment" in Oct. 1970. The files at the Gettysburg National Military Park include reams of material on the 1913 and 1938 reunions.

Walt Whitman's description of hearing the news in Washington of the victory at Gettysburg is included in McElroy, *The Sacrificial Years*.

President Wilson's address was reprinted in the *New York Times*, July 5, 1913.

The anecdote of the two soldiers reuniting at the site of Pickett's Charge was told in the *New York Times*, July 2, 1913.

The story of the Gettysburg Hotel brawl was reported by the *New York Times*, July 3, 1913.

The seventy-fifth anniversary reunion was covered extensively by the *New York Times*, beginning June 29, 1938. *Prologue Magazine*, a publication of the National Archives, ran a retrospective by archivist Mitchell Yockelson, "The Great Reunion: The Seventy-Fifth Anniversary of Gettysburg," in the summer of 1992. Another magazine, *Gettysburg*, also looked back at the reunion in its July 1, 1992, issue.

Paul L. Roy recounted his efforts to coordinate the seventy-fifth anniversary in his book *The Last Reunion of the Blue and Gray* (Gettysburg, Pa.: Bookmart, 1950).

The *Gettysburg Times*, Sept. 10, 1935, reported that many Union veterans opposed the flying of the Confederate flag at the reunion. The *New Orleans Times-Picayune*, Feb. 6, 1938, told of the defiance of Confederate veteran David Corbin Ker.

The *Gettysburg Times*, June 30, 1938, reported that P. Guibert had walked to Gettysburg from Pittsburgh.

Harry Rene Lee's passion for the Stars and Bars was reported in *Gettysburg* magazine, July 1, 1992.

John W. Weaver's death was reported in the *Gettysburg Times*, July 7, 1938.

President Roosevelt's address was reprinted in the *New York Times*, July 4, 1938.

Overton H. Mennet was quoted in the *Gettysburg Times*, June 28, 1938, as was John Milton Claypool. Mennet also was quoted in the *New York Times*, July 2, 1938.

The *Gettysburg Times* of June 3, 1938, told the story of Charles W. Eldridge turning 107 at the reunion.

Gettysburg magazine of July 1, 1992, reported Louis Quint's drive from Minnesota to the Gettysburg party.

A photograph of the Harris father-and-son duo was printed in the *New York Times*, July 1, 1938.

The stories of Warren Fisher, his wife, Daisy, and Alvin F. Tolman were told by the *Gettysburg Times*, June 16, 1938.

On July 1, 1938, the *Gettysburg Times* reported how M. A. Loop scaled the observation tower.

The *Washington Star*, July 3, 1938, printed the comments from Samuel B. Hanson.

James Handcock's trip to a Philadelphia ball game was recorded in the *Gettysburg Times*, July 11, 1938.

The telegram from veterans asking Washington officials for permission to remain forever at Gettysburg was printed in the *Gettysburg Times*, July 7, 1938.

3. OLD AGE AND STOLEN VALOR

Sources on Helen Dortch Longstreet are bountiful. Her books include *Lee and Longstreet at High Tide: Gettysburg in the Light of the Official Records* (self-published, 1904). Her essay "Wooed to the Warrior's Tent" can be found in the Helen Dortch Longstreet Papers at the Atlanta History Center. Further information regarding the widow of General Longstreet is included in Sarah E. Gardner, *Blood and Irony: Southern White Women's Narratives of the Civil War, 1861–1937* (Chapel Hill: University of North Carolina Press, 2004). Stories about her wanderings around upstate New York were published in the *Savannah Evening Press*, May 2, 1956; the *Atlanta Journal*, May 3, 1956; and the *Atlanta Constitution*, May 3, 1956. Her work as a reporter/columnist at the two Gettysburg reunions was carried in the *New York Times* on July 2 and 4, 1913, and July 3, 1938. Her battlefield posts also were published in the *Atlanta Constitution*, July 4, 1938, and the *Gettysburg Times*, July 1, 1938. The *Gettysburg Times* also quoted her in a June 27, 1938, article. *Life* magazine featured her at the Bell plant in Atlanta in its Dec. 27, 1943, edition. Her experiences as a riveter also were covered by the *Atlanta Journal* on Oct. 12, 1943, and Dec. 20, 1943. She also can be found in a *Time* magazine article, July 22, 1935. One of the best obituaries of this remarkable Southern woman was published in the *Atlanta Journal*, May 4, 1962.

LaSalle Corbell Pickett's obituary ran in the *Washington Post* and the *New York Times*, both on Mar. 23, 1931. Her autobiography is titled *What Happened to Me* (New York: Brentano's, 1917). The online *Encyclopedia Virginia* also includes material on the widow of George Pickett (http://www.encyclopediavirginia.org/Pickett_LaSalle_Corbell_1843-1931), as did *Time* magazine, Apr. 6, 1931.

Dr. Paul White's study of Charles Thiery was published in the *New England Journal of Medicine*, Jan. 8, 1959. The Boston Globe ran Thiery's obituary on Mar. 17, 1958.

J. P. Moore's reminiscences about Henry Dorman and other aged Civil War veterans appear in his narrative *This Strange Town—Liberal, Missouri* (Liberal, Mo.: Liberal News, 1963). Dorman also was covered in the *New York Times*, Feb. 11 and 12, 1910; the *San Jose (Calif.) Evening News*, Mar. 16, 1914; and the *Hayti (Mo.) Herald*, Mar. 26, 1914. He also can be found in the *Herald of Gospel Liberty* magazine, published by the General Convention of the Christian Church, Mar. 31, 1910.

For more on J. Frank Dalton, aka Jesse James, a good read is Dale L. Walker, *Legends and Lies: Great Mysteries of the American West* (New York: Forge Books, 1997). The columns by Robert C. Ruark in the *New York World Telegram* ran on July 5, 6, and 7, 1949. His trial in Union, Mo., was covered by the *St. Louis Post-Dispatch* on Mar. 10, and 11, 1950, as well as the *Washington (Mo.) Citizen* of Mar. 17, 1950; the *Washington Missourian*, Mar. 16, 1950; and the *Franklin County (Mo.) Tribune*, Mar. 17, 1950.

Walter Urwiler's remarkable ability to manipulate his heart rate was documented in J. B. Harris, H. E. Hoff, and R. A. Wise, "Diaphragmatic Flutter as a Manifestation of Hysteria," *Psychosomatic Medicine* 16, no. 1 (1954) 56–66, and in the *Journal of the American Medical Association*, Mar. 21, 1936, Apr. 1, 1939, Apr. 12, 1941, and Aug. 4, 1951. His adventures in hospitals in Nevada, California, Washington State, and Texas were reported in the *Nevada State Journal*, July 21 and 26 and Aug. 3 and 8, 1951; *Stars and Stripes*, Aug. 4, 1951; *Time* magazine, Aug. 13, 1951; the *Tacoma News Tribune*, Aug. 6, 7, and 8, 1951; the *Seattle Times*, Aug. 8, 1951; and the *Idaho Falls Post-Register*, Oct. 18, 1951.

Every war collects its share of pretenders. After World War I the future novelist William Faulkner, who would write so truthfully about the Civil War, the Confederacy, and the emerging New South, leaned on a cane and hobbled about the town square in Oxford, Mississippi. He said he had been injured in aerial dogfights over Europe, even though the war had been over before Faulkner could get to it.

In Korea, Ferdinand W. Demara posed as a physician and performed operations on the battlefront. He was serving in the Canadian navy as a lieutenant surgeon and had enlisted as "Dr. Joseph Cyr" after the real Dr. Cyr's medical papers were stolen. Authorities placed Demara in a state mental hospital in Boston.

Others, most peculiarly politicians, have inflated their service during the Vietnam years, boasting of jungle battles when in truth they never left their National Guard posts in the States. Medals and battle ribbons from the Gulf War, Iraq, and Afghanistan have been awarded to veterans not entitled to wear them. In 2005 Washington passed the Stolen Valor Act, which outlawed false claims of military honor. But in June 2012 the Supreme Court struck down the act, ruling that the First Amendment "protects the speech we detest as well as the speech we embrace."

The Stolen Valor Act was triggered in part after Rick Duncan stood in front of television cameras and traveled the country reliving his time at the U.S. Naval Academy, his tours of duty as a Marine Corps captain, and his efforts sponsoring homeless shelters for military veterans. He told audiences he was in the bombed Pentagon during the September 11, 2001, terrorist attacks, and later suffered a brain injury from a roadside explosion in Iraq. "I have a plate roughly about the size of a cup and saucer on this portion of my skull," he said in a CNN interview. "Right here, I have a scar that runs back here and then down here."

None of it was true. His real name was Richard G. Strandlof. He was a drifter, mental patient, and petty crook. Eventually he was questioned by the FBI and charged by authorities. "Sometimes I don't know where, basically, what reality I am in," he confessed. He reappeared on CNN and admitted he had been home in San Jose, California, on the morning of September 11, watching the airplane attacks on television. He did not attend the Naval Academy, he did not serve in the Marines, and he did not fight in Iraq. Why the lies? "It came to be a combination of things," the disgraced thirty-two-year-old Strandlof said. "One, some severely underdiagnosed mental illness. And two, being caught up in the moment."

William Faulkner masquerading as a disabled World War I veteran comes from Joseph Blotner, *Faulkner: A Biography* (New York: Random House, 1984). Ferdinand W. Demara was unmasked as a counterfeit surgeon in the *Pacific Stars and Stripes*, Aug. 1, 1956. Richard Strandlof's fall from grace as a phony decorated Marine Corps captain in Iraq was reported in the *New York Times*, May 15 and June 8, 2009, and May 20, 2011; in the *Los Angeles Times*, July 8, 2009; and the *Stars and Stripes* Middle East edition, June 9, 2009. The CNN interviews aired at various times in June 2009.

4. ALBERT WOOLSON

The best sources for Albert Woolson's life come from the man himself, especially his short but helpful autobiography, "My Reminiscences," a separate memoir titled "Personal Remarks," and a third called "The Baldwins," all available in the H. N. (Bert) Woolson collection on Albert Woolson at the Whitman College and Northwest Archives, Walla Walla, Wash. Many of his numerous letters are housed there as well. A separate letter he wrote July 14, 1943, to the family of Albert Sweet is included among the Albert Burbank Sweet and Family Papers at the Minnesota Historical Society in St. Paul. The Whitman College and Northwest Archives also has several recorded interviews with Woolson. The one I found most intriguing was housed at the Veterans' Memorial Hall for St. Louis County and Duluth, Minn., especially because it includes his dubious story that he and his father once met Abraham Lincoln. Also of tremendous value is Steven Aaron Passon, "Last of the Union Blue: A Biography of Albert Henry Woolson" (PhD diss., University of Minnesota, 1967). Upon Woolson's death, the *New York Times* printed a lengthy and useful front-page obituary on Aug. 3, 1956. *The Banner*, a publication of the Sons of Union Veterans of the Civil War, ran a lengthy tribute to Woolson in its Fall 1956 issue. His and his father's Union army records can be found in the Adjutant General's Report, Minnesota Military Service Records, 1866, Minnesota Historical Society, Division of Archives and Manuscripts. The National Archives in Washington, D.C., also retains copies of Albert Woolson's service record. His father, Willard Woolson, is listed in Alonzo L. Brown's *History of the Fourth Regiment of Minnesota Infantry Volunteers during the Great Rebellion, 1861–1865* (St. Paul: Pioneer Press, 1892). Also of note is Richard Moe, *Last Full Measure: The Life and Death of the First Minnesota Volunteers* (St. Paul: Minnesota Historical Society Press 2001).

The death of Civil War veteran Henry T. Johnson, which prompted Woolson to join the Grand Army of the Republic, was reported in the *Duluth News-Tribune*, Nov. 12 and 13, 1928.

An outstanding source for the Grand Army of the Republic is the Grand Army of the Republic Museum and Library in Philadelphia. It houses not only abundant materials on Woolson but also records and reports from the national organization and the various state chapters around the North, including Minnesota. These documents include transcripts of the yearly encampments, where I found Woolson's recollections after visiting the Gettysburg reunion and his report on closing the Minnesota chapter. Similar documents can be found at the Library of Congress in Washington, D.C., including the *Final Journal of the Grand Army of the Republic, 1866–1956* (Washington, D.C.: U.S. Government Printing Office, 1957). That report includes Woolson's photograph prominently displayed, and his title as the "solitary sentinel" of the GAR at its end.

The feud between Woolson and Orrin S. Pierce was reported in the *Minneapolis Star Tribune*, Nov. 12, 1945; the *Minneapolis Tribune*, July 6, 1946; and the *Minneapolis Star*, June 27, 1947. *Minnesota History* magazine ran a lengthy treatment on the dispute in its Winter 1980 edition. Pierce's obituary was published in the *Minneapolis Tribune*, Feb. 24, 1948.

The disbanding of the Duluth chapter of the Grand Army of the Republic is covered in the *Duluth News-Tribune*, Mar. 19, 1932.

The closing of the Minnesota chapter was reported in the *Sheboygan (Wis.) Press*, June 5, 1947.

The dispute over the Grand Army of the Republic encampment held in 1936 in Washington, D.C., was covered by the *New York Times* on Apr. 14, 1935. The parade and encampment itself was covered by the *Washington Evening Star* on Sept. 23, 24, and 25, 1936. The *Washington Post* also covered the event on Sept. 23, 24, and 25, 1936.

The Grand Army of the Republic gathering in Columbus, Ohio, was recorded by the *Columbus Dispatch* on Sept. 13, 15, and 16, 1941.

A report on the Des Moines encampment of the Grand Army of the Republic can be found in the *Des Moines Register*, Sept. 10, 1944.

The second reunion in Columbus, Ohio, of the Grand Army of the Republic was covered by the *Columbus Dispatch* on Sept. 30 and Oct. 1, 3, and 4, 1945.

The Grand Army of the Republic's activities in Indianapolis were recorded by the *Indianapolis Star* on Aug. 25, 26, 27, 28, 29, and 30, 1946. The *Duluth News-Tribune* reported on Aug. 26, 1946, that Woolson was attending the encampment. Fremont Power, the Indiana reporter, wrote a recollection of his meeting Woolson at the gathering, which was published upon Woolson's death a decade later, in the *Indianapolis News*, Aug. 2, 1956.

The Grand Army of the Republic's meeting in Cleveland was covered by the *Cleveland Plain Dealer* on Aug. 10, 11, 12, 13, and 14, 1947.

In Grand Rapids, Michigan, the Grand Army of the Republic's encampment was covered by *Stars and Stripes* on Nov. 14, 1948. Included was a photograph of several surviving veterans, including Woolson.

The final encampment of the Grand Army of the Republic was held in Indianapolis. The *Indianapolis Star* reported the last joint activities on Aug. 28, 1949, in an edition that included a lengthy *Indianapolis Star Magazine* retrospective feature titled "The G.A.R.—Forever in Memory." Other coverage by the newspaper appeared on Aug. 29, 30, and 31, 1949 (with a photograph of a group of veterans including Woolson), and Sept. 1, 1949. The *Duluth News-Tribune*, Aug. 27, 1949, ran a photograph of Woolson smoking a cigar as his train left Duluth for the encampment in Indianapolis. The *Saturday Review* column by John Mason Brown appeared in the magazine's Sept. 24, 1949, issue. The recollections of Nancy Baxter are from conversations with the author.

5. WALTER WILLIAMS

Unlike Woolson, Walter Williams apparently did not write down his reminiscences or memoirs. He did, however, speak randomly of his past adventures both in the Civil War and herding cattle up the Chisholm Trail. These stories can be found most often in newspaper and magazine accounts around the times of his birthdays, including the following: *Dallas Morning News*, May 10, Oct. 16, Nov. 16, and Dec. 20, 1953, July 10, 1954, Nov. 13 and 15, 1955, Aug. 12 and Nov. 1, 2, and 4, 1956, Jan. 8 and 10, June 16, Sept. 6, and Nov. 14 and 15, 1957; the *Austin American-Statesman*, Nov. 27, 1953, Mar. 26 and 29 and Nov. 1, 1954, Nov. 14, 1956, June 16 and 19 and Nov. 3, 6, 12, 15, and 26, 1957; the *Houston Post*, Nov. 3, 1957; the *United Daughters of the Confederacy* magazine, Sept. 1951, May 1954, July 1954, and Dec. 1954; the *Port Arthur (Tex.) News*, Aug. 5, 1953; the *Los Angeles Times*, Nov. 16, 1953, Nov. 15, 1954, and Nov. 15, 1957; and *Stars and Stripes*, Nov. 17 and 20, 1953, Mar. 31 and Nov. 17, 1954, Oct. 10, 1955, and June 20, 1957. Copies of many of these newspaper accounts are kept in the collections of the Center for American History at the University of Texas, Austin. More background on Williams was recorded by his daughter, Carrie Williams James, in her chapter "Walter W. Williams," in *Father Wore Grey*, ed. Lela Whitton Hegarty (San Antonio: Naylor Co., 1963).

Walter Williams's pension records were obtained from the Texas State Archives and Library Commission in Austin.

The Frank X. Tolbert interview in the *Dallas Morning News* ran Apr. 15, 1954.

The 1937 reunion that Williams attended in Corsicana, Tex., is reported in the *Navarro County Scroll*, vol. 15 (1970), and also is housed with the Navarro County, Tex., Historical Society.

Life magazine's feature on Walter Williams was published in the June 1, 1953, issue.

A useful summary of the lives and activities of Confederate veterans in Louisiana after the war is Herman Hattaway, "The United Confederate Veterans in Louisiana," *Louisiana History: The Journal of the Louisiana History Association* 16, no. 1. (Winter 1975): 5–37. This article also details the 1903 reunion in New Orleans.

The *Confederate Veteran* magazine of Dec. 1915 reported the creation of Memorial Day in Louisiana to honor former Confederate President Jefferson Davis.

The Little Rock, Ark., convention and President Taft's letter were reported by the *Arkansas Gazette*, May 16, 1911.

W. P. Park's letter to Jefferson Davis, written June 3, 1888, and Davis's 1888 speech in Mississippi City, Mississippi, are both included in *Jefferson Davis, Consti-*

tutionalist: His Letters, Papers, and Speeches, collected and edited by Dunbar Rowland, director of the Department of Archives and History of the State of Mississippi, and secretary of the Mississippi Historical Society (Jackson: Mississippi Department of Archives and History, 1923).

Confederate Veteran magazine reported in July 1928 and Aug. 1928 on the reunion that year in Little Rock, Ark.

The 1933 reunion at Baton Rouge, La., was covered by the *State Times of Baton Rouge* on Oct. 19, 1933.

The reunion there five years later was covered by the *State Times* on Oct. 13, 1938.

The 1939 Baton Rouge reunion was covered by the *State Times* on Oct. 12 and 13, 1939.

The *State Times* reported on the 1940 convention on Oct. 1, 17, and 18, 1940.

The 1942 convention in Baton Rouge was covered by the *State Times* on Oct. 15, 1942.

The 1945 reunion at Baton Rouge was covered by the *State Times* and *Sun Advocate* on Nov. 24, 1945.

William D. Townsend recalled his war stories in the *United Daughters of the Confederacy* magazine, May 1951.

The *Shreveport (La.) Times* ran a lengthy profile of Townsend and his wife on Apr. 16, 1950.

Townsend's antics at the 1951 reunion in Norfolk, Va., were reported by the *Virginian-Pilot* on June 2, 1951.

Townsend's obituary ran in the *Baton Rouge State Times* on Feb. 14, 1953; in the *Shreveport Times*, Feb. 24, 1953; in *Stars and Stripes* Europe, Feb. 24, 1953; and in the *United Daughters of the Confederacy* magazine, Apr. 1953.

Townsend's funeral was covered by the *Shreveport Times*, Feb. 25, 1953, and the *Baton Rouge State Times*, Feb. 24 and 25, 1953.

Townsend's pension records were obtained from the archives maintained by the Louisiana secretary of state in Baton Rouge.

The letter from Willie Mae Bowles regarding the daily routine of her dying father, Walter Williams, was included in Jay Hoar, *The South's Last Boys in Gray* (Bowling Green, Ohio: Bowling Green State University Popular Press, 1986), as well as in *Confederate Veteran* magazine, May–June 1987.

6. OLD MEN IN BLUE

Albert Woolson's daily life and birthdays in snow-bound Duluth, Minn., were described in the *St. Paul Pioneer Press* Sunday magazine, May 14, 1953; the *Duluth News-Tribune*, May 31, 1953; *Stars and Stripes Pacific*, Feb. 6, 1953, and June 12, 1954; and *Stars and Stripes Europe*, Feb. 13, 1953, and Feb. 12, 1955.

The vignette of the Duluth schoolchildren collecting pennies for Woolson is recounted in *Time* magazine, Mar. 23, 1953.

The 1953 Memorial Day parade and ceremonies are reported in the *Duluth News-Tribune*, May 31, 1953.

Woolson's letters to his son Rob and his family come from the H. N. (Bert) Woolson collection on Albert Woolson at the Whitman College and Northwest Archives, Walla Walla, Wash.

The Cora Gillis and A. B. Kapplin letters are housed in the H. N. (Bert) Woolson collection, Whitman College and Northwest Archives.

The letter from President Eisenhower is stored at the Eisenhower Presidential Library and Museum, Abilene, Kans.

Researchers wishing to trace the lives of Union army veterans would be well served to start with Jay Hoar, a New England professor who has dedicated much of his professional life to tracking down stories about Civil War veterans and contacting their descendants. He has compiled these narratives in his two-volume work, *The North's Last Boys in Blue* (Salem, Mass.: Higginson Book Co., 2006 and 2007).

The *Portland Oregonian* ran a full obituary on Theodore Penland in its Sept. 15, 1950, edition. The newspaper also published an accompanying editorial marking Penland's passing.

The *Manchester (N.H.) Union* featured James Lurvey in a profile on Dec. 3, 1949. His obituary ran in the paper on Sept. 18, 1950. The *New York Times* marked his passing on Sept. 18, 1950, as did the *Boston Globe*, the *Concord (N.H.) Daily Monitor*, and the *New Hampshire Patriot*. For further reading, there is *Gettysburg* magazine, Jan. 1, 1997.

Lansing Wilcox appeared in the *Wisconsin State Journal*, Mar. 4 and 5, 1951. He was also featured in the Mar. 16, 1951, edition of the *Milwaukee Sentinel*. His obituary ran in the *Milwaukee Journal* and the *Wisconsin State Journal*, both on Sept. 30, 1951.

Material on the life and wartime experiences of James A. Hard was compiled in a six-part, first-person account that ran in the *Rochester (N.Y.) Times-Union* from July 7 to 14, 1950. In addition, more material from the interviews conducted by *Times-Union* reporter Andrew Wolfe is housed in scrapbook vol. 2, 1951, nos. 1–3, at the Rochester Historical Society. A fine example of the pageantry of parades and funerals that Hard attended and officiated at is described in the *Rochester Democrat and Chronicle*, Oct. 16, 1938. Obituaries ran in the *Democrat and Chronicle*, the *Chicago Tribune*, the *Binghamton (N.Y.) Press*, and the *Youngstown (Ohio) Vindicator*—all on Mar. 13, 1953. The *Democrat and Chronicle* of Mar. 17, 1953, covered his funeral.

Albert Woolson's comments upon the death of James Hard were printed in the *Democrat and Chronicle*, Mar. 13, 1953.

The telephone conversation between Woolson and John Salling, as well as an account of how the chat was organized, were summarized by Lewis Gough in the *American Weekly*, the magazine of the American Legion, on May 24, 1953. Gough was the legion's national commander.

7. OLD MEN IN GRAY

Stories abound concerning Walter Williams's ailments and his unconventional home health care. Examples can be found in the *Dallas Morning News*, Aug. 8, and Sept. 8, 1956, and June 21 and 22, 1959; and the *Houston Post*, June 21, 1959.

A feature story on the Confederate Soldiers' Home in Raleigh, North Carolina, ran in the *News and Observer* on Dec. 5, 1920. Also of great value is Herbert Poole, "Final Encampment: The North Carolina Soldiers' Home," *Confederate Veteran* magazine,

July–Aug. 1987, which also covered the protest by home residents. The story of Joe Carpenter's problems at the home comes from the *News and Observer*, Apr. 24, 25, 26, and 27, 1935.

Just as he did for Union veterans, Jay Hoar also compiled biographical sketches of Confederate veterans and included them in *The South's Last Boys in Gray*.

John Graves's pension records are maintained by the Missouri secretary of state's office, specifically the state archives. He also appears in Walter Williams, ed., *A History of Northeast Missouri* (Chicago: Lewis Publishing, 1913). He is cited prominently in the *Higginsville (Mo.) Advance*, Jan. 2, 1942, and May 12, 1950; the *Kansas City (Mo.) Star*, July 22, 1949, and May 9, 1950; the *Anniston (Ala.) Star*, May 9, 1950; the *Sedalia (Mo.) Democrat*, May 9, 1950; the *Fayette (Mo.) Democrat-Leader*, May 12, 1950; and the *United Daughters of the Confederacy* magazine, June 1950 and July 1950

The Missouri Confederate Home is best presented in Wade F. Ankesheiln, *The Heart Is the Heritage: The Story of the Founding of the Confederate Home of Missouri* (Coral Springs, Fla.: Llumina Press, 2007). It also was featured in *Missouri Resources* magazine, Winter 1997–98, in "Resources to Explore: Confederate Memorial State Historic Site," by Jill G. White, the historic site administrator. Also of interest is a photograph in the *United Daughters of the Confederacy* magazine in July 1954.

Pleasant Crump's pension records are housed at the Alabama Department of Archives and History. His presence at Appomattox is verified in William Marvel's *Lee's Last Retreat: The Flight to Appomattox* (Chapel Hill: University of North Carolina Press, 2006). Additional information can be found in the *United Daughters of the Confederacy* magazine, Feb. 1949 and Feb. 1952; the *Montgomery (Ala.) Advertiser*, Jan. 2, 1952; the *Talladega (Ala.) Daily Home*, Jan. 1, 1952; the *Anniston (Ala.) Star*, Jan. 1, 1952; and the *Dothan (Ala.) Eagle*, Dec. 23, 1949.

The *Birmingham (Ala.) News*, Apr. 26, 1950, covered the visit by "Gen." James W. Moore to the Crump farm. More on Moore can be found in the *Birmingham News*, Feb. 26 and 28, 1951; the *United Daughters of the Confederacy* magazine, Feb. 1950, Mar. 1951, Apr. 1951, and May 1951; and the Alabama Department of Archives and History, whose Civil War Service Database includes remarks Moore made upon his election as commander in chief of the Sons of Confederate Veterans on Sept. 27 and 28, 1944.

The Confederate service pension file for William J. Bush is located in the Georgia Department of Archives and History. In addition, the Blue and Gray Museum in Fitzgerald, Ga., has more material on Bush. His theatrics at the Atlanta museum were reported in his obituary by the *Florida Times-Union* on Nov. 12, 1952. Reports about how he reacted to his wife's college degree can be found in the *Milledgeville (Ga.) Union Recorder*, Aug. 23 and 30, 1951, and the *Richmond (Va.) Times-Dispatch*, Aug. 26, 1951. The *United Daughters of the Confederacy* magazine ran his obituary in Dec. 1952, and additional material in its editions of Aug. 1953, Feb. 1989, and Feb. 2000. His antics at the 1951 Confederate reunion in Norfolk, Va., were described with great flair in the *Norfolk Virginian-Pilot*, May 30, 1951, as well as in the *Florida State News*, Nov. 12, 1952; the *Milledgeville Union-Recorder*, Aug. 23 and 30, 1951; and the *United Daughters of the Confederacy* magazine, Feb. 1989. Bush's obituary also appeared in the *Atlanta Journal*, Nov. 11, 1952, and his funeral tributes were described on Nov. 12, 1952.

Confederate Veteran magazine ran a sketch of Bush in its July–Aug. 1987 edition.

The congressional visit at Walter Williams's home is related in Robert J. Cook, *Troubled Commemoration: The American Civil War Centennial, 1961–1965* (Baton Rouge: Louisiana State University Press, 2007). It is noteworthy that Cook believes Williams's claim that he served in the Confederacy "was probably fraudulent." The visit also was reported in the *Houston Post* on Apr. 27, 1958.

8. CENTENNIAL

A selection of General Ulysses S. Grant III's writing and speeches were included in *Civil War History* 2, no. 2 (June 1956), a quarterly then published by the State University of Iowa. A profile of Grant ran in the *New York Times*, Jan. 9, 1961. Material about Sam Willett, the letter to Maine veterans, and the GAR pallbearers at President Grant's funeral can be found in Charles Bracelen Flood, *Grant's Final Victory: Ulysses S. Grant's Heroic Last Year* (Cambridge, Mass.: Da Capo, 2011).

The most thorough work on the U.S. Civil War Centennial Commission and its leadership difficulties is Cook's *Troubled Commemoration*. A complete file of the commission's papers and documents is preserved at the National Archives in Washington, D.C. An example of the holdings is the commission's Jan. 1958 "Statement of Objectives and Suggestions for Civil War Centennial Commemorations." For timely records of their work, consult the monthly bulletins titled "100 Years After," which were printed and distributed during the late 1950s and early 1960s. I found a complete set of copies at the National Museum of the U.S. Navy Yard in Washington, D.C. Other Centennial Commission research was published in the "Notes & Queries" section of the *Quarterly Journal of Studies in Civil War History* 4, no. 2 (June 1958): 197–98. More information is available in W. Fitzhugh Brundage, "Commemoration and Conflict: Forgetting and Remembering the Civil War," *Georgia Historical Quarterly* 82 (1998): 559–74.

Eisenhower's admiration for Robert E. Lee is discussed in John S. D. Eisenhower, *General Ike: A Personal Reminiscence* (New York: Free Press, 2003), 138.

The president's recollections about Civil War veterans in his hometown of Abilene, Kans., can be found in his memoir, *At Ease: Stories I Tell to Friends* (New York: Doubleday, 1967).

Grant's election to the head of the Civil War Centennial Commission was reported in the *New York Times*, Dec. 21, 1957.

Virginia Livingston-Hunt's letter is contained in the National Archives holdings of centennial records, as is Bruce Catton's Nov. 1958 speech to the Civil War Round Table in Washington, D.C. So is the Dallas couple's letter to Sen. Lyndon B. Johnson.

The *New York Times* published an overview of the Centennial Commission's preparations on June 9, 1957.

President Eisenhower's proclamations regarding the Civil War Centennial are among his official papers at the Eisenhower Presidential Library and Museum in Abilene, Kans. The key dates are Dec. 7, 1960, and Jan. 5, 1961. More can be found in the *New York Times*, Dec. 8, 1960.

Newspaper coverage of the ceremonies kicking off the centennial at Grant's Tomb and Lee's burial site ran in the *New York Times*, Jan. 9, 1961.

9. LAST IN BLUE

The correspondence from the Florence Guards in Chicago, as well as that from Frederic Bauer of the Sons of Union Veterans of the Civil War, is housed at the Eisenhower Presidential Library and Museum, Abilene, Kans.

Coverage of President Eisenhower's wreath-laying ceremony at the Lincoln Memorial appeared in *Stars and Stripes Europe*, Feb. 13, 1954.

News of free medical care for the remaining Civil War veterans appeared in *Stars and Stripes*, Jan. 18, 1956.

Coverage of the special gold medals for the remaining Civil War veterans appeared in *Stars and Stripes*, May 23 and July 14 and 21, 1956.

The Duluth parade and ceremonies honoring Woolson on Memorial Day 1953 were reported in the *Duluth News-Tribune*, May 31, 1953, and the *Stars and Stripes Europe*, May 31, 1953.

Woolson's hospitalization for bronchitis was noted in *Stars and Stripes Europe*, Dec. 6, 1953. Doctor C. H. Christensen's memories of Woolson in the hospital were shared by his son, Anders Christensen, in a Feb. 28, 2011, online comment (http://attic.areavoices.com/2011/02/28/last-union-civil-war-vet-dies-in-duluth-1956/).

Woolson's 107th birthday celebration was reported in *Stars and Stripes Europe*, Feb. 13, 1954.

The Woolson family's decision to taper off his public activities for Memorial Day 1954 was reported in *Stars and Stripes Europe*, May 30, 1954.

Woolson's determination to "be around" for several more birthdays was cited in *Stars and Stripes Pacific*, June 12, 1954.

The *Duluth News-Tribune* reported about the new Woolson bust on Aug. 9 and 10, 1954; *Stars and Stripes Europe* carried a news item on Aug. 16, 1954. The Woolson interview with reporters and the visit by Maj. Gen. Ulysses S. Grant III was reported in the *Duluth News-Tribune*, Aug. 10, 1954. The *News-Tribune* also covered the installation of the bust at the city hall on Feb. 12, 1955.

Stars and Stripes Europe covered Woolson's 108th birthday on Feb. 12, 1955. The Eisenhower and MacArthur letters are housed among records at the Gettysburg National Military Park.

Woolson posing for sculptor Avar Fairbanks was featured in the *Daily Utah Chronicle*, Feb. 17, 1955.

Woolson's hospitalizations for lung congestion were noted in *Stars and Stripes Europe*, Feb. 28 and Apr. 20, 1955.

Woolson's Memorial Day 1955 message to remaining Confederate veterans was reported in *Stars and Stripes Europe*, Apr. 28, 1955.

The family's decision to sit out the Memorial Day 1955 activities, and instead to take a lake trip, was reported in *Stars and Stripes Europe*, May 30, 1955.

The June 1955 hospitalization was reported by *Stars and Stripes Europe*, June 1, 1955.

Woolson's birthday greeting to Walter Williams in Texas was covered by *Stars and Stripes*, Nov. 9, 1955.

Williams's Feb. 1956 birthday greeting to Woolson, the letter from Charles Edison, and the greetings from President and Mrs. Eisenhower are all housed among the records

at the Gettysburg National Military Park. The park also has copies of greetings from
Secretary of the Army Wilber M. Brucker and former Minnesota Gov. Harold E. Stassen.

Woolson's next hospitalization was reported by the *Duluth News-Tribune*, Mar. 17,
1956, and *Stars and Stripes Europe*, Mar. 17, 1956.

Tim Johnson's remembrance of meeting Woolson was shared in an online comment on Mar. 19, 2011 (http://attic.areavoices.com/2011/02/28/last-union-civil-war-
vet-dies-in-duluth-1956/).

Woolson's final hospitalization, struggle for life, and his death were reported by
Stars and Stripes Europe, July 31 and Aug. 1, 1956; *Stars and Stripes*, Aug. 3, 1956; the
St. Paul Pioneer Press, Aug. 2 and 3, 1956; the *Minneapolis Morning Tribune*, Aug. 3,
1956; the *Duluth News-Tribune*, Aug 3, 1956; the *Sheboygan Press*, Aug. 3, 1956; and the
New York Times, Aug. 3, 1956. A separate tribute to Woolson appeared in the *Washing-
ton Post*, Aug. 3, 1956.

His funeral was reported in the *Duluth News-Tribune*, Aug. 5 and 7, 1956; the *Min-
neapolis Morning Tribune*, Aug. 7, 1956; the *St. Paul Pioneer Press*, Aug. 4, 1956; the *Daily
Oklahoman*, Aug. 7, 1956; *Stars and Stripes*, Aug. 7, 1956; and *Stars and Stripes Pacific*,
Aug. 8 and 12, 1956.

The federal court's order officially closing the Grand Army of the Republic was
reported by *Stars and Stripes Europe*, Oct. 19, 1956.

Dedication of the Woolson statue at Gettysburg was reported in *Stars and Stripes
Europe*, Sept. 3 and 14, 1956.

Bruce Catton's elegy appeared in *Life* magazine, Aug. 20, 1956.

Reactions to Woolson's death from the three living Confederates, including Walter
Williams, were recorded in *Stars and Stripes Pacific*, Aug. 4, 1956.

10. DEBUNKED?

Louis Baker's claim as the last veteran in blue appeared in the *Oklahoma City Times*,
Aug. 3, 1956, and *Stars and Stripes*, Aug. 7, 1956.

The *Daily Oklahoman* of Sept. 24, 1945, and Sept. 19, 1948, described him loafing
and whiling away his days on the downtown stoop in Guthrie, Okla.

The *Daily Oklahoman*, Sept. 4, 1949, reported his disinterest in Grand Army of the
Republic activities.

The Haskin Service Report was composed in Washington, D.C., for the *Daily Oklahoman* and is dated Nov. 8, 1956; it was made available from the newspaper's files.

Baker's obituary, noting his claim to be the last Union army soldier, ran in the
Daily Oklahoman on Jan. 19, 1957.

The *United Daughters of the Confederacy* magazine, Apr. 1952, published a profile of
William Lundy.

Photographer Bruce Roberts, who took pictures of Lundy in 1954, was interviewed
by the author, Sept. 21, 2010.

Lundy's deer hunting trip was reported by Stars and Stripes, Nov. 22 and 24, 1954.
Sports Illustrated mentioned him in its "Pat on the Back" column on Dec. 13, 1954.

The *Boston Traveler*, Jan. 18, 1955, reported Lundy's television appearance on his
107th birthday, as well as his comments that he was "always sorry" he did not shoot a

Yankee. This clipping can be found in the McCain Library and Archives, University of Southern Mississippi, Hattiesburg.

Stars and Stripes Europe, May 31, 1955, told how Lundy was awarded an honorary diploma, along with his nieces.

William Lindsey McDonald, *Civil War Tales of the Tennessee Valley* (Killen, Ala.: Heart of Dixie, 2003) includes the interview Lundy granted, on the condition that he could hold the author's two small daughters.

Stars and Stripes, Oct. 8, 1956, and the *United Daughters of the Confederacy* magazine, Jan. 1957, each reported that Air Force Chief of Staff Gen. Nathan F. Twining awarded Lundy a special gold medal.

Stars and Stripes, Jan. 20 and 23, 1957, recorded Lundy's 109th birthday.

Lundy's gallbladder problems, surgery, and recuperation were reported by *Stars and Stripes*, Mar. 3, 6, and 9 and Apr. 1 and 16, 1957.

Stars and Stripes, July 4, 1957, reported that the military had named Lundy an honorary plane spotter.

Progressive Farmer magazine carried Lundy on its Aug. 1957 cover, with a profile featured inside.

The *Houston Post*, Sept. 2, 1957, reported that Lundy had died, as did the *Chicago Tribune*, Sept. 2, 1957; the *Reno (Nev.) Evening Gazette*, Sept. 2, 1957; and *Stars and Stripes*, Sept. 3, 1957.

Lundy's Confederate pension file records are maintained by the Florida State Library and Archives, Tallahassee.

His funeral was covered by the *Tampa Morning Tribune*, Sep. 5, 1957, and *Stars and Stripes*, Sept. 6, 1957.

John Salling was often interviewed and featured in profiles, and he rarely passed up the opportunity to impart his mountain-home wisdom. The more notable articles include the *Cincinnati Enquirer*, Nov. 8, 1958; the *Washington Post*, May 15, 1955; the *Richmond (Va.) Times-Dispatch*, May 15, 1955; and *Stars and Stripes Pacific*, Oct. 9, 1956, and Nov. 11, 1958.

Salling's appearance at the Confederate reunion in Norfolk, Va., was covered by the *Norfolk Virginian-Pilot*, May 31 and June 1 and 2, 1951.

Pension application and other related records for John Salling, James Salling, Lydia Salling, and Elisa Salling are all maintained by the Library of Virginia, Richmond.

The George A. Smathers Libraries, University of Florida Digital Collections, Gainesville, houses a transcript of M. J. Hansinger's Jan. 30, 1959, interview with Salling in Slant, Virginia.

A good primer on the role of saltpeter miners during the Civil War can be found in the Nov. 2001 issue of *Virginia Minerals* magazine, published by Virginia's Division of Geology, Charlottesville. It notes that "the identity of the last surviving Confederate veteran is a hotly disputed topic."

The *Washington Post* article quoting Salling on war was published Mar. 11, 1951.

The *Richmond (Va.) News Leader*, Apr. 4, 1951, included Salling's story about the visit from federal revenue agents, his daughter Nancy Thompson's comments about how he acted after taking a "spoonful of likker," and his trip to the veterans' hospital in Johnson City, Tenn.

Salling's airplane stop in Richmond appears in the *Richmond News Leader*, July 17, 1953.

His trip to Washington, D.C., was covered by the *Kingsport (Tenn.) Times News*, July 19, 1953.

Salling's soldier bonus was recorded by the *Richmond Times Dispatch*, Apr. 1, 1954.

His cold and pneumonia, and his joke about an eighty-two-year-old woman, come from *Stars and Stripes Europe*, Feb. 27, 1956.

Salling's 110th birthday was reported by the *Richmond News Leader*, May 12 and 15, 1956; the *Washington Post*, May 13 and 16, 1956; the *Kingsport News*, May 16, 1956; the *Independent Press-Telegram* of Long Beach, Calif., May 13, 1956; and *Stars and Stripes*, May 15, 1956. The gifts he received were noted by the *Richmond Times-Dispatch*, Nov. 2, 1956, and the *Washington Post*, Nov. 2, 1956.

When he turned 111, his birthday was reported in the *Richmond News Leader*, May 15, 1957; the *Richmond Times-Dispatch*, May 16, 1957; the *Kingsport News*, May 16, 1957; and *Stars and Stripes*, May 19, 1957.

His 112th birthday brought the proclamation from the Civil War Centennial Commission; it can be found among the commission's records housed by the National Archives in Washington, D.C. The records also include the press release and speeches given by the commission in his honor. Salling's birthday celebrations were reported by the *Washington Post*, May 9, 1958; *Stars and Stripes*, May 13 and 17, 1958; and the *New York Times*, May 16, 1958.

When Salling died, his passing was reported by the *Richmond News Leader*, Mar. 16, 1959; the *New York Times*, Mar. 17, 1959; the *United Daughters of the Confederacy* magazine, Apr. 1959; the *Richmond Times-Dispatch*, Mar. 17, 1959; the *Washington Post*, Mar. 17, 1959; the *Washington Daily News*, Mar. 16, 1959; *Stars and Stripes*, Mar. 17, 1959; and the *Knoxville (Tenn.) Journal*, Mar. 17, 1959.

His funeral was covered by the *Richmond News Leader*, Mar. 18, 1959; *Stars and Stripes*, Mar. 21, 1959; the *Kingsport News*, Mar. 17, 1959; and the *Richmond Times-Dispatch*, Mar. 18, 1959.

The funeral wreath sent by Walter Williams was reported by the Associated Press on Mar. 17, 1959, as was Williams's statement upon learning of Salling's death: "Am I the last one? Well, I always wanted to stay here until they were all gone, to see what happened."

11. IN HIS MEMORY-CLOUDED MIND

Walter Williams's reaction to the death of William Lundy was reported in the *Los Angeles Times*, Nov. 15, 1957. Dr. Russell Wolfe's statement that "anything can happen" to Williams was reported in the same article.

Williams's ride in the 1957 Veterans Day parade was reported by the *Austin (Tex.) American*, Nov. 12, 1957. His 115th birthday celebrations were recorded by the *Los Angeles Times*, Nov. 15, 1957; the *Dallas Morning News*, Nov. 14, 1957; and the *Austin American*, Nov. 15, 1957.

The correspondence between Cooper Ragan, Maj. Gen. Ulysses S. Grant III,

Edmund Cass, Willie Mae Bowles, and Dr. Russell Wolfe is housed in the Civil War Centennial Commission files at the National Archives in Washington, D.C. Also there are documents related to the Apr. 1958 tribute the commission awarded Williams, including statements from President Eisenhower and Representative Schwengel's remarks at the home in Houston. The poem is from "Paul Revere's Ride," by Henry Wadsworth Longfellow. The event was covered by the *Houston Post*, Apr. 24 and 27, 1958, and the *Houston Chronicle*, Apr. 27, 1958.

News of extra pension assistance for Williams was reported in the *Dallas Morning News*, June 16, 1957, and the *Austin American*, June 16 and 19, 1957.

Walter Williams's 116th birthday was covered by *Stars and Stripes*, Nov. 16, 1958.

The *Life* magazine feature on Walter Williams ran in the May 11, 1959, issue.

Stars and Stripes reported on June 12, 1959, that Williams had been promoted by the Confederate High Command.

Williams's stroke was covered by the *Chicago Tribune* and *Stars and Stripes*, both on June 21, 1959, and again by *Stars and Stripes* on June 24, 1959.

The *New York Times*, Aug. 12, 1960, quoted Willie Mae Bowles as saying her father's condition was "just up to the Lord, now."

The correspondence between Bill Elliott, Thomas Stephens, Andrew Goodpaster, and Maj. Alfred Kitts is stored at the Eisenhower Presidential Library and Museum in Abilene, Kans.

The *Dallas Morning News*, June 21 and 22, 1959, reported that Williams's health was deteriorating, as did the *Austin American*, June 10 and 22, 1959; the *Washington Daily News*, Aug. 11, 1959; and the *Houston Post*, June 21, 1959.

The telegrams between Frank Vandiver and Maj. Gen. Ulysses S. Grant III are part of the Civil War Centennial Commission files at the National Archives in Washington, D.C.

The internal White House memo is housed at the Eisenhower Presidential Library and Museum, as are drafts of the presidential proclamation honoring Williams and instructions for Fort Sam Houston on how to proceed upon Williams's death.

The Lowell Bridwell story appeared in newspapers around the nation, most notably in the *Post and Times-Star* in Cincinnati.

The *Dallas Morning News*, Sept. 5, 1959, quoted Willie Mae Bowles defending her father. That same day, the newspaper published reactions from Williams's neighbors in Franklin, Tex., about whether he truly was a Confederate veteran.

Williams's pension application files are housed by the Texas State Archives in Austin.

Robert S. Harper, a fellow at the American Association of Historians at Princeton University, was quoted by the *Columbus (Ohio) Evening Dispatch*, Sept. 4, 1959. Also quoted in that article were Warfield W. Dorsey, commandant of the Mount Vernon, Ohio, Sons of Union Veterans Fife and Drum Corps, and Mrs. Marcus Crocker, past Ohio president of the United Daughters of the Confederacy. The article further quoted Willie Mae Bowles defending her father, as did a piece in the *Austin American*, Sept. 4, 1959, and another in the *Washington Post*, Sept. 4, 1959.

The *Austin American*, Sept. 5, 1959, quoted Gov. Price Daniel, state comptroller Robert Calvert, Veterans Affairs commissioner Charles Morris, and Ethel Everitt, all defending Williams.

The *Houston Post*, Sept. 6, 1959, quoted Sen. James Eastland defending Williams, as well as Vick Lindley of the Bryan (Tex.) Eagle, explaining the old Hood's Brigade roster.

Tom Crigler of the Sons of Confederate veterans was quoted in the *Austin Daily Texan*, Sept. 16, 1959.

Charles Morris was quoted in the *Uvalde (Tex.) Leader News*, Sept. 12, 1959.

Mrs. G. W. Chambers was quoted in the *Austin American Statesman*, Sept. 6, 1959, defending Williams.

Lester Fitzhugh was quoted in the *Houston Post*, Sept. 8, 1959, about a roster of Hood's Brigade that he had uncovered.

Mrs. Fisher Osborn was quoted in the *Houston Post*, Sept. 11, 1959, about other brigade records.

United Press International, Sept. 5, 1959, reported Willie Mae Bowles's comments that "my daddy is the type of person that never lied." She also said she never told him about the controversy accusing him of dishonesty.

12. LAST IN GRAY

Stars and Stripes, Sept. 28, 1959, reported that Walter Williams had recovered from his illnesses of July and August. The paper's feature article, "We're Catching up with Methuselah," ran on Sept. 24, 1959. On Nov. 13 and 15, 1959, the paper described Williams's upcoming birthday plans.

The birthday extravaganza was reported in the *Houston Post*, Nov. 15 and 16, 1959; the *Houston Chronicle*, Dec. 13, 1959; the *Dallas Morning News*, Nov. 11, 1959; and *Stars and Stripes*, Nov. 17, 1959.

On Dec. 11, 1959, *Stars and Stripes* reported that Williams was in critical condition. *Stars and Stripes Europe* reported Dec. 12, 1959, that his doctor had predicted Williams might have only "48 hours left."

The *Chicago Tribune*, Dec. 13, 1959, quoted Willie Mae Bowles saying, "I think he's in a coma." The *Austin Daily Texan*, Dec. 13, 1959, reported his condition as critical.

Stars and Stripes, Dec. 15, 1959, reported a slight gain in Williams's health, and then on Dec. 18, 1959, that he was "losing ground again."

News of Williams's death appeared in the *Houston Post*, Dec. 20, 1959; the *Austin American-Statesman*, Dec. 20, 1959; the *Dallas Morning News*, Dec. 20, 1959; the *New York Times*, Dec. 20, 1959; the *Gettysburg Times*, Dec. 21, 1959; the *Sacramento Bee*, Dec. 20, 1959; and the *Nevada State Journal*, Dec. 20, 1959.

The comments from Stephen Jones are from an interview with the author on May 4, 2010.

Maj. Gen. Ulysses S. Grant III's telegrams to Frank Vandiver are contained in the Civil War Centennial Commission's files at the National Archives in Washington, D.C.

The White House correspondence, including the instructions from Colonel Schulz and President Eisenhower's statement on the passing of Williams, are all housed in the Eisenhower Presidential Library and Museum, Abilene, Kans.

The *Time* magazine story, "The Unquenchable Legend," was published Jan. 4, 1960.

There were two Robert D. Price appreciations, both in the *Austin American-*

Statesman. One was a tribute to all the Civil War veterans, which ran on Dec. 20, 1959; the other was a tribute to Williams, Dec. 21, 1959. A separate appreciation was published in *Stars and Stripes*, Dec. 21, 1959.

The Bruce Catton eulogy in *Life* magazine appeared on Jan. 11, 1960.

Williams's funeral and burial were national news. Among numerous media outlets, they were covered in the *Houston Post*, Dec. 21, 22, and 24, 1959; the *Cincinnati Enquirer*, Dec. 21, 1959; *Stars and Stripes*, Dec. 24, 1959; and the *United Daughters of the Confederacy* magazine, Feb. 1960.

13. OF THE DEAD, SPEAK NO EVIL

Texas State Senate Resolution 4 was printed in the *Journal of the State of Texas*, Regular Session for the Fifty-Seventh Legislature, convened Jan. 10, 1961, and adjourned May 29, 1961.

The federal pension rolls were released from the Veterans Administration on Dec. 19, 1959—the day Walter Williams died in Texas.

An overview of the South's reaction to the centennial commemorations can be found in Robert Cook, "(Un)Furl that Banner: The Response of White Southerners to the Civil War Centennial of 1961–1965," *Journal of Southern History* 68, no. 4 (Nov. 2002): 879–912. Another overview is provided in chap. 4, "The Civil War Centennial," of Robert G. Hartje's *Bicentennial USA: Pathways to Celebration* (Nashville: American Association for State and Local History, 1973). Also of great interest are the monthly reports called "100 Years After," issued by the U.S. Civil War Centennial Commission. A complete set is housed at the National Museum of the U.S. Navy Yard in Washington, D.C. Further, as previously noted, is Cook's book *Troubled Commemoration*. A complete file of the commission's papers and documents is available at the National Archives in Washington, D.C.; examples of their holdings include the Jan. 1958 "Statement of Objectives and Suggestions for Civil War Centennial Commemorations" and the commission's initial summary report of May 1961, titled "Centennial Observance Unfolds: Faithful to Past and Present." Of further interest is chap. 8 in John Bodnar, *Remaking America: Public Memory, Commemoration, and Patriotism in the Twentieth Century* (Princeton, N.J.: Princeton University Press, 1992).

The anecdote about Gen. Daniel Sickles can be found in Thomas Keneally, *American Scoundrel: The Life of the Notorious Civil War General Dan Sickles* (New York: Nan A. Talese/Doubleday, 2002).

The 1884 Memorial Day address by Oliver Wendell Holmes Jr. is reprinted in *American Speeches: Political Oratory from Abraham Lincoln to Bill Clinton* (New York: Library of America, 2006).

The anecdote about Joseph "Fighting Joe" Wheeler comes from William Manchester, *Controversy and Other Essays in Journalism, 1950–1975* (Boston: Little, Brown, 1976), 81.

The Kansas speech is covered in Robert S. La Forte, "Theodore Roosevelt's Osawatomie Speech," *Kansas Historical Quarterly* 32, no. 2 (Summer 1966): 187–200. It is reprinted in full in *American Speeches: Political Oratory*. The *New York Times* reported on the speech in its Aug. 31, 1910, editions.

John Clem's retirement was announced in the *New York Times*, Aug. 8, 1915.

Henry Adams's recollections of old Civil War soldiers and sailors crossing Lafayette Square in Washington, D.C., can be found in his memoir, *The Education of Henry Adams* (1907; repr., New York: Modern Library, 1996), 325–26.

The Confederate adventures and postwar life of William Henry Lafayette Wells come from her niece, Elizabeth Teass, in a July 1998 interview with the author. A Wells profile also appeared in the *Plano (Tex.) Daily Star-Courier*, Apr. 20, 1979.

The *New York Times*, June 9, 1957, described preparations around the nation for the coming centennial observations.

The Montgomery, Ala., celebrations were reported by the *Montgomery Advertiser* on Jan. 8, 1961 and Feb. 3, 8, 18, and 19, 1961. The letter to the editor from William Martin was printed Feb. 3, 1961, in the *Montgomery Advertiser*. The W. J. Mahoney column, "As I See It," ran in the *Montgomery Advertiser* on Jan. 8, 1961.

Stories of the celebrations and protests in Jackson, Miss., ran in the *Jackson Clarion-Ledger* on Mar. 26, 27, and 29, 1961.

News of the celebrations and protests in Charleston, S.C., were published in the *Charleston News-Courier*, Mar. 14, 15, and 25, 1961; the *Boston Globe*, Apr. 13, 1961; the *New York Times*, Apr. 12, 1961; the *Atlanta Constitution*, Apr. 12, 1961; and the *State* newspaper in Columbia, S.C., Apr. 12, 1961. President Kennedy's comments about the furor over hotel accommodations were made during a press conference and are contained in his public papers at the John F. Kennedy Presidential Library and Museum in Boston.

Vice President Lyndon Johnson's speech at Gettysburg is noted in Robert A. Caro, *The Passage of Power* (New York: Alfred A. Knopf, 2012), and Taylor Branch, *Pillar of Fire: America in the King Years, 1963–65* (New York: Simon and Schuster, 1998).

The resignations by Maj. Gen. Ulysses S. Grant III and Karl Betts from the Civil War Centennial Commission are covered in depth in Cook, *Troubled Commemoration*.

Laurence D. Reddick's speech at the Waldorf-Astoria Hotel in New York was reported by the *New York Times*, Apr. 23, 1961.

Allan Nevins's appointment to head the Civil War Centennial Commission was reported by the *New York Times*, Dec. 5, 1961.

Accounts of the commemorations at Bull Run, the Lincoln Memorial, and Gettysburg were included in the "100 Years After" reports by the Civil War Centennial Commission.

The May 1965 gathering at Gettysburg was described at length by the Illinois Civil War Centennial Commission in its "Final Assembly of the Civil War Centennial Commission and the State Historical Society's Spring Tour," housed in the national commission's files at the National Archives in Washington, D.C.

Allan Nevins's address, "The Challenges of 1864 and 1964," was reproduced in the Civil War Centennial Commission's final report and can be found in the commission's records at the National Archives in Washington, D.C.

The commemoration in Fitzgerald, Ga., was reported in the "100 Years After" report for June 1965, as were highlights of the final gathering at Gettysburg. More on Fitzgerald is included in Brundage, "Commemoration and Conflict."

William Marvel's investigation was published as "The Great Imposters" in *Blue and Gray* magazine, Feb. 1991. The files at the Gettysburg National Military Park include a copy of a letter Marvel sent on Jan. 23, 1991, suggesting that the Woolson statue at the battlefield be renamed in his honor as "the last participant in that war."

The Mark Twain quote comes from Twain's *Autobiography*, vol. 1 (Berkeley: University of California Press, 2012), 30.

The Huck Finn quote comes from Twain, *The Adventures of Huckleberry Finn* (New York: Modern Library, 1993), 3.

The investigation by the Texas Civil War Centennial Commission into Williams's authenticity is summarized in J. W. Baker, *A History of Robertson County, Texas* (Franklin, Tex.: Robertson County Historical Survey Committee, 1970). It is available at the Franklin, Tex., public library. The Texas Historical Marker stands at the front gate of the Mount Pleasant Cemetery, just outside Franklin. The debate over its placement is recounted in the files of the History Programs Division of the Texas Historical Commission.

Willie Mae Bowles's grave and marker can be viewed at Memorial Oaks Cemetery, Houston.

POSTSCRIPT

The "Recollections of Sylvester Magee," by Eva Velma Davis Betts of Columbia, Mississippi, are located in the Mississippi Department of Archives and History in Jackson, under her name in box 2 of her records. Among the other holdings is her article "The Oldest Story," published in *Dixie Roto Magazine*, Aug. 29, 1976.

Magee also appeared in the *Jackson (Miss.) Clarion-Ledger*, June 6, 1965, and Oct. 16, 1971; the *Los Angeles Times*, June 1 and Dec. 10, 1966; the *Birmingham (Ala.) News*, Dec. 10, 1966; and the *Toronto Globe and Mail*, May 30, 1967.

INDEX

⟫◆⟪

Page numbers in *italics* indicate photographs